SEX IN THE THERAPY HOUR

Sex in the Therapy Hour

A Case of Professional Incest

CAROLYN M. BATES
ANNETTE M. BRODSKY

Foreword by Gary Richard Schoener

THE GUILFORD PRESS
New York   London

© 1989 Carolyn M. Bates and Annette M. Brodsky
Published by The Guilford Press
A Division of Guilford Publications, Inc.
72 Spring Street, New York, NY 10012

Printed in the United States of America

Last digit is print number: 9   8   7   6   5   4   3   2   1

Library of Congress Cataloging-in-Publication Data

Bates, Carolyn M.
    Sex in the therapy hour: a case of professional incest / by
Carolyn M. Bates and Annette M. Brodsky.
        p.   cm.
    Includes index.
    ISBN 0-89862-726-5
    1. Psychotherapist and patient—Sexual behavior—Moral and ethical
aspects. 2. Psychotherapist and patient—Sexual behavior—Moral and
ethical aspects—Case studies. I. Brodsky, Annette M. II. Title.
RC480.8.B38 1989
174'.2—dc19   88-19032
                                                                CIP

We dedicate this book to the loving memory of our fathers,
Neal Adams Craig and Morris Nathan Ratner.

CAROLYN MAY CRAIG BATES

ANNETTE MAE RATNER BRODSKY

Acknowledgments

We would like to acknowledge our sincere gratitude to Suzanne Brown and Bill Whitehurst for their professional handling of the civil case with which this book deals. We also wish to thank Alex Caldwell for the blind MMPI interpretations; Gary Schoener for the technical review of the manuscript; our developmental editor, Nancy Worman; our copy editors, Abigail Winograd and Judith Grauman; and our chief editor, Seymour Weingarten, for their guidance in turning the manuscript into a polished book. We thank Stuart and Karla Wugalter for feedback on the readability of the manuscript, and Arlene Zayne, Patricia Williams, LeVena LeDay, Rose Lopez, Lori Comparo, and Lisa Campbell for their share in typing drafts of the manuscript over the years of its development.

Carolyn's personal acknowledgments: I am especially grateful to Evelyn Hammond, Ph.D., for her willingness to go the distance with a patient involved in a civil suit, and for her outstanding therapeutic skills. She helped me rediscover the meaning of joyful and courageous living. I am also grateful to my graduate school mentor, June Gallessich, Ph.D., for her unfailing guidance, and to many friends: Donna Odle, whose support and insight never waivered over the past decade; Trisha Myers, whose fresh approach to life helped me to discard my last remnants of bitterness; and T. J. Anderson, Georgia Cotrell, and my "grad school pals," for their candid support throughout the writing of this book. I also want to thank my mother, Virginia Craig, who never stopped believing in me, even when she seriously doubted the wisdom of my actions. My brothers Michael and Richard Craig and my sister, Debbie Craig Schumann, willingly stood by me throughout this unhappy ordeal, and I cannot express how much this meant to me. Finally, I thank my husband, Ken, whose love and calm strength helped me through many of the tearful and anxious moments that taking a stand and writing about it brought forth.

Annette's personal acknowledgments: I want to acknowledge the subtle contributions of my mother, Sadie Ratner Danziger; my son, Michael Brodsky; and my daughter, Rachel Brodsky, by staying healthy, normal, cheerful, and understanding, freeing me to indulge in the intense professional life style that enabled the extraordinary efforts needed to accomplish this book and the work upon which it was based, mostly in the evening and weekend hours. I am grateful for the encouragement of such comments as, "Mom, stop procrastinating and get back to work on that book!"

Carolyn M. Bates
Annette M. Brodsky

Foreword

The telling of Carolyn Bates's story represents a significant break with a harmful taboo. The sexual abuse of patients by professionals has long been a topic cloaked in silence, with a few exceptions only rarely and reluctantly discussed within the professional community itself. This troubled reserve on the part of the professionals, in conjunction with the considerable coverage given to "sex therapy" on the part of the popular press, has given rise to public confusion regarding the advisability of sexual contact between patient and therapist. Perhaps the most disturbing results of this taboo and subsequent confusion are the continued occurrences of this form of sexual abuse and the absence of laws prohibiting its practice. Carolyn Bates's experiences demonstrate amply the extent to which consumer ignorance and professional silence can allow for abuse with impunity, extreme client vulnerability, tortuous or absent legal recourse, and a lasting sense of shame and confusion. Why has it taken so long for this age-old problem of a highly damaging nature to be addressed adequately?

"First do no harm" is one of the earliest precepts of medicine. More specifically, the 2,400-year-old oath attributed to Hippocrates focuses on a telling aspect of this prohibition:

> . . . with purity and holiness I will practice my art. . . . Into whatever houses I enter I will go into them for the benefit of the sick and will abstain from every voluntary act of mischief and corruption and further from the seduction of females or males, of freemen and slaves.

Sexual intimacies were not mentioned in the Code of Hammurabi compiled 15 centuries earlier, but by the time of Hippocrates the power of the physician and the possibility of sexual exploitation had been recognized as harmful and necessary to curb.

During the middle ages, the treatise "De Cautelis Medicorum," thought to have been authored by Arnald of Villanova, read in part:

> . . . Let me give you one more warning: Do not look at a maid, a daughter, or a wife with improper or covetous eye and do not let yourself be entangled in woman affairs for there are medical operations that excite the helper's mind; otherwise your judgment is affected, you become harmful to the patient, and people will expect less from you.

Here again, the writer of the proscription considers sexual excitement during the course of treatment a serious danger, and specifically warns against its potential to affect the physician's judgment and the public's confidence.

Unfortunately, more recent codes of ethics have failed to forbid specifically sexual contact with patients. The preface to the code adopted by the American Medical Association at its first meeting in Philadelphia in 1847 revealed that it was based in part on the code published by Thomas Percival in 1803. Neither addressed the issue of sexual seduction or contact. Various revisions of this code also failed to mention sexual seduction, even after the field of psychiatry began to evolve.

In 1973 "Principles of Medical Ethics with Annotations Especially Applicable to Psychiatry" was published in the *American Journal of Psychiatry* (Vol. 133, pp. 1058–1064), containing the explicit prohibition: "Sexual activity with the patient is unethical." In 1977 the American Psychological Association followed with a similar explicit prohibition in the revised code of ethics for psychologists: "Sexual intimacies with clients are unethical." This was more than a year after Carolyn Bates began seeing the abusive psychologist Dr. X. Against the background of ancient prohibitions and modern ambiguities, the chronicling of abuse and its consequences as accomplished by Carolyn Bates and Annette Brodsky brings to light the issues involved in heightening public awareness of and professional attention to a problem too long ignored.

A Yiddish proverb says: "Don't ask the doctor; ask the patient." *Sex in the Therapy Hour* is the first book to be co-authored by an expert in the field of psychology and a client who has been victimized by an unethical therapist. Bates's articulate, nonvindictive presentation of her experiences and Brodsky's in-depth professional analysis set the book apart from the few other books of its kind, while simultaneously giving voice to the concerns of all such victims and the professionals who treat them. For a number of years staff at our center suggested the book *Betrayal,* by victim Julie Roy and writer Lucy Freeman, to clients who had been similarly victimized by therapists. Many clients, however, had difficulty relating to the book because Roy's problems tended to be far more severe than those common among the more than 1,000 clients who have contacted us. An additional barrier to identifying with the book was the fact that it described a lawsuit conducted at a time when even the professional community was confused about the issues.

In 1985 Ellen Plaisil wrote the book *Therapist,* which detailed her abuse by a prominent psychotherapist. She indicated that it was written in part for catharsis; since the civil suit settled out of court she never had a chance to tell her story publicly. Hers is a somewhat brief account, and the book is primarily focused on the therapy relationship, devoting almost no description to the legal actions that followed the abuse. The next year Evelyn Walker, in collaboration with T. D. Young, wrote *A Killing Cure,* a detailed account of the Walker v. Parzen civil suit that resulted in the largest cash settlement on record in a sexual exploitation case. The book contains considerable descriptive information that emerged during the trial about Dr. Parzen, the therapist.

While these exposés have helped to heighten public awareness, their various foci have remained limited in audience identification and incomplete in the chronicling and assessment of the effects of the sexual abuse of patients by therapists. This is precisely the point at which Bates and Brodsky make a significant contribution to the literature. Literally hundreds of our clients have repeated Dr. X's words "trust me" when they tell us of their abuse. Carolyn Bates's story functions as that rare medium that is both a point of identification and a provider of additional insight, especially in her unprecedented examination of the gradual transition from a professional relationship to an exploitative one. Her description of her emotional history provides a context that makes clear to the reader why clients in such relationships become confused about the therapist's motives and even about what is therapy versus seduction or exploitation.

The loss of self-esteem, the heightened sense of mistrust, the depression, guilt, and anger that Ms. Bates describes are all symptoms of abuse described by the majority of victims we treat, as is the impact of discovering that one is not the only patient being abused. Many clients are quite ambivalent about taking action until they find that they are not the only victims. Up until that point a client may persist in the nagging belief in the back of her mind that she was "special," that her experience was an aberration and thus incapable of inspiring empathy, or that she is somehow solely or primarily responsible for her abuse. Ms. Bates's insights regarding her own discovery of other victims and her subsequent decision to act provide the reader with a valuable frame of reference and a more thorough understanding of the trauma and frustration that result from acting on one's recognition of the extent of the victimization. The process of seeking redress is often an extremely difficult and lonely experience; victimized clients often find other therapists reluctant to aid or support such an action, and the procedures themselves demeaning and inefficient. As Ms. Bates's story so eloquently reveals, even when the client prevails there is not a magical release from the effects of the abuse, which can haunt an abused patient for years to come.

Through Carolyn Bates's first-hand account and Annette Brodsky's subsequent analysis, a picture of Dr. X emerges that allows for a much-needed consideration of how abusers like Dr. X might be identified and thus prevented from misconduct. Dr. Brodsky has written articulately on this subject in Chapter 9. As she emphasizes in her discussion in Chapter 13, it is imperative that training programs, licensing boards, and the professional community itself pay far stricter attention to the screening of professionals. Dr. Brodsky's wealth of experience in this area and her professional insights afford her observations a clarity of perspective that is extremely welcome in the face of the disturbing public ignorance of the abusive therapist.

As her descriptions of Dr. X and her own reactions to him so well illustrate, clients like Carolyn Bates, after they realize that they have been victimized, struggle to understand why their therapists did what they did. Ms. Bates speaks to and for such victims as she recounts her devastating sense of confusion and betrayal, raising questions regarding therapist motives and underlining the necessity for some degree of patient understanding to allow for a coming to terms with the abuse. It is a sad fact that the client often never receives sufficient explanation for her therapist's actions, perhaps in part because the professional community has not yet given enough consideration to the determining of why such abuse occurs and with whom. *Sex in the Therapy Hour* makes abundantly clear the directions this increased concern must take to reduce the incidence of a situation debilitating to patient and therapist alike.

Via a detailed history and extensive analysis Ms. Bates and Dr. Brodsky alert both the professional and the consumer to the harmful effects of patient abuse and the silence with which it has been surrounded. As the public becomes more aware that some therapists have sexual contact with clients, and why such conduct is improper, more consumers will be forewarned of the danger. Although there has been increasing evidence of public displeasure with the apparent inability of any of the organized psychotherapy professions to remedy the situation, legislative condemnation of sexual misconduct by professionals is still limited to a few jurisdictions.

Where abuse involves a minor or where drugs or other means have been used to facilitate the abuse, criminal charges have been filed under existing statutes in a number of states. In 1983 the Wisconsin State Assembly passed a law making it a first class misdemeanor for a psychotherapist to have sexual contact with a client. In 1986 the law was amended, making the crime a felony. Thus far several psychotherapists have been prosecuted under the 1983 statute and charges have been brought against others under the 1986 statute. In 1985 the Minnesota State Legislature amended the Criminal Sexual Conduct Code to make sex with a psychotherapy client a felony, punishable by up to 10 years in prison and a $ 20,000 fine. A number of therapists have been charged and prosecuted under this statute. Colorado criminalized sex between client and therapist in 1988. In addition, other states, among them California, Michigan, Pennsylvania, and Massachusetts, have considered similar legislation.

Some states have created special statutes governing civil suits against therapists for sexually exploiting their clients. For example, statutes in Minnesota, Wisconsin, and California have made it easier for clients to sue therapists for this type of malpractice by limiting access to the plaintiff's sexual history and defining sexual contact with a psychotherapy client as malpractice per se.

There has also been an increase in the number of statutes mandating the reporting of abuse of this type. For example, in Minnesota all licensed health professionals and health care facilities are required to report abuse of a sexual nature to various licensing boards. In addition, abuse in certain types of facilities must be reported to the Adult Protection Unit of the Division of Human Services.

So, while criminal prosecution of doctors for sexual contacts with patients has a long history in the United States (cf. Pomeroy v. State, 94 Ind. 96 1883) and England (cf. Queen v. Williams, 1 Den C.C. 580, Eng 1850), there have been few reported cases until the implementation of the new criminal laws in a few states. Likewise, the more recent experience with civil suits for sexual exploitation by a therapist, dating from Zipkin v. Freeman (436 S.W.2d 753, Mo. 1968) in 1968, has shown a great proliferation in reported cases in the 1980s. However, the percentage of cases that result in lawsuits, criminal action, or li-

censure complaints is probably still quite small. Whether psychotherapists will avoid such conduct when faced with a greater
likelihood of discovery or consequences is difficult to know.

In Chapter 13 of this book Dr. Brodsky points to the difficult
problem of checking the references of prospective employees or
students. This age-old problem has become worse in recent years
due to a growing case law involving suits by students or former
employees against past employers or training programs, alleging
that they passed on defamatory information when providing a
reference. Minnesota Statute 148.A, made law in 1986, attempts
to turn the tables in such situations, creating a statutory duty to
check with past employers about any history of sexual contact
with clients (including solicitation for sex) as well as a duty to
pass on such information. The employer who fails to check an
employee's records and the past employer who fails to supply the
requested information are held directly liable for future damages.
The employer who passes on such information in good faith is
immune from suit for having done so (should, for example, the
employee not be hired as a result of this information). This statute
attempts to put client safety first through a common-sense
approach to an old dilemma. With or without this statute, our
center advises all employers of psychotherapists to obtain a broad
release from them permitting a "no holds barred" background
check by providing protection for persons contacted who share
information about the applicant in good faith.

It should be noted in closing that two state legislatures have
funded task forces to study this problem. The Minnesota Task
Force on Sexual Exploitation by Counselors and Psychotherapists
functioned from 1984 to 1987, producing a legislative report in
1985, a host of new laws, and a major national conference in
1986. This year it has published a booklet for consumers to
augment a large-scale statewide education program as well as a
major manual for professionals entitled *It's Never O.K.* The California Senate Task Force on Psychotherapist and Patients Sexual
Relations functioned from October 1986 to March 1987 and
produced a legislative report as well as a number of new laws. In
the state of Wisconsin there is a large-scale watchdog effort,
originally begun by the Wisconsin Psychological Association in
1984 but now an interdisciplinary coalition with broad consumer

involvement called the Wisconsin Coalition on Sexual Misconduct by Psychotherapists and Counselors. Within the various psychotherapy fields some state associations have work groups or task forces addressing sexual abuse of patients by professionals.

Carolyn Bates's experiences should not go unaddressed. Her dramatic and forthright account and Annette Brodsky's clinically expert analysis do much to ensure that a situation too long ignored will receive the attention it warrants. It is time for all mental health professionals and the general public to recognize the wisdom of the Hippocratic Oath as a binding statement of ethical responsibility, an oath to aid rather than harm, the promise central to *all* helping professions. *Sex in the Therapy Hour* is an invaluable reminder of the importance of affirming this oath and a compelling testimony of the ramifications of a failure to do so.

Gary Richard Schoener
Executive Director
Walk-In Counseling Center
Minneapolis, Minnesota

Contents

Introduction

This book is about sex between a patient and her therapist. The case of Dr. X was exposed to the public in 1978 through a malpractice lawsuit brought by Carolyn Bates and two other women against the therapist. Ten years later, many consider the resolution of the case to be no more than marginally satisfactory.

Soon after the end of the litigation described in this book, Dr. Annette Brodsky, a clinical psychologist who served as the expert witness for the plaintiffs, approached Carolyn with the idea of presenting the story at the 1984 annual convention of the American Psychological Association. In that panel discussion Carolyn was joined by other participants in the case: the plaintiffs' attorneys, a therapist from whom Carolyn had subsequently sought treatment, and Dr. Brodsky herself. The audience was appalled at the lack of resolution of the case and gave Carolyn a standing ovation for her presentation. That presentation became the first step of a collaborative effort between us to document the details of the story and its implications for professionals.

Our purpose here is to examine through Carolyn's experiences as a victimized patient the legal, moral, and ethical issues involved in the phenomenon of sexual contact between therapist and patient. We consider not only the perspective of the patient, but also the concerns of the attorneys, the subsquent therapists, the evaluators, the licensing boards, and the ethics committees— all of whom played a part in the litigation of the malpractice claim. This story offers an account of the personal situation that led Carolyn to enter therapy, the incidents of sexual intimacy with her therapist, the aftermath of those incidents, and the problems within the system that permitted at least two repetitions of history after resolution was supposedly reached. This is a true case, and the data come directly from the participants themselves or, in the case of the perpetrator, from court records and other documented evidence.

We have chosen to provide aliases for two characters in the story. The name of Carolyn's boyfriend during her early 20s is disguised for the protection of his privacy. The name of the sexually abusive therapist in this case has also been withheld. Our decision to refrain from identifying him was made only after great consideration. We have supplied him with the alias of Dr. X, because he could be any one of a number of people in any one of a number of places. With respect to the real Dr. X, it is our hope that in telling this story we shall neither promote him nor cause him unnecessary difficulty. We do not identify the location of the events in the story because the phenomenon of harmful sexual contact between a psychotherapist and a patient is not indigenous to any one region or state.

In short, we have chosen to tell this story in order to inform members of the helping professions, and those of the public who seek their help, of the many ramifications of sexual activity between psychotherapists and their clients. Understanding the unwarranted harm that sexual contact between therapists and patients can bring to the lives of everyone involved is crucial to the goals of valid mental health care.

I

CAROLYN'S STORY

1

The Naive Client and the Therapeutic Alliance

I face a dilemma in putting down in print facets of my life that I wish I could erase rather than feel compelled to resurrect—the years of my initial therapy, the sexual abuse therein, and the emotionally scarred aftermath. I am left with a sense of grief as I review the time when I cared so little for myself that I felt that what happened to me was of little consequence, when I sacrificed my well-being to glean acceptance in whatever form it was offered. But as I write today, I care more for myself than I did then, and perhaps this is the single greatest difference beween who I am now and who I was over a decade ago, when I first entered therapy with an unethical psychologist.

I have wondered for some time how I could best tell this story. I suspect some readers will voice the predominant question I encountered while making legal depositions and from friends, acquaintances, colleagues, and psychologists: How could a person with your upbringing, intelligence, and insight have collaborated, repeatedly, in an offense against your own being? I attempt to answer this question from two perspectives: how I managed to become Dr. X's victim, and how he managed to victimize me. For while my sheltered life, self-doubt, and uncritical respect for authority rendered me an ideal subject for exploitation, I must credit Dr. X for his own skillful manipulations. He made no mistakes. He was very, very good at what he did.

Another question asked of me periodically is whether, in spite of the abuse, my 20 months of treatment with this therapist left me with anything beneficial. My answer is no. What personal growth did occur in the early months of therapy was either undone or buried when Dr. X began to exploit me. After leaving therapy with him, I continued to deteriorate, but I did not attend to the damaging effects of his actions until I became miserable enough to risk seeking help again. Fortunately, my second attempt at therapy led me to a competent psychologist.

Mine is not a story about those therapists who, during an emotionally disruptive time in their lives, succumb to their own wishes to have sex with their patients. Nor is it about those therapists who honestly and sincerely fall in love with and communicate that love to their patients. It is not a story about therapists and patients who mutually agree to have affairs, nor is it about a coincidence in which several women in succession attempt to seduce one particular therapist. Finally, this is not a story about patients who have affairs with their therapists and then, in fits of vindictive rage, sue them.

This is the story of my experience—and that of other patients—with one psychologist who exploited his female patients and discounted the emotional repercussions of his behavior. I felt his behavior showed blatant disregard for the professional ethics of psychotherapy and profoundly poor judgment. Throughout the battle of civil litigation, which resulted from claims brought against him by abused patients, Dr. X time and again took full advantage of the legal and licensing loopholes afforded him. It was finally through the courts that the abused patients labored to expose his behavior in an attempt to remove him from his powerful vantage point, so that he could never again harm a vulnerable patient.

This is a true story.

GROWING UP WITH STRICTNESS AND LOVE

A: Dr. X told me that if I wanted to develop emotionally, if I wanted to have any kind of emotional barriers broken down so that I could have relationships with men, I could not let having sex with [the men I dated] get in my way.

Q: Well, do you think that's right?

A: I do not think that I can stay healthy and at the same time apply that philosophy to every man that I go out with.

How did I ever come to this place, where my feelings and ideas about my private sex life were being scrutinized and logged into a public record? How did I arrive at a place where my integrity as a victimized patient was to be measured against the integrity of an unethical psychologist? A knowledge of who I am and the forces in my young life that contributed to my becoming that person will facilitate a better understanding of the dilemma I found myself facing in 1978.

I was the youngest of five children, each of us separated by three to four years. My mother's pregnancy with me had been difficult as well as unexpected. At 38, she had not planned on another child. When I was an adult, she shared with me how angry she had been when she first learned of her pregnancy, but how she fell in love with me at first sight: Fat, hungry, already sucking my thumb, I had no need to be coaxed or taught to nurse.

Within a week of my birth, however, my mother experienced a dangerous hemorrhage that rendered her hospitalized for at least two weeks and semibedridden for the first year of my life. During my first 6 weeks, and periodically throughout the first year, my mother's mother stayed with my family and assumed the role of my primary caretaker. I remember her only as stern, distant, and cold (in marked contrast to my father's mother, who was warm, tender, and gentle). She was an unhappy and stoic woman who had grimly born many hardships in her life. She rarely laughed spontaneously, and all of us children seemed to know instinctively that we must behave cautiously and respectfully around her.

From photographs taken at that time, it is evident that this last pregnancy left my mother exhausted beyond a point she had previously known. My father, however, then 43, took me, as he did many things, in steady but humorous stride. I can characterize my early childhood as one of curiosity, learning, and a serious approach to everything I did, including playing.

My mother freely encouraged my curiosity from an early age, talking at length with me about things I thought important and reading stories to me almost nightly. Both of my parents accepted and encouraged my creative side, supporting my imagination and my desire to learn. At 4 years of age, I fascinated my mother when I approached her with a lumpy sock. Upon her query as to what I held, I ran off a single sentence: "I got me a sock and in my sock is a doll and on the doll is a nose and in the nose is a nostril and in the nostril there's a bug and in the bug is a skeleton and in the skeleton is blood and in blood there's mineral and in mineral there's strength, in strength there is goodness, and in goodness there's God and in God there is holiness—and I don't know what's in holiness." I calmly demonstrated this spiraling discovery by extracting my doll from the sock, holding up a button for the bug and a kinked-up rubber band for the skeleton. Beyond this I could not produce concrete evidence of my assertions. She was sufficiently enthralled to write down what I had said and has since told me that my rendition of this soliloquy marked the day from which she felt she had a creative child on her hands. I began writing short stories and poems when I was 6, stretching A. A. Milne's story into my own version of Pooh Land, an odd hybrid between stuffed animals and the cowboy heroes from "Rawhide," with a dash of Tarzan's Africa thrown in for good measure.

My parents also tried to guide me along the traditional female course, with conservative expectations of career and family. They somehow communicated to me that college was a nonnegotiable expectation. It never dawned on me to question it as a part of my education. But when careers were discussed, only the three my mother had viewed available to her generation were brought to my attention: teacher, nurse, and secretary. I was never told that other fields were beyond my reach, but no other career was promoted, nor was the idea of choosing between career and family.

Like any child, I fantasized about my future. According to a letter my mother wrote to one of her friends I had chosen to "marry a rancher so I can take care of his horses." Her humorous skepticism of my tomboyish nature was evident in her comment, " 'His horses.' It looks like I have my work cut out for me."

Finally, my parents demanded strict obedience. They would not stand for my testing their authority, particularly if I did so angrily, for the expression of anger was forbidden in our home. I seemed far less able to keep my anger under control than did my sister, Debbie, whom I never remember expressing extremes of either anger or joy when we were children. My explosions of temper warranted punishment that took two forms: I was sent to my room until I could promise to show only calmer, more positive emotions, or if I dared to direct my anger toward my mother, I was spanked. My parents, like their parents before them, believed in the judicious use of corporal punishment when their children strayed farther out of line than they felt was tolerable. I would do what I could to avoid switching, but often enough my temper or my restlessness would lead me to be taken from the church pew to the car, where the familiar old switch lay. It stung me, it shamed me, and it most certainly made me aware of my parents' definition of acceptable behavior. The smarting dissipated quickly enough, and the feelings of contriteness vanished soon after—but the lessons remained. I learned that authority is absolute and not to be challenged. If I dared to challenge it, anger from those I loved—and, with it, the risk of rejection and the feeling of shame—descended upon me. In adulthood, these lessons were manifest in my skillful avoidance of conflict and, for some time, my willingness to sacrifice myself to appease the anger of authority figures.

The form of punishment I regret, however, the one that I wish had never been a part of my mother's heritage, was being slapped across the face. On rare occasion—but not rare enough— I would cross my mother in such a way as to make her angry enough to slap me. A blatant lie on my part guaranteed this response. My father never slapped me, to my relief. In fact, I never remember him laying his hand on me—a switch, or a belting if the crime was great enough; more often, a stern look or a brief and firm command from him sufficed. I do not know why my parents differed in their use of this form of punishment. Perhaps using one's hands to inflict pain was not the way my father had been raised. Perhaps my father did not have the opportunity to mete out much discipline; since my mother ran our home, she was generally the witness to our misbehavior.

The slapping was a form of punishment that, unbeknownst to my mother, struck at the heart of my being and evoked a humiliation that far exceeded any shame for having misbehaved. It reinforced a growing sense of shame I felt as a living being. I realized much later that this form of punishment was meant to enforce respect for what was considered right and good, and I have no doubt that my mother was only repeating what had been done to her when she herself had misbehaved or blatantly challenged the authorities in her life. But I left these encounters feeling an anger far greater than that which I felt after the less humiliating switchings.

None of the punishments, however, was ever administered arbitrarily or impulsively. They were meted out for a disobedience of action that arose from my angry feelings. Speaking angrily, stomping a foot, slamming a door, or even glowering brought about corporal punishment or isolation. The punishment for disobedience was harsh, and I learned that expressing anger was a violation of my parents' values.

My recollection of misbehavior and subsequent punishment is that neither occurred with great frequency, and one spanking was generally good for a couple of months' worth of tolerable behavior. As I grew older, the time between punishments naturally increased—both because my parents believed suspension of privileges to be more appropriate punishment for older children and because I learned to hide my disobedience more skillfully. By the time I was 11, I would not experience corporal punishment again, although in an impatient, angry moment when I was 16 I feared my mother would slap me for uttering a curse in her presence. I was relieved to receive no more than a shaking by my shoulders.

In this atmosphere, I learned a respect for and an obedience to authority that was so great it preempted the establishment of my own sense of authority. I imagine that my parents intended to loosen their hold on me as I advanced toward adulthood—as I remember their doing with my older brothers—so that I might begin to make decisions for myself and thus develop an independent sense of control over my life. But something happened to ward off this probability, and for many years to come I would not know what it would be like to let go of my parents' authority in lieu of my own.

My home felt safe, but I was fearful of the world beyond my sheltered surroundings. My anxiety at leaving home to begin school manifested itself in severe migraine headaches the first school day of each new year. I remember little contact with any other children besides my quiet, introspective sister, Debbie, 4 years older than I, and those children I saw while in school and church. When I was 9, my brother Michael described me as "a serious little old lady who didn't know how to play."

We lived in a small, blue-collar town on the U.S.–Mexico border. It was a dusty, hot, economically depressed community. My father eked out a living as the town's sole provider and installer of venetian blinds.

My father was also a lay preacher in a young and close-knit fundamentalist church that he had been instrumental in forming. My parents' commitment to the church was a serious one, and I took to heart its biblical teachings of faith and salvation. Unfortunately, this belief also seemed to entail the attitude that Christians held unique answers to emotional troubles. Rather than problems being discussed openly, they were handled through prayer or kept to oneself. Thus, our family appeared to be relatively free of emotional upset: In reality, however, my siblings and I had merely learned to harbor our anger, dislikes, and disappointments within ourselves, well shielded from our parents.

My father was not a businessman at heart, and after 19 years of running his venetian-blind shop, he sold it for $2,000. In 1964, when I was 9 years old and the last of my three brothers had left home, we left the town of my childhood, my parents' home for 20 years. We moved to a college town so that my father could complete undergraduate and graduate school at a state university, a Depression-thwarted dream that he was at last able to realize.

Throughout my preteen and early teenage years, my father

went through his own metamorphosis as he was exposed to higher learning and more progressive thought than he had ever known before. The university campus was caught up in the volatile mood that was evident throughout the country in the late 1960s, and Dad became enthralled with the city, the campus, the youth he worked with, and the professors he studied under. His own intellectualism had been stifled in the border town we had lived in; he himself had been sheltered, his own horizons limited despite his continual reading and study. A full 20 years older than the average student, he became a mediating element between students and faculty. He was a sounding board for the former, trusted by the latter. On the day Martin Luther King was assassinated, my father spoke eloquently on the issues of civil rights, riveting the attention of many on campus.

It was, I believe, a blossoming transition that he was making, from a venetian-blind salesman in a semiliterate, impoverished border community to a graduate student and teaching assistant at an energetic university campus teeming with controversy. Its effect on me, a child of 12, was only to increase my idealization of him—he was a good man, and he was doing good things. I relished the books he brought me to read, the same ones that he assigned to his freshman English classes. He let me spend time in his office, and when he proctored his final exams, I would play chess with him to pass the time. As young as I was, I was falling in love with the idea of college and graduate school, too. I was, however, too young to recognize the near-poverty level at which we were living as my parents struggled to feed and clothe us on my father's small salary.

I matured socially more slowly than many of my peers, feeling comfortable in the tomboy role and shunning makeup and activities that reinforced femininity. My friends accepted my behavior, though they encouraged me to groom myself in more conventional ways. With hindsight, I have come to suspect that exchanging my tomboy role for the more stereotypical "young lady" role might have allowed me to interact with my peers more easily. But I was hesitant to venture into the world of adolescence, perhaps because I had grown up a reserved child with little self-confidence: I had always been disinclined to interact with people outside of my family.

In my early teenage years, I remained easily intimidated by

my peers and highly self-conscious of being some 20 pounds overweight. I saw myself as plain but not unattractive. Although I had friends in the youth group at the church my family joined, I had few at school. In junior high, my weight, clumsy social skills, and ignorance of makeup and dating earned me the stinging nickname of the Moose. I fled to the refuge of my typewriter, writing in lieu of social interaction, creating short stories in which a petite heroine held her own against various challenges and dangers in her life.

By the time I reached high school, I had come to dread the lunch periods, the students' time to socialize. I would retreat from the cafeteria, where I dismally failed to befriend others, and hide behind a bush or tree on the grounds outside. Eating alone in public was an embarrassment to me—I felt like the unwanted "big girl" who ate in spite of her size.

My most treasured relationships in high school were primarily with teachers. They didn't seem to mind my size: They appreciated my inner strengths, my eagerness to work for them. I loved my teachers and believed that they cared for me. I even loved homework, for the most part, because it not only occupied my time but offered me something in which I could excel; it was a means by which I could ensure approval and appreciation. My grades were consistently above average, except when I tackled physics, as a senior, and earned my first C. I assuaged my guilt over this, a failure in my mind, by earning awards in writing—I was an English teacher's dream student.

I was also discovering that my few friends found me a willing listener and at times sought me out to talk with them about their problems. This, coupled with my curiosity about why people behave the way they do, sparked my first interest in considering a career in psychology; and my unabashed hero worship of my father, who was then working toward his doctorate, cemented graduate school as a goal for me.

Perhaps my shyness was due in part to a thorough preoccupation with my father's progressively debilitating illness during my early teenage years. When I was 13, he was diagnosed as having Lou Gehrig's disease, a degenerative nerve disorder. His doctors estimated that he would live another 2 to 5 years. He had begun teaching English to university undergraduates as he proceeded with his own degree. But as his health waned, he was forced to stop his education. My mother and he decided that he would stay home for the course of his illness, and she bravely attempted home nursing. Over the next 21 months I watched as he went from using a cane to crutches to a wheelchair. Debbie, fluent in Spanish, spent some of this time in Guatemala helping our church's missionaries with the Quiché dialect; while she was away, I was Mother's only help in caring for Dad.

My father had always been a strong, gregarious man. His words and interactions, though drained of their physical energy, were alive with a spirit of faith that never left him. Through stilted dictation to my mother, he wrote his resignation letter to his colleagues at the university in which he said:

> For most of my life I have known myself to be in the hands of the Lord, and I am certainly no less so now than in more promising days. The doctors, I think, have no hope at all for my recovery, at least they offer me none. But like Cyrano de Bergerac, I have no surrender in me, and will flail about with my puny sword, to the last awkward stroke, if it comes to that—not as fighting an enemy, but simply as not giving up a contest.

Only with hindsight can I put words to what I felt as I helped my father in his last months of life. As he was dying, so too was my place in the world as his child dying , and deep within me I knew that our relationship would soon be totally irretrievable. He weakened so rapidly—this strong, intelligent man whom I had never dreamed was destructible. For the last months of his life, I was too stunned to feel anything but a dull pain. But I clearly knew, even then, that there would soon be no father to come home to, to feel safe near.

My family did not talk about the fact that Dad was dying. No one admitted it inside the walls of the house until some days before his death, when it became impossible for him to swallow. I had never seen him frightened until the day his doctor told us that it was time for him to go to the hospital. His ability to speak had seriously deteriorated, but he could still communicate with us; this intelligent, warm man who had spoken four languages fluently now blinked once for "yes," twice for "no." The blinks flew as he told my mother and his doctor, a longtime friend, that he would not go to a hospital to die. So the doctor taught us how to feed Dad by means of a tube inserted through his nose and how to use an aspirator to keep him from choking on his saliva.

Within the week, the church elders of our congregation anointed Dad with oil in a poignant ceremony made calm by his peaceful acceptance of his own death. The family gathered about him. I remember standing at the foot of his bed holding onto his feet, watching him look at each of us; his gaze finally rested on my mother, where it stayed until he died.

COPING WITH EMPTINESS

My father's death came in the spring of 1971, in his 59th year. It was less than 2 years after the initial diagnosis. I had not nursed Dad to the total exclusion of my social life, but I had preferred to devote a substantial amount of my attention and thought to him. This was so because I adored my father, because my parents needed my help, and because I found staying home safer than venturing out into the world of adolescence. But his death catapulted me from the secure orbit I had known into a frightening unknown. At 15, I experienced his death as a lesson in utter helplessness. I threw myself into the escape of my short stories, but there was a desperation to my efforts now, as I tried to write understanding and hope into my heroine's experience of *her* father's death.

I survived the next 2 years, staving off the depression that would later descend in its darkest form, by immersing myself within the middle of the church youth group, which was itself caught up in the Jesus movement of the early 1970s. There was a monthly newsletter to write, retreats to the country to plan, friends to help as they struggled with problems of boyfriends, drugs, and crises in school. And there was the warmth of fellowship, a feeling of belonging and purpose that served as a glue, literally holding my life together and giving structure to my time. The youth group was my haven, a place where I found spiritual and intellectual challenges for my mental energies, social challenges to my self-conscious reticence, outlets for my love for others, and multiple sources of love from others. It was the place where I could, at least for the remainder of my high school years, feel safe from the world.

When I was a senior in high school my security crumbled, seemingly overnight, as my four closest friends left town for college. Suddenly I was alone again, and going to church soon became an experience of grief and longing and nothing more. The very next retreat after their departure was my last. Sitting alone beside a mountain stream, I felt that all that was left of that integral part of my life was myself and my guitar. Other kids were there, wonderful kids, from the younger ranks of the youth group, but I did not have the same connection to them that I had come to have after three years of growing up with my other companions, now gone. I felt the odd one out, somehow disconnected. And for the first time in my life, I felt disconnected from God. Prayer only made the sense of distance seem greater, and I engaged in it with lessening frequency after that year.

At the same time, my relationship with my grieving mother oscillated between close talks, mutual withdrawal, and angry interactions. My mother had always shown a sense of rootedness and well-being in raising her children; she seemed to know herself and her purpose with respect to her family and to be content in that knowledge. I never saw her in despair, until my father died, and then her own anguish—over both the loss of her beloved and the subsequent ravaging of her own identity—was such as I had never seen in anyone, and I felt powerless to ease it.

Mother faced the grim task of returning to the world of employment, from which she had been absent for 35 years, in order to support herself and her two daughters. She found a clerking job within a few months of Dad's death, and I contributed $100 a month from the Social Security check I had begun to receive, saving the rest for college. For the remainder of my high school years, we supported each other with our physical presence, but emotionally the distance between us grew—what we could not talk about lay between us, a mass of hurt and grief that hardened the longer we avoided it.

I suspect that what would have been the normal tumultuous course of mother–daughter separation was made all the worse by the depression that descended upon the whole family after my father's death. Prayer was not sufficient, and yet we had no other recourse through which to cope. We each sought the reason for his death, holding tightly to the belief that it existed somewhere, just beyond our ability to understand. My sister and

18-year-old freshman, and I was far from ready for it. Prior to that, I had dated only three young men in high school for any substantial length of time, most often going to movies or attending activities connected with my church youth group. In spite of my limited experience, I had begun to recognize a distressing pattern. I felt frightened by the boys' emotional and sexual expectations, and then I felt guilty for having engaged in any kind of sexual contact. I would inevitably break off these relationships after 6 months to a year.

At the same time that I began this first affair, which would continue off and on for more than 5 years, I stopped attending church altogether. Though I was drawn to the momentary security, warmth, and sense of connection that sex provided, premarital sex without even the illusion of commitment was antithetical to the values of my childhood. Thus warring emotions left me feeling totally ungrounded, uncertain of my values: I could not reconcile the sexual activity with Steve and what I knew the church to teach. I recognized the teachings of forgiveness, but I did not want to be continuously reminded of my need to be forgiven. My guilt was too strong, and being in church grew harder to endure—disapproval and condemnation of my sins seemed to permeate the air. Certainly these were all my own imaginings, because the members of the congregation knew nothing about this aspect of my life and in fact warmly embraced me when I would attend. No, it seemed to be my father's disapproval I felt—or that of his God, which was, by then, one and the same to me.

As the tenuous relationship between Steve and me progressed through the first year, my control over these newly emerging, volatile emotions began to break down. I brimmed over with disillusionment, anger, frustration, and, above all, a pervasive sense of desperation. My reactions to any hints from Steve of ending our relationship were of such inordinate proportions that, in hindsight, I know they were related to my ongoing grief over the separation by death from my father. At the slightest insinuation of separation from my first lover, I would succumb to hysterical outbursts and tantrums of a dimension I had never known before. I engaged in behavior previously foreign to me: lying, pleading, spying, ranting, and grasping to hold onto this only-sometimes-willing man. When he was with me, I

mother and I had struggled, each within our own private wo
with the guilt that arose from our belief at the time that, had
own faith been greater, Dad's life might have been spare
would be years before we would tell one another how we
faced this guilt.

In the meantime, I found some respite from my depres
in the more immediate conflict between Mother and myself.
approached my 18th birthday, the distance between us gre
wanted freedom; she was frightened to give it to me. This cor
was aggravated by the fact that my sister, 22 years old
wanting to exercise more independence, had gotten her ⌐
apartment. Debbie's presence had served as something of a bu
between my mother and myself, and with her absence, the
sion at home increased. Thus, in spite of my attachment to
mother and my home, after one semester of college I felt m
imprisoned than secure. I moved out, aware of both Moth
disapproval and my own fear of leaving home. Yet I was ⌐
aware that my leaving brought both of us a sense of relief.

My first home away from home was a disaster. I ⌐
supporting myself and could not afford to live alone. I paired
with the first young woman I could find to share an apartm
with. We were utterly mismatched: She chain smoked, worke
night, and valued loud music and drinking parties far more t
serious studying. My home was truly not a home—week ⌐
week, I found myself in a sterile apartment with a woman I
not like. My sole form of transportation was a ten-speed bic
so escape after dark was nearly impossible. Contrary to my
pectations, moving out of my mother's house had not made
any better. I needed an escape, and found one, in Steve.

I met Steve, a man 4 years my senior, in a freshman ⌐
class at the university. He was a veteran of the Vietnam War,
in the States for only 3 years before we met. Our attractio
each other was immediate and intense. In spite of the fact th
was only 22, he seemed far older than the other men I had ⌐
By our second date I decided I wanted to see him exclusivel
he gave no indication that he intended to reciprocate. Nor
less, I continued to see him, becoming more dependent upc
time together to ward off the feelings of depression that
nearly always encroaching upon me now.

My first sexual experience was with Steve when I v

experienced a curious combination of safety, hope, and whole-ness. But the feelings would disintegrate the moment we parted, and I would be left with an emptiness that I could not face.

During my sophomore year of college, I attempted the first of several half-hearted escapes from my relationship with Steve. I left town to attend another university in the same state. Prior to this move, I had never ventured beyond my hometown, but had stayed put, unable to bear the separation of leaving the familiar places I knew. Now, only 4 hours away, I nonetheless felt as though I was at the end of the world, and I spent most evenings in tears and most nights sleepless. And with this move, I learned that if I ran away, Steve would follow in pursuit. I realized then I had not left the relationship, Steve and I had merely exchanged roles.

I was unable to endure the pain of being away from home for more than a semester. It seemed that only my grades survived the move; I conscientiously maintained a four-point average. At the end of the semester, I returned to my hometown and found an apartment of my own, reenrolling in the university my father had loved.

My relationship with my mother continued its painful downhill course: Both of us wanted closeness and peace; neither of us was able to understand the antagonism and friction that arose whenever we were together. In my rebellion, I experienced her as smothering, authoritarian, and unyielding. Yet she knew that my lack of social experience had left me ill prepared to cope with the adult life I was entering headlong. She was witness to my destructive acting out and remained helpless to do anything about it.

The return to my hometown also meant a return to my relationship with Steve. In spite of the fact that I had grown up in this town, I found myself without a life there that I could really call my own. I had let my sense of self come to depend totally on my relationship to Steve; if I were not with him, I was in a void, groundless, not knowing what to do with the incredible sense of emptiness that was always with me now, just beneath the sur-face. I was seeing fewer and fewer people and making almost no new friends at the university. I went to classes, returned to my apartment, studied if I could concentrate, and ruminated over where Steve was and when he might next call.

Steve's ambivalence about our relationship manifested itself in our dating pattern. We either spent time with his family members, to whom he was deeply attached, or spent evenings alone at his apartment. We never attended group functions or went out with our few mutual friends, as he was unwilling to convey to other people that we were dating. Above all else, Steve had a need to appear unattached, an indelible fact of his life that I seemed unable to accept as evidence that I should get out of the relationship permanently. I stayed with him, and I stayed unhappy, living always with the feeling that our next minutes together would be our last.

After 2 years of this, I had had enough of myself and my bounding between extremes of depression and emotional outbursts. At the smallest suggestion of Steve's interest in dating other women or wanting to spend less time with me, I was catapulted into a black depression—living for the moments he would call, obsessively counting the days between hearing from him. I had no motivation to be with other people. More and more, the time we spent together was given to arguments that quickly grew to hysterical proportions, spurred by my suspicion and possessiveness, which I had never experienced with my other boyfriends. I found myself weeping and dragging through the days.

Oddly, Steve always came back to me, as if in search of a reprieve from an ongoing sense of agitation that he seemed at a loss to calm. In hindsight, I suspect that his spending energy on the turmoil between us was, for him, preferable to focusing on the turmoil he had felt since his time in Vietnam. His inconsiderate behavior toward me seemed to increase his need for my forgiveness. One day, for example, he informed me that he had decided to marry his high school girlfriend (a woman who—I later learned—was at that time refusing even to see him). As he indicated to me that she was his current conquest, he attempted to rest his head in my lap, his common expression of a need for comfort. Perhaps there was within me then a seedling of self-respect, for I was able to push him away and leave. For once, I refused to see him—for a while, at least.

Yet my misery seemed never ending. I felt overwhelmed by a sense of hopelessness that seemed to disallow any ability to enjoy life. I knew I had to find help.

ENTERING THERAPY

Q: During your psychotherapy with Carolyn were you encouraging the transference phenomenon? To try and build up her trust in you in the therapeutic relationship?

A: There wasn't a necessity for encouraging it. My recall is that Carolyn trusted me almost from the word go.

After our second major breakup in what would ultimately become a series of separations from Steve, I felt frighteningly lost, confused as to who I was and what I should be doing with my life. I had isolated myself from my family, unable to bear my mother's emptiness and hurt, helpless to do anything about it. My college grades were dropping as my inability to concentrate increased. For the first time in my life, I was ambivalent about being alive. One of my friends told me of a colleague of hers who was in therapy with a psychologist who apparently really cared for her well-being. He would call her at work to "check up on her and see how she was doing." His name was Dr. X. On this recommendation, in the early fall of 1975, I entered therapy. I was 20 years old.

I remember walking into Dr. X's office feeling absolutely humiliated that I needed psychological help and, at the same time, feeling out of control emotionally. The first words this therapist ever spoke to me engendered within my naive self a sense of his omniscience. He gazed at me from head to foot and said, "Well, what's his name?" I was amazed, awed. In less than 5 seconds, he had deduced the source of my agony. I knew, with the certainty provided me by his rapid and correct assessment, that I had been right to seek help and that I had sought help from the right person.

After our first session, I took the Minnesota Multiphasic Personality Inventory (MMPI; see Chapter 12); our early meetings involved his learning about me. His notes indicate that he wrote down the facts he deemed important: family history and present family environment; my having been a relative "loner" all of my life: that I had not had sex for several months; the method of birth control I had used; that I had lied in order to maintain a relationship with Steve; that I felt deserted; and my

"4+" depression. Furthermore, he described me as a parasitic, highly dependent person for whom "godliness" was important.

My first impressions of Dr. X were based as much on his self-confident presentation as they were on my preconception of what a mature, wise, professional psychologist would be. He was a middle-aged, slightly graying man of average height and weight, a heavy smoker who wore a three-piece suit; his after-shave permeated the office, as did his air of confidence. Having come from a background wherein the older men I met were family friends and the incarnation of trustworthiness, I willingly and unquestioningly accepted Dr. X. I assumed that his interest would be in helping me get well.

NINE MONTHS IN THERAPY

I remember long periods of silence during the early sessions, when I struggled to understand the emotional emptiness and deadness I was experiencing. I was completely unaware of what therapy was about—what was I supposed to say and do in this office? Sometimes I felt completely lost as to how to cope with my ever-present pain, and I would simply sit with it in Dr. X's office. But in spite of the pain, I felt a sense of hope and safety now, especially from the frightening suicidal feelings that had been stirring within. This feeling of safety seemed to emanate from the room: a safety in the dark wood of the walls and desk, the shelves filled with prestigious-looking professional books I believed he must have studied in depth.

I tried to determine what Dr. X wanted me to say so that I might say it and thereby feel secure in his acceptance and affirmation of me. I held no assumption of equality between us. I was unable to assert myself on *any* level: When he asked if I minded his smoking, I could not tell him that I would have preferred he not smoke. I was unable to voice my resentment at paying for full sessions that frequently ended on time after beginning 10 minutes late because the previous patient had stayed beyond the allotted time. I was a passive, withdrawn patient, erroneously believing that therapy was like medical treatment: The doctor would give me some magic formula to bring about emotional health.

After some 2 or 3 months, I slowly began to realize that I

had to interact with Dr. X actively, that I must sincerely disclose my thoughts and fears. My attempts at confessing my anger with and resentment toward Steve were positive steps, and Dr. X stayed with me, unretaliating and indestructible in the face of a realm of emotions that I considered unacceptable and even dangerous but could no longer control.

I wanted Dr. X to take care of me—the way my father had not been able to do after the onset of his illness, or perhaps even before then. The kind of caretaking I wanted seemed so foreign yet so irresistibly inviting that I may have only imagined it was part of my life before Dad's death. But Dr. X *did* take care of me in his own way: He was very kind—never insincerely or sweetly kind, just calmly and quietly. His presence was self-assured but also warm, supportive, and steadfast. And in spite of feeling ashamed of needing to seek help, I never once, in those early months, doubted that I had done the right thing in entering treatment with him.

I was frightened to take emotional risks in therapy. For example, Dr. X once suggested that I might talk to my father, as I imagined him sitting in an empty chair, and tell him just how angry I was with him for dying. There it was, that chair in the corner, and for a brief moment I could indeed imagine my father there, weakened, pale, and with an odd look of questioning in his face. "What would you like to say to him?" Dr. X asked me, and suddenly I was flooded with grief. There was my father, smaller than I remembered him even in his illness, but strong in his heart, wondering how I had come to this point in my life, how I could have forsaken my mother, my church, my faith. And at that moment, I felt the first conscious whisperings of resentment and anger for his having deserted me, feelings that were only to be swept aside by shame for having them.

I seemed to live with shame for weeks during that part of my treatment, not only for being angry with my father for something beyond his control, but because I was living a life he would never have condoned. I had turned away from everything he had lived for; I had not kept myself pure of heart or body. I was bringing my mother pain when I was near her, or I was deserting her. And in spite of all the conflicting feelings about being sexually active, I continued my involvement with Steve; the idea of facing another loss was too painful to consider.

In December of that first year, Dr. X encouraged me to keep a journal and allow him to read it. This, too, proved to be therapeutically beneficial for me. This self-reflective activity enabled me to focus on how I felt about myself when I was alone or around others. At a time when I felt incapable of self-support, this exercise provided me with a sense of my therapist's support of me while I was away from him. I wrote directly to him in the entries. One of my early entries reflected my feelings of desolation:

> With myself, I feel lost, without direction, wanting some kind of help to know who I am and what I can do with myself. . . . I do not feel in control at all, I feel powerless. . . . I'm scared that inside me I am not being honest with myself. . . . I want to be honest, and healthy, and trusting—but I don't know where, or how, to begin.

Over the months, in my weekly 45- to 50-minute sessions, I have no doubt that much of the trust and love I had for my father was directed toward Dr. X, for I perceived him as having both wisdom and an unconditional concern for my well-being. I did not recognize at the time that this transference of feelings was occurring, but I did come to perceive him as a parental figure. And so I remained very dependent, working hard in therapy, in my eagerness for his acceptance and approval, believing him to be my sole source of affirmation.

Undoubtedly, Dr. X recognized my ongoing dependence on him, but we did not work to resolve it at this point in treatment. Rather than work on how I perceived him, Dr. X worked with me on the ongoing issues in my life: my feelings of confusion and despair in my relationship with Steve, my insistence that I remain in a relationship with a man who clearly did not want an exclusive relationship with me, my conviction that I could not survive without him. An earlier journal entry written to Dr. X had demonstrated to him how I interacted with Steve:

> I listened to what Steve said, feeding back what I think he wanted to hear . . . needing his approval so desperately . . . and scared that I'm not good enough . . . but I felt tense and wary . . . futile and angry . . . and I wanted to be distant . . . Insulated—since you used that word in a therapy session, I can't find a better word to describe how I feel so much of the time—and there's nothing that

feels lonelier . . . a gnawing ache in my gut . . . I can't be any kind of a companion—I don't know how to be. I was never "there" when I was around Steve—I want to know how to be "there." . . . I feel out of place and ugly—like extra baggage . . . like a mechanical doll—just saying what was expected of me . . . not a being, just hollow.

My grooming—such as my reluctance to use makeup—was a source for discussion in therapy. Clearly, I was resistant to taking on the female role that had been presented to me when I was a child; but we did not explore the implications of this resistance in terms of either my relationship with my mother or the covert negative value of being female that I had learned from my religious upbringing. Instead, Dr. X interpreted my tomboy manner as a means of avoiding intimate contact with men, and he challenged me to leave the "unfeminine" nature behind.

In an attempt to help me lessen my dependence on Steve, Dr. X frequently encouraged me to confront the independence I feared, to date other men and not hesitate to become sexually active with them. He praised me as I overcame my ambivalence toward having sexual affairs; he suggested that my behavior indicated I could now "take or leave" the monogamous relationship I had so much wanted with Steve. But my insecurity continued to give way to shame, and my inability to discern healthy relationships from unhealthy ones worsened. My judgment of what was destructive for me was terribly poor. I grew less able to say no to men who would gladly and readily have sex with me without the promise of any substantial commitment. I began to settle for the paltry sense of being loved that these short-lived affairs seemed to offer. Still, casual sex with the men I dated left me feeling even less in control of my life, less able to know with any certainty just what I wanted from these relationships and from myself. Nonetheless, I felt that I needed Dr. X's praise of my apparent independence; and lacking sufficient self-love and self-assurance, I clung to the immediate, though transient, affection I gleaned from the few affairs I had.

In late winter Dr. X read journal entries regarding trust in him and the wisdom he offered me in therapy. He also saw evidence of my entrenched tendency to take any anger with or mistrust in him and place it on myself:

> With you, I felt warm but at the same time, very vulnerable. . . . I felt relieved and able to relax, because while I know you've "been on to" my act for a long time, I think I finally believe that you're not out to shaft me with that knowledge. Anyway, although I'm at a loss as to what to be without my script, I didn't feel angry or uptight or defensive towards you today. . . . But most of the threat's gone—although I still don't know why you were a threat to me—unless it's because you are trying to kill parts of me—and even when those parts are full of shit, they're still me. . . . I just feel tired and worthless and ignorant of myself and things to do . . . ignorant about how to be a real person, and see you as one.

During the first 5 months of treatment, Dr. X taught me that my feelings of discomfort during our sessions were really signals of my resistance to a possible truth about myself. When he introduced a disturbing idea into therapy, I learned to listen to it in spite of the emotional discomfort it might produce. Then, in the sixth month of therapy, I complained about feeling sexually loose, a statement that required daring courage because it implied that I disagreed with his prescriptions, that I was hesitant to continue accepting his formula for mental health. I timidly stated that casual sex might not be as helpful for me as he had suggested. His response to my first attempt to stand up to him was his most disturbing suggestion to date. He wondered aloud if I was denying my sexual attraction for him.

2

Sex Enters the Therapeutic Relationship: "Trust Me," He Says

I remember quite clearly my spontaneous reaction to Dr. X's suggestion that I might be sexually attracted to him: astonishment, followed by a sense of uneasiness and confusion. He was so much older than I, or so he seemed to me. I felt like a child around him, like a struggling, searching, hurting child. This man was my surrogate father. A sexual attraction toward him was unthinkable, taboo, incestuous. Yet all of these reactions neatly fit my pattern of resistance to any of his therapeutic suggestions, and he patiently assured me that I needed to think about the two of us, and how we interacted, and whether or not there was some sexual attraction to him that I was denying. The session ended with my feeling a sense of distrust in the validity of my own reactions.

I still wanted a monogamous relationship with Steve, but

Dr. X insisted that my wanting such a relationship with a man as noncommittal as Steve indicated that I was just too frightened to explore other relationships. Monogamy, he stressed, could foster clinging, symbiotic relationships and was unhealthy for me since it further encouraged my dependency. He openly encouraged me to reach beyond my fears and insecurities. I was to continue my attempts to involve myself with men other than Steve and not forbid myself sexual encounters with them.

I dated very few men for any length of time, and I had especially brief relationships with the men with whom I had sex. The one relationship that lasted more than a few months was with a man living out of town, with whom I had infrequent dates. This pattern disallowed the development of anything beyond the superficial, even with the men who cared for me and wanted more than a casual relationship. I would inevitably break off with a man I was dating and return to Steve, who was never far from the center of my attention. He would grow more interested in me—to the point of proposing marriage from time to time—if my involvement with another man showed any signs of becoming serious. Our one formal engagement lasted a month, but we both managed to keep in check any real commitment to each other or to anyone else.

Significantly, I refused to have intercourse with Joe, the one man who fell deeply in love with me and who earnestly pursued a commitment from me for nearly 2 years. Dr. X would not explore this platonic relationship in therapy, although in more than one session I brought up my puzzlement concerning my fear of committing myself to Joe and the lack of sexual attraction I felt for him. This was of great concern to me because I enjoyed myself around Joe—of all the men I dated, only he could make me laugh and help me to forget my problems. Instead, Dr. X and I focused on the relationships in which I was sexually active. With each sexual relationship I had, however, I felt progressively insulated from all the men I dated. This in turn appeared to provide Dr. X with evidence of my "resistance" to him, which we worked on in therapy.

The stated goal of therapy became my evolution into a less depressed and more emotionally open, alive, reachable woman. Dr. X reassured me that my resistance to this was evident in my discomfort with being in more than one ongoing sexual relationship—my hesitancy to share myself sexually with men was my way of putting up emotional walls. Dr. X drew a parallel between my reluctance to polygamous sexual encounters and my denial of a sexual attraction to him. If I insulated myself from him in therapy, I would continue to insulate myself from others outside of therapy. I came to understand that my conflict was born exclusively of my own insecurities, that I had not only to trust Dr. X but somehow to show him that I trusted him.

Dr. X explained to me that sexual intercourse was like a handshake: a way men and women came to know one another. At one point in therapy, he talked about his own sexual encounters, indicating their value in increasing human contact. In describing to me one of his own brief affairs, he spoke of the value of having a sexual encounter without emotional attachments, an encounter wherein two people came together, had intercourse, and went their separate ways. Convinced that I needed to experience this kind of honesty, I continued having sexual affairs. We did not examine my diminishing self-esteem, my inability to assert myself and say no when I didn't want to be sexually active. We did not consider the ever-present fear that challenging the men I dated would cause them to abandon me. As we further explored the therapeutic goal of sexual openness, I began to have numerous anxiety-laden dreams. I recorded a very vivid one around this time:

> Steve left me at this place that was obviously a butcher shop, painted up to look sterile. The focus wasn't on him, although I experienced the feeling of desertion and/or rejection and helplessness that I so often experience in dreams about him or Dad. The focus was on the surroundings and my wanting out, because it was a butcher shop, but they said I had to stay. Then the dream changed, and some young people were taking me through an old, ghetto-like ghost town. I stopped at an old, half-torn-down shack and said, "This is the place," and they said, "No! It's haunted! You can't go near there!" and there was the child again—not the same one that overdosed in the other dream, but still a shabby child, she was in rags and her hair was scraggly—she resembled me physically when I was about ten years old, but she was wild, with haunting eyes, and she frightened me terribly. I approached her, although the others continued to protest, and I knew, if I go into this shack, the things I find will be bizarre and frightening.

We never connected my anxiety with the fact that engaging in numerous superficial affairs was in opposition to the religious values of my upbringing. We never discussed the possibility that the conflict and pain I experienced were natural responses to my promiscuity. We never looked at how a part of me had stopped growing when my father died. Yet the very part of me that remained a 16-year-old, mired in a childlike relationship with a father long dead, was feeling a child's shame for the young woman's promiscuity. Rather, Dr. X used dream interpretation to label my conflict an overt indication of my unwillingness to simultaneously trust him and take risks in sexual relationships with other men.

THE SEXUALIZATION OF THE THERAPEUTIC RELATIONSHIP

In the fifth month of therapy, I had depleted my savings, most of which came from Social Security checks I'd been receiving since my father's death. Dr. X was willing to charge me less to see him; he reduced his fee from $45 a session to $35, then to $20. I was indebted to him for his generosity, especially in light of the expense of running his private practice, which, he explained, was quite high.

I also felt grateful to him for his help in showing me how insecure I was with Steve and how that insecurity often led me to be manipulative and "phony" with people. We discussed, on many occasions, what Dr. X described as various "tricks" I could pull out of my "grab bag of manipulations." I used these tricks to avoid honesty, because I did not know how to recognize my own honest feelings, much less communicate them to Steve. I believe that Dr. X was right, and this part of my therapy was helpful to me. What was not helpful, however, was Dr. X's own refusal, or inability, to help me get in touch with my feelings about him. I did not dare to say what I felt about him when I knew it was not what he wanted to hear.

By the eighth month of therapy, the issue of my sexual attraction to Dr. X took a central place in therapy, and the sexualization of the relationship was underway. Dr. X hugged me after one session, prior to opening the door to his office. I experienced this physical contact as caring and paternal. But at the end of the next session, he briefly kissed me good-bye on my lips.

I walked out of his office feeling stunned, uncertain of what the kiss had meant. As with everything Dr. X did and said in therapy, I accepted this action without rebellion; and as with other men in my life, I did not feel empowered to express my own desire. That desire, had I been able to verbalize it, doubtless would have been a plea for a sexual moratorium. But I could not even consider what I wanted, or needed, in relationships with men. I felt and behaved like a chameleon with them, and with Dr. X most of all, searching for what they wanted and expected and never questioning my belief that defining myself by their wants and expectations was normal.

I had always talked with Dr. X from this chameleon-like orientation, looking to define myself in terms of what he indicated I should be. But I first overtly acted out this orientation during one of our next sessions. At this meeting, Dr. X told me that he once had a female patient who would come to therapy dressed in a skirt and wearing no underwear. She would sit with her legs spread apart in what he told me was "a very inviting manner." He had challenged her, he said, suggesting that she was trying to express her attraction to him in a passive, indirect way and that this was seductive but manipulative. A healthier way would be to express her feelings more directly. He then said, with an approving smile on his face, "And Carolyn, do you know what she did? She came in the very next session and stood right here by my desk and took her clothes off in front of me." That, he said, was a direct and healthy way of showing her feelings for him.

One wonders now whether it would have been therapeutic for Dr. X to have covertly challenged me at any point to compete with another of his patients, especially when the prize was what I valued so desperately—his powerful approving smile that said, "I condone who you are." But certainly at this point, I see with hindsight, that Dr. X's own personal problems were emerging in our sessions. And I, not knowing the difference between my own health and illness, much less his, took up the gauntlet. The following session, I entered the room, nervous and nearly dizzy at what I was going to dare to do to master the challenge he had issued. I stood by his desk, said hello, and quietly took my clothes off. And I did win the challenge. Dr. X smiled his gentlest and most approving smile and told me I was very pretty; then we talked about how I felt about behaving "in such an honest way" with him. It did not take long for me to be able to say that I felt exposed and that I was grateful when he nodded his assent to my question of whether he would not mind my getting dressed. When I left that session, I had the first experience of feeling more numbed after the hour than before.

For several meetings following this, Dr. X held me for longer moments at the end of each hour until one time he pulled my hips up against his genitals, an action that both frightened and confused me. As with everything he did in therapy, however, I did not challenge this action.

During this time, Dr. X repeated his interpretation of my response—that my inability to warm to his advances was indicative of my deliberate attempts to put up barriers in our relationship. I was, according to him, averse to attaining emotional well-being. We had long since decided that I was more comfortable in an unhealthy state, for that was the way I knew how to be. Emotional sickness was a companion, safe and controlling. Believing him, I felt my illness to be totally self-induced, and I grew even more despondent. Dr. X was aware of my tendency to assume total responsibility for my confusion, as indicated in sections of my journal:

> The thought, or feeling, or fear keeps coming out at me in the middle of times when I'm with friends: I'm unstable—and I feel hopeless—and I hate myself. . . . I almost felt listless when I left, but decided that was a cop out. So I went on and thought about what you said. I don't understand why I'm afraid to trust you and/or why I'm afraid of you. But I know I feel formless—without shape—and valueless (without values—and maybe without *value*, too). . . . I feel like masses of tangents right now—not a solid thing to my personality at all.

The no-win situation was not apparent to me then. Not to be attracted to Dr. X automatically labeled me sick. I could not doubt his interpretations of my resistance without doubting the doctor himself, and our entire therapeutic relationship. So I remained, unwilling to discount the trust I had spent 8 months building. I did not challenge him. I did not dare assert myself and state that I wasn't sexually attracted to him. And while I most often tried to gauge what he wanted to hear, and felt depressed if I thought I was saying the wrong thing, I could not go so far as to agree with his assertion that I was attracted to him. I chose the option I knew best: resigned muteness. And throughout it all, Dr. X never highlighted or challenged my need for acceptance, a need so intense that I would, in its service, forfeit my own feelings, opinions, and actions to his.

Finally, during a session not long before Dr. X began relaxation techniques with me, he stated that my denial of attraction to him, coupled with my growing uneasiness and resistance to having casual sex with the men I dated, suggested that I possessed a homosexual orientation. He suggested that I needed to consider exploring sexual relationships with women. It was, after all, in the company of a few college girlfriends that I felt safe, accepted, and cared for. I could share with them insecurities about my relationship with Steve, which was still going along its rollercoaster way. I could talk with them, too, about the spiritual loneliness and uncertainty I experienced after leaving the church at age 18.

At this time, lacking any substantial understanding of my own sexuality, the suggestion of lesbian encounters frightened me. I had been raised in a strictly heterosexual, homophobic culture. Yet now I faced this never-to-be-doubted doctor, an expert in the knowledge of the human mind, who was suggesting that I might be gay. The message was clear: My failure to feel sexually attracted to him proved that my heterosexuality was questionable.

SEDUCTION

In the summer of 1976, during my ninth month of therapy, I came to a session agitated and tearful. The swings between my feeling out of control and emotionally deadened had increased. Dr. X asked me to lie down on the floor of his office and relax; he remained in his chair and talked with me. I remember feeling greatly exposed as I lay belly up on the floor. I covered my face with my right arm for the entire session.

The next week, he repeated his request. Again I lay on the floor, my face covered. He sat beside me this time and rubbed my stomach, asking me if, and if so, why, that action made me nervous. I was frightened of his impatience with, and disapproval of, my unresponsiveness. My only response was not to object.

In the next session we went through the same ritual. I lay on the floor, feeling tense and exposed; my eyes were closed and again covered by my arm. He sat beside me, rubbing my stomach. This time, he unzipped and lowered my slacks and touched my genitalia. I felt simultaneously frightened and incredulous, then overcome with a helpless sense of resignation as I began to realize that these actions were leading to sex. As with everything else that Dr. X had done with which I felt uncomfortable (his smoking, his interpretations and suggestions, his more intimate physical contact), I could not confront him and express my discomfort with or dislike of his actions. I tried to think of other things: my schoolwork, my parents, my boyfriend. Not a word was spoken by either of us. In less than a minute, Dr. X rolled on top of me, penetrated me, and, moments later, climaxed.

In that moment I experienced, for the first time in my life, the absolute terror of dissociation. I found myself floating in the upper reaches of the room, unable to abide what I saw on the floor. I tried to envision that this was not going on, that I did not feel the utter humiliation of being used sexually while I lay there, frigidly unresponsive.

Dr. X talked of other things while pulling on his pants, as if what had happened were an experience neatly encapsulated unto itself that was to have no effect upon him or me. He ignored the message of my physical passiveness as he had ignored my resistance to his suggestions earlier in therapy. This first episode of sex with him was so alien to what I had expected from older men, doctors, and father figures that my image of who he should be clashed irreconcilably with what he was doing. During intercourse I felt nothing. Afterward, I felt ashamed, like a dirty little girl who could do nothing to clean herself up. And somehow I knew that I could not talk to anyone else about what had happened.

The deposition taken 2 years later reveals my frame of mind during that first occasion of intercourse:

Q: Did you in any way tell him to stop?
A: No, sir, I did not.

Q: And did you in any way struggle to stop him?

A: I was incapable of that.

Q: Why do you say that?

A: Because to have stopped him would have been the same as saying that his therapy was something I disagreed with. I did not feel competent to say I disagreed with any kind of therapy he was going to use.

Q: Well, had you ever heard at that point of psychologists using intercourse for therapy?

A: I had not heard of any kind of therapy before.

Over the next 12 months, sexual intercourse occurred during eight or ten sessions—nearly once a month. They were wordless, compartmentalized encounters, never more than 4 or 5 minutes long, always at the start of the session. On some occasions, Dr. X would begin with the relaxation approach; on others, he would methodically escort me into his office, lock the door, close the drapes, and pull me down to the floor. If he did not intend to begin the session with intercourse, he would not touch me at all. I don't know what determined his choice of when to have sex with me and when not to. I don't know how he saw himself during these episodes: as party to a fantasy love affair, as a helpful friend, as a therapist throwing caution to the wind, or as an exploiting individual who didn't give a damn about the powerful and painful consequences of his actions. I don't know how he saw himself because I never asked him. He never asked me what I thought of the sexual encounters. He never seemed concerned that I was growing more closed and automaton-like as the months passed.

Where Dr. X's first kiss had rendered my feelings simply evasive, intercourse with him now made my feelings race from me, beyond a point where I could retrieve them. And even though this numbing was deadening, it was also a relief. Unfortunately, perhaps, the numbing was only episodic. As Dr. X and I continued to have intercourse, my feelings would sometimes erupt in a sudden flood, tumbling forth into my awareness. I once felt special that he would consider me attractive; I more often felt confused that this was happening and ignorant of what to do. I felt angry because I saw no choice and guilty because this was premarital sex. And always, always, I felt shameful, because he was a father.

When these feelings did surface, I consciously refused to think about the sexual encounters. When I did, I was overwhelmed by vague and confused feelings: anger and loss, and a sense that Dr. X had meant to show me how much he cared for me. At the same time, I felt unbearable anger that I turned toward myself, rather than toward him, and fear born of a powerless sense that it would happen again and I would not be able to stop it. I felt more lost than I had when I began therapy. And rather than acknowledge these feelings, I pushed them aside, convincing myself that he, the professional, could be trusted to help me, regardless of his methods. It was easier for me to believe in him, to try to understand that whatever he was doing was in some way meant to help me, than it was to deal with my guilt for participating in what felt so unclean.

During that year of sexual encounters, Dr. X talked about his own interpersonal problems. He spoke frequently of his anger with his estranged wife, his sense of helplessness in the face of the divorce that was underway, and his own unhappiness in his relationships with his parents and colleagues. Discussion of my problems grew less frequent, but I did not challenge this: His misery was evident, and I both cared for him and felt a sense of obligation to him—even though he continued to charge me for sessions in which discussion of my issues was replaced by discussion of his own. Nonetheless, I held to my basic hope that he could provide the answers that would lift my depression and make sense of my confusion.

Yet as the sexual encounters continued, it became less difficult for me to see the inappropriateness of the situation. What I had resisted believing slowly grew more conceivable to me: Dr. X had capitalized on both my dependence upon him and my inability to trust my own feelings. More than anyone in my life, he understood that my relationships with men were driven by a fear of separation and rejection, and he acted on that knowledge deliberately. He took what I now believe was a natural and normal resistance to having sex with a paternal figure and set it up as an obstacle to be overcome. I believed his advances to mean that my having sex with him was a legitimate action in the process of changing the immature and unhealthy way I related to men. This interpretation was supported when, immediately following one of our last sexual encounters, he offered me a therapeutic hope with these words: "I felt a breakthrough—like I finally got through to you."

I had not been able to leave therapy. To do so would have meant that I would never get well. I could not reject Dr. X, the authority upon whom I relied, and was paralyzed by the notion of confronting him directly. In my first indirect attempt to stop the sexual intercourse, I discontinued taking birth control pills. Dr. X's angry response to this was that it was an adept maneuver to close off emotional relationships with men. But he would not stop his sexual advances, and when intercourse occurred, he would withdraw as he climaxed and ejaculate on the floor.

My next move was to lessen the frequency of office visits to twice a month. The sessions had become little more than anxiety-producing experiences in preparation for which I would emotionally anesthetize myself. Hours before going to Dr. X's office, I would clamp down on my confused feelings and angry thoughts. I could not turn to Dr. X for help, and whatever other outlets I may have had in friends or family were made inaccessible by the desire not to reveal my shameful participation in my own exploitation. Mine was a self-imposed isolation, as I tried to push further from my mind the growing awareness of Dr. X's betrayal.

In the midst of this aberrant relationship, with so many of the unresolved issues concerning my father and my own sexuality mixed up with the new issues created by my having sex with Dr. X, any chance of productive therapy was undone. I felt increasingly that my efforts at getting well were futile, and as the months went by, I knew I was getting no better. I began to feel a greater sense of responsibility for Dr. X's sexual advances toward me. And I found myself growing resentful of the other men in my life: My reactions to sexual intercourse with Dr. X—dissociation to another time or place or a blanket numbing of my feelings—began occurring when I would have sex with my boyfriends. My ambivalence about continuing to be sexually intimate with Steve, upon whom I was still emotionally dependent, was intensifying. Therapy was giving me no effectual way to cope with my problems, and I was beginning to feel as though I were paying to service Dr. X sexually as well as to listen to his problems. Even so, I still did not possess the strengths I needed to challenge him openly about the validity of his therapeutic methods; I was not yet willing to risk losing not only the one person I had totally trusted, but also the illusion that he was trustworthy to begin with.

TERMINATING THERAPY

Earlier in treatment, I had been hesitant to broach the subject of ending therapy, convinced that my lack of sexual responsiveness toward Dr. X and my decreasing sexual responsiveness toward other men were symptoms of emotional illness. I had sincerely believed that therapy was essential and could work.

Fortunately, outside experiences helped me to raise my self-esteem. In my senior year of college, I began student teaching high school students, who, en masse, possessed the disarming ability to care for me unconditionally. This stimulus reawakened an embryonic self-caring that had lain dormant for 6 years. With this self-caring came the realization that, by contrast, the confused, disoriented feelings surrounding my sexualized therapy sessions were irreconcilable with emotional health. Rather then assert myself, however, I started seeing Dr. X every other week. After another episode of intercourse, I dropped back to 30-minute sessions, but I claimed the reason to be due to financial troubles. I would not directly address Dr. X with my feelings about his behavior. But I had finally acknowledged the conflict to myself. Although I did not want to believe that Dr. X would use me, I realized that I was, in fact, being sexually exploited.

My actual decision to stop treatment with Dr. X seemed to force itself upon me, as though the part of me wanting to be healthy would no longer be denied, regardless of how much I numbed my feelings. The event that led to the decision occurred when I called Dr. X at home one evening, distraught after Steve and I had broken our one formal engagement to be married. I was weeping, angry, overcome by fear of impending desertion. Dr. X told me to come to his home immediately, and we would talk there. When I arrived, he met me at the door, took my hand, and, without a word, led me into a bedroom. He closed the door behind us, and began kissing me. Before another minute had passed, he was taking my clothes off. I was still in tears, still wanting to talk about Steve, still fantasizing that Dr. X would empower me in some way to make Steve be the person I wanted him to be. I did not object when he pushed me back on the bed and entered me. The physical act was identical to what had occurred in his office—brief, nonmutual, mechanical. I retreated into what was now a familiar emotional shell and confused my numbed feelings that always accompanied sex with Dr. X with the calming down of my anxiety about Steve.

But the numbing did not last long, and I finally allowed myself to see the very cold and very harsh truth of what was happening to me. I was being used, and I knew I did not want to be used anymore. I knew then that I would not have sex with Dr. X again. This insight gave me the much needed strength to consider terminating therapy. I was determined to end what I finally understood to be an abuse of the fundamental principle of psychological treatment—trust.

Still, I couldn't reconcile Dr. X's actions with my perception of him. I could not understand his motivation for deliberately harming me, for causing me to feel a kind of shame and hurt that I had not known before. This paradox haunted me at the time, and in some ways, it haunts me still.

I remained emotionally unequipped to challenge Dr. X. I still could not confront him with my realization that his therapy was at once inappropriate, unprofessional, unethical, and—above all else—harmful to me. Instead, I told him that I didn't think the school district, my employer-to-be, would keep me on if I were undergoing psychological treatment. Although he must have known that this would be highly unlikely and that it was a questionable reason for terminating treatment, he never questioned me about it, never encouraged me to challenge him honestly.

He did tell me, however, that he felt jealous of the latest sexual relationship I had just entered. I remember feeling confused—I still wanted to please him and assure myself of his approval, yet I found that my actions toward that end now made him jealous. I felt responsible for his jealousy and at once was angry for the double bind in which I again found myself with him. At last my first sense of conscious anger with Dr. X began to emerge. Perhaps it was this anger that helped me to realize that the last beneficial shreds of the patient–doctor relationship were lost. Dr. X had traded them for his warped preference of acting out his own needs with a self-doubting patient.

The disillusionment I experienced, necessary though it was and too long in coming, also brought me grief. I was only beginning to realize the implications of my neediness. I had settled for an abusive form of contact rather than risking no contact at all. I was ashamed of myself. But I was also angry with Dr. X. He had methodically sabotaged my self-trust. He had disabled my sense of direction and my judgment. I had lost any chance of resolving the problems I brought to him initially. I had lost the opportunity to deal with the additional conflicts that had emerged in the course of therapy. And I had lost another father.

THE AFTERMATH

I terminated therapy in the summer of 1977, almost 2 years after I'd begun. Within a mere 2 months, the combined effects of the sexual abuse and the unresolved problems that had originally prompted me to enter psychotherapy made life seem unbearable. I was burdened with an unending depression, and my thoughts progressed from occasional ideas about suicide to a studied contemplation of it. I experienced a pervasive sense of having no control over my life. I felt helpless to affect the world around me, helpless to affect my inner world. I was torn between caring for the once-trusted Dr. X and hating the therapist who had used me sexually. My confusion emerged in the form of violent dreams that brought me screaming into wakefulness. They were recurring nightmares that would haunt me during this period of my life: visions of Dr. X chasing me with a knife through large houses full of dark passages and unknown rooms, nightmares of finding myself in a war-besieged city, where he offered sanctuary to women as they passed by while my warnings to them not to go with him went unheeded; dreams of dancing while paralyzed from the waist down, wanting to trust someone to carry me because I could not carry myself, and knowing that I was lost when I saw the face of Dr. X.

My depression and confusion seemed beyond hope. My

unresolved fear of, and anger with, my father's helplessness over his death became enmeshed in my anger at my ex-therapist, which in turn was enmeshed in my own personal shame. I desperately wanted to love myself at the same time that I perceived myself as completely unlovable. And though I wanted to trust others, I could not overcome my fear of being emotionally maligned again.

I was viciously angry with myself that my own naiveté had left me unable to recognize Dr. X's duplicity soon enough to save me from further emotional scarring. I believed I would always be unable to choose and maintain a healthy relationship. Staying in what was a contemptible excuse for therapy after the first sexual encounter further validated this self-distrust. Not surprisingly, I continued to isolate myself from my family. If anyone in our family had sought psychological treatment before, I had not known of it—I thought I was the first to be in enough trouble to need help. Two years earlier, when I told my mother that I was in therapy, there had been a tearful episode, and I had felt shame at my weakness. Telling her what had happened in treatment—how my wonderful doctor had not been a savior but an exploiting sham—was beyond me.

I carried with me a dark secret—I believed myself a failure in therapy, a failure for reasons that I was too ashamed to share. I dismissed Dr. X's responsibility in the matter and blamed myself for what had occurred between us.

My shame was compounded by immense guilt as I clung to my involvement with Steve. I acted out my anger over his affairs by having affairs myself, realizing even as I did that I did not love these men but exploited our relationships to hurt Steve. Had I been more stable, perhaps more at peace with myself, perhaps freer of the impact of my experience with Dr. X, I might have been able to see that some of these men were actually in love with me, but in my tenacious and obsessive clinging to Steve, I remained emotionally distant, untouchable.

There were very few healthy relationships in my life; suspicion and distrust characterized most of them. I held at arm's length many of my friends, lovers, and members of my family. The issue for me had become one of not trusting again unless my judgment could be infallible: a tidy guarantee of emotional insulation from any other exploiters I might run into. I suspected the loving, caring people in my life just as I did everyone else, and was just as likely to push them away.

In my more self-scrutinizing moments I realized—and despaired over—the psychological labor that lay ahead. If I were to resolve the emotional chaos that I felt within, I would have to get help. But I had neither enough love for myself nor trust in others to seek out another therapist as soon as I should have.

THERAPY AGAIN

I entered therapy once again, after about 3 months of increasing despondence. Relying on my trust of men of the church, I sought a recommendation from my preacher. He put me in touch with a minister trained in family and marriage counseling. My only self-admitted reason for returning to therapy was—again—the relationship with Steve. My disabling fear of separation from Steve had not lessened, and his own ambivalent attraction toward me kept him returning to me after countless breakups. When he threatened separation, I wept uncontrollably, and my grief for my father surfaced at the same time. I could not stop my overreactive, hysterical behavior upon each breakup, nor could I act on my own slowly emerging wish that each separation would be final.

As I entered treatment with this minister, and slowly began to trust him, we occasionally spoke of my past treatment. I had not revealed to him my reasons for having left therapy, and if he wondered, which I believe he did, he did not ask. During a session some 2 months into treatment, however, he began pushing me to explore my extreme reluctance to really trust him. Then, before either one of us was aware of what was happening, I cried out at him in anger, unaware that I was calling him by Dr. X's name. We were both surprised, I believe, at the outburst, and when he gently reminded me that he was not Dr. X, I began to weep with a force I had known only once before—when grieving alone the day after my father died.

The floodgates were opened, and the sense of shame that I had for this incestuous-like relationship was overshadowed by a greater sense of relief that I could share it with someone. My counselor grieved as he learned of the sexual exploitation. But it did not surprise him—he had heard of this before, with Dr. X. I have no doubt that it was his concern for me that led him to suggest that I not pursue the matter legally. He tried to assure me that sooner or later someone would "blow Dr. X's cover." My own fears also kept me still: I knew that the victim was inevitably suspect in a crime of this type, and my sexual exploitation by Dr. X had not been a solitary episode but had occurred repeatedly over a period of 12 months.

My ability to share my dark secret, to experience a sense of unconditional trust in him, led me to explore my difficulties in trusting other men. Although I voiced my wonder as to whether or not I had gained anything whatsoever from therapy with Dr. X, I was not ready to explore in any depth the effects of the incestuous relationship. Instead, I worked intensely to confront my grief and confusion over my ongoing relationship with Steve. The minister helped me to start looking at the anger I was holding in. His straightforward approach helped me clarify my confusion and release some of the rage that neither of us had quite expected to find. Becoming aware of my anger in its unsuppressed strength was a beginning to the process of healing. The minister's validation of my right to be angry was a great help. I became aware, slowly and painfully, of what Dr. X had done to me and what I had allowed to happen. I was not ready to forgive him or myself for this, and I would not be ready to do so for many years.

After 3 months of treatment, I could no longer afford to see the minister and was unwilling to go into further debt for therapy. I had paid Dr. X $2,200 and was still paying off a $1,500 bill, $10 and $20 at a time. But I felt a fondness and gratitude for this religious counselor. He had helped me through the point in my life when I was most suicidal—a hideous New Year's eve I spent alone after Steve told me he was taking another woman with him to spend the evening at his parents' home. In desperation I called my counselor, whose stern words to me let me know just how angry he would be with me if I threw my life away over someone like Steve. For this more than anything else, I have felt grateful to him. During my work with him, I had tried to understand my dependence on Steve, to determine ways I could experience myself as an individual separate from him. I did not reach these goals then, but I took my first steps in their direction.

3

The Discovery of Other Victims: I Am Not Alone

After the minister and I first discussed the possibility of my filing a complaint against Dr. X, we gave the matter no further consideration. Within 2 months after I ended my treatment with him, however, during my first year as a high school teacher, one of my students served as a catalyst for my taking legal action. She told me one day that she was seeing a psychiatrist at her mother's insistence, to resolve some emotional concerns. The psychiatrist who was treating her practiced across the hall from Dr. X. I realized that this 16-year-old child might just as easily have ended up in Dr. X's office. What would stop another child—or another adult, for that matter—from entering therapy with Dr. X? What would deter him from exploiting another naive woman? I found myself unable to face this trusting youngster until I had made the silent commitment to do what I could to bar this unethical therapist from further practice, to call him to account publicly.

VARIATIONS ON A THEME

Two weeks later, in the early spring of 1978, I learned through friends that Suzanne Brown, a local attorney practicing family law, was representing another of Dr. X's ex-patients in a malpractice suit against him. I was not surprised that someone else was suing him. I had never entertained the idea that I was the only patient whom Dr. X had approached sexually. I even felt a sense of relief in this realization.

I made an appointment with Suzanne Brown the day I was given her name. She later told me that as she listened to me tell my story, she felt a sense of eeriness because it was so strikingly similar to that of her first client. There were, at best, minor variations on the same theme. Had Brown not known better, she could have picked up my story whenever I paused and filled in the details herself. What I told her affirmed her suspicion that Dr. X had a systematic *modus operandi,* wherein he developed and subsequently exploited at least two patients' trust and dependence.

THE FIRST PLAINTIFF: BREACH OF CONTRACT

As I talked more with Brown, I learned briefly of the other case involving Dr. X and one of his female patients. Three months before, the young woman had contacted her and stated that she had been sexually abused by a psychologist during treatment. The first client's reaction had been quite different from mine. She recognized the sexual intercourse as misconduct by a therapist. Feeling that she should not have been billed for the session in which intercourse occurred, she directly confronted Dr. X, who refused to refund her money. She then sought an attorney, to take action on what she considered to be a breach of contract, wanting Dr. X to reimburse her for the session.

Brown learned that Dr. X had told her client he would publicly deny her accusations. They decided she should return to his office with a concealed microphone, hoping he might admit his actions in a taped conversation. I learned about the general outcome of the meeting from Brown. The first client had asked Dr. X why he engaged in intercourse with her and why in his office. He admitted to her that the sexual intercourse had been destructive on his part, but that his life was troubled and that he himself felt victimized, believing that he cared too much for people and thus got himself into trouble.

Brown believed that the overall content of this first transcript did not give her sufficient bargaining strength. Thus the client, quite bravely I thought, returned to Dr. X's office. During this visit, Dr. X again admitted that he had engaged in intercourse with her. He also admitted his breach of ethics in having had sexual contact with her. And he declared that he would lie to keep his license.

Upon hearing about what Dr. X had said, it seemed to me that he recognized his inability to exercise competent judgment as the woman's therapist at the time: He had stated that he felt caught between wanting to be her friend and her therapist. But I was astonished when Brown told me Dr. X had promised that there was absolutely no chance that he would repeat his sexual advances with another patient.

SEARCHING FOR CO-COUNSEL

In deciding to take my case, Suzanne Brown considered not only the similarities between my story and her first client's, but also the differences. She recognized that she now had two clients sincere in their wish to pursue both a licensing complaint and civil litigation. Thus she wrote to Dr. X, telling him of the existence of the tapes.

In spite of the incriminating evidence, Brown suspected that the ensuing legal battle would cost far more than she could afford. She accepted both the cases against Dr. X on a contingency basis but needed the assistance of co-counsel to help defray the anticipated costs. She contacted several lawyers in town. The first attorney she approached was unwilling to take the case because he thought it would not be personally remunerative. The second attorney required that Brown front part of the money, something her small firm could not afford. Finally, she called Bill Whitehurst, a young, successful attorney who was rapidly gaining experience in malpractice and personal-injury suits. He was immediately interested and became intrigued by the taped evidence.

In the meantime, Dr. X read the transcripts and quickly acknowledged their veracity. Soon thereafter, he was on the phone to me, calling several times in one day. My roommate intercepted the calls, while I tried to reach Brown or Whitehurst. At one point, I listened in on Dr. X's plea to my roommate that she put me on the phone. He told her that I would destroy his practice and ruin his life if I continued with the litigation. It was incredibly painful to hear the distress in his voice. I again retreated into that emotional shell—the shell I had first known during therapy with him—where I was safe from my feelings. Within the hour I reached Whitehurst, who quickly demanded that Dr. X's attorney "call him off."

Through his attorney, Dr. X offered a settlement that included an agreement not to see any female patients for 1 year, and a pledge to enter some form of therapy himself. He further offered the plaintiffs the opportunity to police his practice on a monthly basis, through the review of his clientele load. On the advice of Brown and Whitehurst, we declined the settlement.

At this point, Whitehurst believed that the case had overcome two potential obstacles. First, the tapes were our defense should we be charged with accusing Dr. X falsely. Second, the taped conversations themselves offered substantial proof that Dr. X took responsibility for his actions.

Although my story and that of the first client differed significantly in several ways—in our initial responses to the seduction and in our manner of dealing with it—our attorneys were greatly impressed by certain similarities—by discussions of an alleged sexual attraction that we had for Dr. X, the gradually increasing physical contact, and his instructing us to relax on the floor. In addition, we both sought treatment in order to resolve similar issues in our heterosexual relationships. Finally, we both perceived Dr. X as a father figure and subsequently grew dependent upon him and trusted his skills and intentions.

Whitehurst envisioned demonstrating Dr. X's liability by proving psychological and emotional damages. In order to prove such damages, psychological data on each plaintiff taken prior to the seduction had to be obtained and compared with data taken afterward. Dr. X's records were procured through a court order, and we were given a new battery of psychological tests. The attorneys initially chose a local psychologist to administer the tests. We completed a life history questionnaire and underwent a diagnostic interview. We were given the revised Wechsler Adult Intelligence Scale, the Bender Gestalt Test, the MMPI, the Forer Sentence Completion test, the Rorschach Test, and the Thematic Apperception Test. The results of these and future tests that I took, required for the purposes of litigation, are discussed in Chapter 12.

THE THIRD PLAINTIFF: ALLEGED ABUSE OF A MINOR

Brown and Whitehurst filed their third client's case against Dr. X the day before the statute of limitations would have run out. This case was far more difficult than—and different from—the first two: It involved drug abuse by the patient and alleged neglect on Dr. X's part.

This young patient had first met Dr. X when, as a teenager, she had been hospitalized after running away from home and displaying aggressive behavior. He had seen her for a psychological evaluation at a time when his behavior, as he described it, was "very macho-istic." She was in group therapy with him during her stay at the hospital and entered individual therapy 3 years later for the treatment of mental health problems and substance abuse. She was a minor at the time the first alleged abuse had occurred. The span of time during which Dr. X was treating her in individual therapy overlapped my time in treatment with him. She had sought out Brown and Whitehurst after reading of the first two suits against Dr. X.

When the third suit was filed, Dr. X expressed his own sense of victimization when he told one reporter: "This is ridiculous. If it isn't clear to anyone by this time what is happening, it never will be. What can I say?"

While he would eventually admit to having engaged in intercourse with me and Brown's first client, Dr. X would only admit to holding this young woman in his lap. His approach to sexual contact with her was somewhat different from his behavior with me and the first plaintiff: He allegedly knelt on the floor in front of her and commented on the size of her breasts. In his deposition, however, at least part of the sexual scenario appeared markedly similar to that documented in the first two suits:

> Q: Did you ask her to lie down on your floor and relax?
> A: I remember her lying on my floor on one occasion. I remember being on the floor. I don't know whether we were lying side by side or . . . sitting on the floor but we were both on the floor in my office.

Nevertheless, Dr. X would never admit to the third ex-patient's allegations, in particular those stating that he had fondled her during her first stay at the hospital, when she was a teenager. To do so would have meant risking the felony charge of sexual abuse of a minor.

FURTHER RESEARCH

Of primary concern to Brown and Whitehurst were previous cases of this nature in the United States. Their search for precedents disclosed that few civil suits had been brought by patients against their therapists for sexual misconduct, and few of those cases had been won. Nevertheless, their search of published material on the subject proved enlightening and forewarned them of the unavoidable publicity that would focus on their clients' private lives. They had struggled for some time over how best to handle the delicate and intimate nature of our cases. They finally decided to offer as much detail as necessary rather than wait for the defendant's lawyers to elicit it from us. They based this decision on three issues brought out in their research.

First, they discovered that the pleading they were to file would need far more detail than a general pleading. In the latter, they need only to have stated, "During the course of therapy, the defendant had sex with the plaintiff." This would have allowed Dr. X to counter with, "But it was just an affair"; "she tried to seduce me"; or "we had a personal relationship outside of therapy." Second, they believed that Dr. X's repetitive *modus operandi* would speak for itself if they could bring to light his unethical behavior through a presentation of our statements. Finally, they hoped to avoid some of the intimate and intrusive questioning during our depositions by offering the information at the outset. Thus the lawyers wrote directly into the pleadings, in explicit detail, our narratives of what had happened in Dr. X's office.

THE OTHER WOMEN

When the story of the lawsuit—including detailed accounts of Dr. X's sexual advances—appeared in the local newspapers, Suzanne Brown was flooded with phone calls from other ex-patients of Dr. X. Some of these women stated that the newspaper accounts were descriptions of what had happened to them. Brown and Whitehurst discussed each woman's story, wondering how it might help the two cases and whether they would have to file a class-action suit against Dr. X. While several women expressed interest in coming forward as witnesses, several could not or would not be able to help. Many feared the emotional ordeal, while others feared the publicity. None was interested in pursuing a case of her own.

Of the women who called, 6 agreed to act as witnesses. Of those 6, the attorneys chose not to use anyone whose alleged experience of sexual abuse had involved notably different methods of seduction. Whether or not they could be used as witnesses in the first two cases, all 6 women shared a single desire: They wanted assurance that Dr. X would not continue to make sexual advances toward his patients.

4

The Labyrinth of Civil Litigation: Where Are We Going, and When Will We Get There?

QUIET NEGOTIATIONS

Prior to filing the first two lawsuits against Dr. X and making the cases public, Brown and Whitehurst negotiated with Dr. X's insurance company. They believed that much of the cases' initial value lay in our capacity to mar Dr. X's reputation. They reasoned that if he were interested in protecting his reputation, he might be interested in negotiating and thus preventing the cases from being filed. Apparently, either Dr. X or his insurance company was not so inclined. Brown and Whitehurst failed in negotiations, so in the summer of 1978 we filed malpractice suits in the state district court, charging professional negligence, assault and battery, deceptive trade practice, fraud and deceit, breach of contract, and intentional infliction of emotional distress. My lawsuit stated in part:

Defendant, as a psychologist licensed to and practicing psychology . . . owed a duty to Plaintiff to exercise the standard of care of psychologists in this community in his relationship and treatment of Plaintiff.

Defendant failed to exercise that standard of care in his relationship with and treatment of Plaintiff, in that Defendant:

a) failed to provide any constructive psychotherapeutic treatment for Plaintiff;

b) sexually assaulted and abused Plaintiff, his patient, under the guise of psychotherapy;

c) failed to terminate his psychologist/patient relationship with his client and refer her for proper psychological care;

d) encouraged dependence on himself as the one trustworthy male figure in Plaintiff's life.

Such conduct specifically violates the ethical standards of Dr. X's profession as set forth in the American Psychological Association's Ethical Standards of Psychologists [1981], which provides in pertinent part:

. . . Psychologists are continually cognizant of their own needs and of their inherently powerful position *vis a vis* clients, in order to avoid exploiting their trust and dependency. Psychologists make every effort to avoid dual relationships with clients and/or relationships which might impair their professional judgment or increase the risk of client exploitation. Examples of such dual relationships include treating employees, supervisees, close friends or relatives. Sexual intimacies with clients are unethical.

CIVIL LITIGATION

Early in the proceedings, Whitehurst warned me that a suit against Dr. X might prove to be the first of two lawsuits. A second suit, against Dr. X's insurance company might be required to prove their responsibility for covering sexual misconduct, something they denied from the beginning. Thus I realized I was getting myself into something that could drag on for years. The temptation to "jump ship" crossed my mind more than once.

Within 2 days of filing the suit, Dr. X's attorney responded in court, "denying each and every allegation made in [the] plaintiffs' petitions." Served with a list of written questions drawn up by Brown and Whitehurst, Dr. X denied many of the allegations. Yet his responses would change, both with time and with the forum in which he was questioned. For example, Dr. X adamantly denied Interrogatory Request 73: "That during the course of your treatment of Plaintiff you violated that section of the American Psychological Association's Code of Professional Ethics which states: 'Sexual intimacies with clients are unethical.'" But the following month, when facing the revocation of his license before the state licensing board for psychologists, he affirmed the chairman's final question: "In your professional judgment are you guilty in your own mind by your own standards that you have internalized and embraced of the profession, that you have committed unprofessional conduct in regard to the specific allegations that [the complainant] makes?" (Dr. X would lose his license, temporarily, as a result of these hearings, as discussed in Chapter 5.)

Nonetheless, early in the civil proceedings, Dr. X attempted to distort the nature of the patient–doctor relationship. He argued first that a dual relationship had existed between himself and each of the two patients and, second, that we were never charged for the minutes in which sexual contact occurred. In response to Interrogatory Request 70: "That you billed Plaintiff for each session of treatment with Plaintiff whether or not sexual intercourse was involved," Dr. X responded: "I can neither admit nor deny the above request for the following reason: She may have been charged for the session but was never charged for the time intercourse took place."

The issue of the context of sexual intercourse would prove to be a crucial argument in these cases. We claimed that he had induced us to have sexual intercourse in his office during psychotherapy sessions for which we had been charged and that we had considered the intercourse to be a part of that therapy. Dr. X insisted that the intercourse was separate from, and in addition to, therapy. He asserted that a personal relationship existed between himself and each of us. Thus, he claimed, we were psychologically free of a patient identity and thereby able to consent to the intercourse.

Dr. X fully refused to answer any interrogatories that might have identified any of his other patients as witnesses. The gist of these unanswered questions is illustrated by Interrogatory Request 50, which would find its way to the center of legal battles that eventually spanned the entire gamut of the state's courts:

> Please state whether you have kissed, touched, hugged, fondled or had any sexual contact of any type, including sexual intercourse, with any other current or former patient you have undertaken to treat.
> If so, please state:
> a) the full name of each such patient;
> b) the date of each sexual contact;
> c) a complete description of each act of sexual contact; and
> d) whether each act of sexual contact occurred in your office or some other location. If at some other location, give the full street address of said locations.

ROUND 1: THE STATE DISTRICT COURT,
THE STATE SUPREME COURT,
THE CIRCUIT COURT OF APPEALS

In October, Dr. X submitted a protective order to the state district court judge attempting to prevent any information regarding his other patients from being presented. He claimed that this information was not relevant and he argued that disclosing other patients' records would violate his constitutional rights of privacy as both a therapist protecting his clients and as an individual protecting himself. Brown and Whitehurst argued that the information was essential to their demonstrating how Dr. X's intentional actions were manifestations of a general scheme of abuse. They were certain that Dr. X used a predetermined plan of action in his seductions of patients.

Interrogatory Request 50 would never be answered successfully. Perhaps its Achilles' heel was in the generalizations that were not exclusive to sexual contact. The words *touched* and *hugged* broadened the behavior under scrutiny, and Dr. X's attorney objected to this. He argued that if such evidence of alleged sexual contact with other patients were to be admissible, then the trial might involve every female patient ever treated by Dr. X. The therapist would then

> be entitled to place on the witness stand every female patient with whom he had no sexual relations, those with whom he had

sexual relations, if any, prior to or subsequent to the period of psychological treatment, and those with whom he had sexual relations, if any, at the time of but in addition to his psychological treatment. . . . Extreme jury confusion and prejudice would necessarily follow.

In response to Dr. X's claim to a constitutional right of privacy, Brown and Whitehurst argued that this right did not include a psychologist's sexual contact with patients. In particular, given the therapist's claim that the intercourse occurred apart from the doctor–patient relationship, they argued that

> under state law, communications between physicians and their patients are not privileged. . . . No statute . . . has been enacted granting such a privilege to psychologist–patient communications. . . . Considering the contention of [Dr. X] that his sexual acts with patients were not a part of treatment, [Dr. X] is inconsistent if he is now arguing that his acts are protected by any type of physician's or psychologist's privilege.

The state did recognize a limited common law right to privacy. Brown and Whitehurst believed, however, that while the information requested was embarrassing, it was of legitimate public concern. Furthermore, it was possible to assure the patients' privacy: Dr. X could submit the names in a sealed envelope, with the court maintaining jurisdiction over the disclosure and over the issuing of subpoenas. In all records, the names could be correlated to letters of the alphabet. Finally, a female mental health professional could make initial contact with the patients upon Brown and Whitehurst's discretion.

The judge ordered Dr. X to provide our attorneys with the answers to Interrogatory Request 50 but restricted the question to the times when Dr. X was treating the complainants. The answers were to be filed with the court in a sealed envelope and a copy sent to the plaintiffs' attorneys, the information therein not to be made public.

Determined not to relinquish the information, Dr. X was held in contempt of court and ordered to jail until the names were supplied. Arrested the following day, he was immediately freed on a $100 bond while he tested the law before a higher court. The state supreme court, however, would not hear either side's arguments and refused to overturn the contempt judgment against Dr. X. The therapist quickly applied for another writ, to the district federal court. Again the judge upheld the order.

Next, Dr. X brought the issue before the appellate court. Although the circuit court of appeals had agreed to hear our arguments, a new obstacle had arisen. While Dr. X's appeal was pending, the state legislature had enacted a statute, to be put into effect in the summer of 1979, that deemed physician–patient communications confidential and privileged from disclosure. The circuit court was unwilling to make a far-reaching decision on Dr. X's claim of a constitutional right to privacy. Instead, it referred the issue to the district court, instructing that court to determine whether the new statute might be applied in our case. We were now in our second year of litigation, and the process was feeling increasingly like a legal merry-go-round.

ROUND 2: THE DISTRICT COURT, THE STATE SUPREME COURT

Reconsidering his previous judgment, the district court judge determined that the statute would not protect Dr. X in the forum of sexual contact with patients. Once again, Dr. X was ordered to jail—although jail amounted only to an afternoon spent in the sheriff's private office. Lawyers for both sides realized that they might well travel the entire judicial course again. This time, the attorneys and judges would have to consider the repercussions of the new statute on Interrogatory Request 50.

Once again, Dr. X appealed to the state supreme court, arguing that the statute should be applied retroactively and, once again, that the patients' constitutional right to privacy precluded the disclosures sought. In the spring of 1981, following a lengthy deliberation, the court rendered its decision. The majority opinion focused on the issue of whether the state legislature had intended the statute to operate prospectively or retroactively. If the statute were found to apply retroactively, then the court had to determine whether the content of the information sought in Interrogatory Request 50 was privileged under the statute's edicts.

Holding that the statute did apply retroactively, the majority of the judges deemed the material privileged and disclosure of it forbidden:

> The general question posed by interrogatory number 50 seeks a simple "yes" or "no" answer to a compound inquiry, i.e., whether [the appellant] engaged in a variety of activity ranging from touching to having sexual intercourse with former or current patients. A "yes" answer thus would be required even if [he] merely touched other patients, but the inference drawn from a "yes" answer might be that [the appellant] had sexual intercourse with other patients. This could prove highly embarrassing or perhaps even destructive of existing family relationships for women who were patients/clients . . . at any time after 1972.

In the dissenting opinion, another justice, joined by three others, strongly disagreed with the conclusion that information about sexual contacts was privileged under the pending statute:

> There is nothing in [the statute] that indicates an intent to extend the privilege to communications that do not relate to the professional relationship between the professional and the patient/ client. . . . The legislative intent is clear that only those *communications* which fall within the professional relationship, i.e., that relate to the diagnosis, evaluation or treatment of the patient/ client are entitled to the privilege. . . . [The appellant] has specifically denied in his answers to interrogatories and admissions that his sexual contacts with the plaintiffs were a part of his professional treatment of the plaintiffs. It follows, therefore, that any sexual contacts he had with any other female patients or clients were likewise not a part of his treatment of them and were not encompassed within his professional relationship with them.

> While one can appreciate [the appellant's] ostensible desire not to "kiss and tell," plaintiffs in this case have alleged that [his] seductions of them were but single sordid chapters in his pursuit of a course of conduct during psychotherapy which was not unusual or unique to him. The interrogatories and admissions on file strongly hint that [the appellant's] defenses to plaintiffs' action will include his contention that each of the plaintiffs initiated the sexual advances. . . . It cannot be denied that under these circumstances it is important, even crucial, to plaintiffs' case to be afforded an opportunity to show a course of conduct of the defendant.

It is difficult to fault the court for its chivalrous desire to protect the unnamed female former patients, but I venture to say that we would not have been as protective of former male patients. This gender-based discrimination, though, is consistent with former decisions of this court. . . . The sad result of this chivalry, however, is the needless mischief inflicted on the time-honored goal of a trial which is to seek the truth. . . . The court's decision commits further injustice, unintended by the legislature. It allows a professional engaged in psychotherapy to inflict serious psychological damage to his patient while it cloaks him with the protection of the privilege to conceal his own wrongs. Finally, it has allowed the privilege to be claimed for the benefit of the wrongdoer, not the wronged.

With its five-to-four vote, the court's judgment released Dr. X from his long-held charge of contempt and protected his right to withhold any information regarding sexual contact with other patients. The far-reaching effects of this decision were positive for the state's community of professional psychologists as a whole; for us, however, it meant our first significant loss.

THE CHANGE OF VENUE

While the cases were being tossed from court to court on the issue of privacy, Brown and Whitehurst battled on a second legal front. Late in 1978, Dr. X's attorney filed a motion for a change of venue. This was the greatest threat, and our attorneys now faced the task of disproving Dr. X's claim that "there existed in the county too great a prejudice" to allow his receiving a fair and impartial trial. The basis for the claim was the newspaper coverage of the story in the four months after the lawsuits were filed.

Brown and Whitehurst hired both a consultant to conduct a public opinion survey and an advertising agency to estimate how many people might have been exposed to the story. Together these two studies suggested that no more than a third of the people in the area had heard of the cases. Our attorneys vehemently argued these points in the change-of-venue hearing.

Precedent was in our favor. Whereas in criminal cases constitutional rights have been zealously defended against the threat of bias, and changes of venue have been granted at the slightest hint of publicity, in civil cases changes of venue have rarely been granted. Nonetheless, the judge chose to move the trial to a small town in a neighboring county because he believed that in civil cases less publicity is needed to "poison the well." He was concerned that the publicity over the nature of the lawsuits, Dr. X's recent loss of his professional license, and the contempt charges might collectively harm his chances for a fair trial.

The change of venue was potentially harmful to our cases. All of the eligible counties were far less urban than ours. And Brown and Whitehurst had little doubt that this was the true reason behind Dr. X's fight to move the trial: His attorneys knew that citizens of small towns tend to make smaller awards for damages. We had hoped that the jurors in our home county would show greater sophistication, that they would more readily interpret severe psychological damages to mean higher compensatory awards.

Brown and Whitehurst also suspected Dr. X's attorneys of wanting the trial to take place in a small town because in such a setting jurors might show less sympathy for female patients, especially female patients who were unmarried and sexually active. Brown admitted that from the start, she and Whitehurst had encountered a disillusioning amount of sex role stereotyping. They repeatedly ran up against people who assumed that women could not be sexually victimized outside of violent rape, and they worried that they might not find jurors free of this bias in a rural town of 2,000. This concern, however, was muted by our sense of relief when, after seven different settings had been considered, the three cases were finally scheduled for trial in the late fall of 1982.

A CLASS-ACTION SUIT

Brown and Whitehurst had originally planned to keep our cases separate. This decision had initiated a 5-year juggling act: The plaintiffs only rarely saw each other and were never allowed to communicate with one another. This strict rule required of

Brown and Whitehurst a balancing act unprecedented in either's law practice—plaintiffs' appointments with them, with diagnosticians, and with the persons taking our depositions could never overlap. The most time-consuming aspect of this precaution was the need for the attorneys to explain everything in triplicate, from legal issues to how the cases were progressing. Protecting the cases from accusations of collaboration between the plaintiffs was essential.

Then, in the summer of 1982, Dr. X's attorney initiated a motion to consolidate the cases. Well aware of the time and expense of trying three cases separately, Brown and Whitehurst offered only a nominal argument. Collapsing the three cases into a class-action suit could even be to our advantage; we could compare the similarities in Dr. X's methods of seduction while contrasting the distinctly different effects that his behavior had upon each of us.

I knew the trial was now likely to proceed as scheduled. In order to have a sense of what my courtroom experience would be like, I attended the hearing to consolidate the cases. The tediously slow pace of the proceedings afforded me a glimpse of the journey our cases had taken through the larger court system. The frustration I experienced with the entire litigation process hit home. I did not know how I would ever manage to sit through 3 or more weeks of the endless bartering between the attorneys that seemed to go on unendingly. The feel of the courtroom was out of sync with the aggravating impatience I experienced. The judge was good-humored, joking quietly with the attorneys, who were like professional competitors rather than bitter adversaries. The state district judge expressed his concern that a jury would be confused by a conglomerate case, with each plaintiff serving as a witness for the other two. Nonetheless, he granted Dr. X's motion, apparently consoled by his attorney's statement, "this won't be a case the jury goes to sleep on, your honor."

In spite of the consolidation of the cases, the three plaintiffs continued to adhere to a strict regimen of noncommunication with one another. Brown and Whitehurst still believed this advantageous: Our vowed silence precluded any possibilities of one case contaminating another. We did not speak at length with one another until the day the case was settled.

SETTLEMENT

By the fall of 1982, both sides were aware that the costs of trying the case would be phenomenal. The trial promised to monopolize at least 3 weeks' time in a small town some 75 miles from home. Our counsel realized they would need to win an extraordinary judgment just to break even. Dr. X's counsel also faced high financial costs. After 4 years and 9 months of litigation, both sides were ready to settle the case. The insurance company's incentive to settle seemed to increase as the probability of proving psychological damages grew.

Dr. Annette Brodsky had been brought into the case as an expert witness several months before. Her role was to evaluate each of us and determine, to the extent possible, whether our sexual relationships with Dr. X had harmed us psychologically. She evaluated us soon after being called into the case and again at a time much closer to the finalized trial date (see Chapters 11 and 12). Her deposition must have left Dr. X's attorneys with the unsettling impression that we would indeed be able to convince a jury that Dr. X's actions had been detrimental to us. Within 4 weeks of Dr. Brodsky's deposition, Dr. X's insurance company initiated serious settlement offers for the first time in all the years of litigation. In my relief, I joyously dubbed the impact of her testimony "the Brodsky Effect."

The negotiations that followed were completed in a few days. Of the $110,000 we won, I left my attorney's office with $26,000. Then and now, I consider this financial award more a token payment and preferable alternative to going to trial than a true form of compensation for the damage Dr. X had inflicted. Part of it went toward my therapy, which I had reentered and would not leave for many months. Part of it would eventually go toward my graduate education in counseling psychology, a goal I had held as a teenager. I would wait, however, to realize this goal, as my experience with Dr. X had poisoned it for me; at the time I could not imagine entering the profession in which he had thrived.

In the meantime, when I received my portion of the award, I wished that the entire ordeal would be over. But it was not. Dr. X's license had been only temporarily revoked, and he could easily practice some form of counseling again. He was "out there," and I knew it. And the effects of what he had done were still within me, and I knew that as well.

THE PERSONAL COST OF CIVIL LITIGATION

Suzanne Brown once told me she could never be certain which aspect of litigation was hardest on her three clients. The frustration caused by the countless court dates that were set and broken was nothing compared with the emotional strain of anticipating the trial itself. And while giving depositions, I endured personal embarrassment at the intimate, sometimes degrading, and often irrelevant questions that were asked. On the occasion of my first deposition, Whitehurst held up the proceedings for 2 hours while trying to find a female court reporter, insisting that there were too many men present, given the intimate nature of the material to be discussed.

I experienced intense emotional discomfort during the hours of Dr. X's deposition, in which he branded me a liar and a seductress yet diagnosed me as emotionally sound and free of any psychological damage. These diagnoses were based on nothing more than his inspection of me as we dealt with the stress of giving depositions:

Q: Now you say in your opinion that no damage has resulted from this?

A: That's correct.

Q: And what do you base that opinion on?

A: My observation of her . . . by looking at her. I've seen her at depositions and I've seen her today, yesterday. . . .

Q: You said you were basing your opinion partly on observations of the women.

A: That's correct.

Q: What do you observe about Carolyn that makes you draw the conclusion that she hasn't suffered any damage because of your actions?

A: Well, she appears physically healthy. Her affect remains appropriate to the situation.

Q: Affect appropriate. Will you tell me what that means?

A: She laughs when something is funny and is serious when things are supposed to be serious, and her mood and demeanor are appropriate to what's going on.

I felt both dismay and grief as I sat across the table from Dr. X through the 3 days of his depositions. On one occasion, he winked at me, as if to say "this is nothing between friends." During his own deposition, he told Brown that he cared for me, even now. Yet I heard him disregard my experience of lacking power in therapy with him, and I heard him discount the impact that his distortions of the therapeutic relationship had on me and could potentially have on any patient:

Q: At some time in your office did you touch Plaintiff's vaginal area?

A: That's correct, yes.

Q: And it was in . . . a regular therapy session or a session when she had ostensibly come there for therapy?

A: I'm going to disagree with that because of the way you worded it. I'm going to say that Carolyn and I were intimate when we agreed to be intimate and we were therapeutic when we agreed to be therapeutic.

Q: And with a patient who was neurotic, who was dependent, who was depressed, who had feelings of insecurity and need for approval you think she was capable of making the decision, oh, well, now we'll have sex and now we'll have therapy?

A: I believe she was capable of consenting.

Q: You still believe that?

A: I believe that that's what took place between Carolyn and I in our relationship.

Q: Do you think you had a responsibility to see that it not take place?

A: I did.

Q: And you did not do that, did you?

A: That's correct.

Q: Do you think you failed Carolyn?

A: Not particularly, no. . . .

Q: I take it it's your position that Carolyn has not been damaged at all by your actions?

A: That's correct.

Q: On what do you base that opinion?

A: The absence of anything to the contrary.

Q: Well, for example?

A: I've seen no documentation or evidence that she has been damaged in any way other than the allegations.

Q: You've seen [the psychological evaluations]?

A: I saw [the] report.

Q: And that doesn't verify to you any damages?

A: Absolutely none.

Q: And since you don't believe that causation can be shown at all you think it would be hard to link you with any damages she might have?

A: Absolutely, via the use of psychological tests. . . .

Q: Do you think that if [Carolyn's] inability to trust a male in the various relationships that she has with males had been permanently hampered that that would be a damage?

A: I don't think that's possible. . . .

I had only one occasion to smile throughout these long hours of depositions. Once during Dr. X's deposition, his attorney, exceedingly frustrated by his client's refusal to answer my attorney's questions simply and then be quiet, threw his hands in the air and sank so far down in his chair that he nearly disappeared under the table. Dr. X would not stop talking about himself, and with many of his answers he gave Brown and Whitehurst substantially dangerous information, until they had far more lines of questioning to pursue than they needed.

Many psychologists in our community had been aware of Dr. X's reputation for sexual harrassment of his staff and female co-workers, and many of them were undoubtedly frustrated that they were powerless to take action. Yet even discreet support from the psychological community for the patients who finally did take action was negligible. Perhaps this was due to a professional interest in remaining neutral and unprejudiced, or perhaps Dr. X's colleagues were frightened by his reputation for threatening lawsuits against anyone who would dare even to write a letter of complaint against him. In 5 years of legal battles, I received a single letter, through my attorneys, from a psychologist at the local university. She thanked me, as well as the other plaintiffs, for the courage and strength to make a complaint against Dr. X and follow it through to its end.

Going public was more a source of humiliation than of pride. I stated publicly that I had not realized that the buyer must beware when purchasing psychological treatment, that in spite of being academically intelligent, I had not been psychologically sharp enough to see what was being done to me, nor to realize how terrible its repercussions could be. It was truly difficult to explain to anyone who had never been a depressed patient in therapy how I had placed my self-protective discretion in limbo, how I willingly deferred my judgment to that of my therapist, how I came to be in so vulnerable a position. More often than not, individuals who had never experienced a dependent relationship with a therapist asked, "But you look like a healthy person; how could you have let this happen to you?"

An ever-present disappointment in myself was terrible enough, but it was only the beginning of a nightmarish struggle I entered when I attempted to help bring to a halt Dr. X's practice of seducing his patients. Proceeding with a civil suit proved to be the final step in wiping out all of the naiveté left from my childhood. Dr. X's lawyers got very personal very fast. In his defense, Dr. X tried various ways to create and maintain the illusion that what had happened was as much our responsibility as his, if not more our responsibility: He had been a victim of three vindictive seductresses.

Throughout the years of the ongoing lawsuit, I encountered many people who expressed the sentiment that the woman can always say no, and if she doesn't say no, then the consequences are hers alone to bear. The fault implied by this sentiment led me to recognize how many victims of sexual assault are affected by such prejudice—and it does not seem to matter who the perpetrators are: rapists, family members, therapists, physicians, dentists, or employers.

Throughout the hours of depositions, it was implied that what happened in Dr. X's office was my fault. Sitting across a table from Dr. X, I was asked the names of my childhood friends, first boyfriends, high school companions, college roommates, and landlords. I was asked the names of the boys with whom I had first engaged in sexual experimentation—boys who were by then men with families of their own. Dr. X's attorney asked me about the kind of sexual interaction I had experienced with each man I had ever dated, how long each relationship lasted, how long sexual contact within each relationship lasted, and whether I was in more than one sexual relationship simultaneously. He asked me whether I had slept with the professor—35 years my senior— for whom I worked as a lab technician when I was in college. I wondered whether the defense was aware of the man's reputation for sexual harassment, about which I had known nothing until I experienced it firsthand, or whether they were merely trying to paint a picture of me as a young woman who was attracted to older men. Fortunately, I was able to answer that I had refused his requests for a sexual encounter.

I was asked to describe in detail the acts of sexual abuse in therapy: Could I mentally control vaginal lubrication? At what angles were my legs spread? Did I have orgasms? Were the sexual encounters in the first or last 5 minutes of the hour? Was I charged for those minutes or only for the therapy itself? And why was it that I never ran out of the office screaming rape? And because I did not respond to the abuse in the stereotypical way of the damsel in distress, I was questioned about my sexual behavior in relationships with other men:

Q: Have you ever had occasion to swap sexual partners with anybody?

A: No, sir.

Q: Have you ever had sex in front of anybody else?

A: No, sir.

Q: And when you engaged in sex, did you just have intercourse with these people or would you have oral sex with them, too?

A: At times I have had oral sex.

Civil action, with all of its insinuated derogation, guarantees its own anguish. The hurt began when my initial attempt to achieve mental health backfired. My subsequent decision to expose the malpractice touched all parts of my life. Family members and friends reacted to my publicized complaint and lawsuit with shame and alienation or by reevaluating their support for me.

Two days before we filed suit, I faced the inevitable, painful task of telling my mother about it. The experience was reminiscent of the shameful conversation 3 years before, when I told her I was seeing a psychologist in the first place, implying a grave deficit in my abilities to cope with my problems. Now I had to tell her that I had been vulnerable enough to be used, too dependent to break away, and angry enough to publicly reveal the whole ordeal. My mother responded to each assertion with tears of pain, confusion, and shame—for herself, for me, and for the dishonor I would bring to our family's name and to my father's memory. Over and over again, she said, "I don't understand how this could have happened." Unable to console myself, I was helpless to console her.

My mother soon learned her own lessons in human nature as she found herself not the subject of her friends' pity, scorn, or shame. Instead, members of her church, people at her job, and neighbors told her how proud they were of her daughter's courage.

In spite of her disagreement with my actions, my mother would never desert me, nor would any member of my family, although my aunts and uncles, members of a more conservative generation, would never bring up the subject of the case against Dr. X. It was like a scandalous divorce, my family's contemporary closeted skeleton.

My mother may have disagreed with my choice of action, and she longed for me to bow out of the fight; but after I told her of my involvement, she immediately called my brothers and sister and requested that they offer me emotional support. All but one did this quite readily, even though they also could not fully understand how it all could have happened. Michael called from Houston to encourage me to stand firm, while Richard and Debbie would meet with me to listen to my concerns that my actions might bring more grief than good to our family. My oldest brother was more reticent to extend support, sincerely believing, I later learned, that I needed to stand on my own in this battle. My closest uncle asked me to drop the case, but his motivation was concern for me, and I knew this.

Steve was quiet about the entire ordeal, except to offer me

encouragement to bow out when I once wavered in my commitment to the lawsuit. Now, however, the periods of time between our breakups were longer, and I was feeling less and less committed to getting back together with him when he would reenter my life. His concern about my involvement in the case, he once stated, was how he would respond to seeing me during the trial after a long separation. This remark served to mark another turning point in our relationship: Steve was no help here, and I finally realized that he would be no help to me in any goal I might pursue that ran counter to his ideas of a woman's role in life.

People I had known for a decade and longer, both intimate friends and acquaintances, became potential witnesses to testify either on behalf of my character or in an attempt to destroy my credibility. The fact that I had briefly dated a young black man in high school was played up by Dr. X's counsel, which concerned my attorneys, since we had anticipated the cases' going to trial in a small, conservative town. Although I experienced a humiliating but nonviolent date rape by a man I had known in college long before I began the litigation, I could not call it that because it would be used to portray me as a woman who cries rape at the slightest whim. And for 4½ years, I had to tell any man I dated that he might be subpoenaed at a later time to testify in court as to whether we had had sexual intercourse.

I discovered that Dr. X had attempted to hire a private investigator to follow me, doubtless in the hope of finding something that would undermine my credibility. Even though I knew I was never followed, there were times I felt that I had sacrificed all aspects of my private life to the case against him.

Finally, the civil action affected my professional life. The superintendent and principal of my school were well aware of the potential problems of a scandal. Within 2 hours of the publication of the story in the newspapers, I was told that, for everyone's sake, I was not to discuss the subject on school property. I accepted this demand without question but was touched beyond measure when other teachers whispered their support or wrote me notes asking how they could help. Whitehurst consoled me when I voiced my fear that I would be asked to resign. "They wouldn't dare," he said; "they know they would face their own lawsuit if they pressured you to do that."

In the 5 years of litigation, there was never a moment when

I did not feel hopelessly entangled. Yet, I sincerely believed that Dr. X's treatment had harmed me: It exacerbated the issues of separation from my father and alienation from men; it led me further away from an understanding of my own sexuality; and it destroyed my ability to trust my perceptions and judgments of other people. I was also convinced that Dr. X was abusing many more patients. These reasons sufficiently justified the price of going public. Moreover, I was buoyed by the support I received from many family members and friends. I also found support within myself: I gained a sense of responsibility in doing my part to prevent other women from being harmed by Dr. X.

5

The Ambivalence of Reporting One's Therapist: Is This What I Want to Do?

MONITORING ETHICS: 1978

From the first moment we filed suit against Dr. X, the other plaintiffs and I as well as Brown and Whitehurst shared a common goal: We wanted Dr. X's license revoked. I was surprised to find that our complaints of ethics violations were the first of this nature that the state licensing board for psychologists had received. Thus there were few precedents for handling a charge of sexual misconduct. Revoking Dr. X's license would require separate hearings for a tentative and final ruling.

Before the licensing board and the attorney general's office could begin an investigation, the plaintiffs were required to submit a notarized, detailed description of the nature of our complaints. In the spring of 1978, I sent the board an affidavit with the required detail. An excerpt follows:

The advances began by his requesting me to lie on the floor of his office and relax. A week later, he sat beside me and rubbed my stomach, asking me if (and if so, why) the action made me nervous. In the next session he began unzipping my slacks and touching my genitalia. I was suddenly aware of his mounting me; however, I had no idea he was penetrating my vagina until he had. Being in a state of extreme dependency upon him at the time, I was too frightened to object.

In many sessions, the "therapy" would take the form of getting me on the floor and having sexual intercourse immediately and then spending the rest of the 45 minutes talking about [his] problems with his wife and their divorce, which was underway at the time. I began to feel as if I was being charged not only for the unsolicited services of a male prostitute, but to counsel him as well.

As the case proceeded, it became obvious that we would get lost in the confusion between issues arising from the licensing hearing and those arising from the civil litigation. Thus, soon after I submitted my affidavit, Brown and Whitehurst decided that pursuing the revocation of Dr. X's license could jeopardize our lawsuit. The harm that negative publicity might cause Dr. X remained one of our bargaining strengths, and a public licensing hearing would render that strength ineffectual. In addition, Brown and Whitehurst were concerned that if the ethics complaints proved successful and Dr. X were deprived of his livelihood, a jury might react in an overly sympathetic manner toward him—Brown and Whitehurst feared the "Hasn't he suffered enough?" attitude. Finally, they discovered that they would be unable to represent us at the board hearings; at best they could only make objections on our behalf. In addition, any testimony we gave to the board could be gathered as evidence by Dr. X's attorneys for use in the civil lawsuit.

In choosing the wisest course of action, Brown and Whitehurst considered the implications of every step in the one process in light of its effects upon the other: How would progress in delicensing affect progress in the civil suit, and vice versa? After consulting with us individually, Brown and Whitehurst notified the board's executive secretary, requesting that the complaints be "held in abeyance" until the legal matters were resolved.

Although none of us was happy with this compromise, we knew we would eventually return to the board with our ethics complaints.

The wait proved shorter than we had anticipated. Dr. X's steadfast denial of all charges coupled with his insurance company's initial unwillingness to negotiate an out-of-court settlement resulted in the filing of the first two lawsuits in the summer of 1978. The subsequent media coverage rendered obsolete our leverage in withholding publicity. Although Brown and Whitehurst remained concerned about the sympathy-building potential of pursuing the revocation of Dr. X's license, we knew that the case might be years in going to trial. We all believed that allowing Dr. X to remain in practice would hold his present and future female patients at risk of sexual abuse. Wanting to ensure that the board was at least aware of Dr. X's activities, we proceeded with our complaints to the licensing board.

A Board Hearing

In the late autumn of 1978, the state licensing board for psychologists held its first administrative hearing to consider the first of two complaints against a fellow psychologist. The meeting was open to the public. This did not please Dr. X's attorney, who had, the previous evening, alluded to the need for protection of privileged materials. At that time, he had also filed a motion for continuance based upon the inaccessibility of two psychologists who were to serve as character witnesses. After some consideration, the board determined that "the essential testimony of these doctors dealt more with the area of litigation than as to the facts of the complaint," and the motion was denied.

When I entered the large auditorium where the meeting was to be held, I saw far more people than I had expected. Dr. Evelyn Hammond, who was in the audience, told me that many of them were psychologists. I had seen Dr. Hammond, herself a counseling psychologist, a few times awhile before when I had sought help in extricating myself from my relationship with Steve. I did not know at the time that I would be seeing her again in the future, nor that the work we would do would move psychological mountains for me. The road to healing and integrating the effects of this entire ordeal, which I would walk with

Dr. Hammond, awaited me at a future date. Now, I joined the audience, nervously praying that I might be inconspicuous. I remained ambivalent—I was responding to my sense of duty, yet I felt ashamed to be in the position of an aggrieved and complaining victim, and I was also frightened.

The photographers from the local press had refused Whitehurst's request that they refrain from taking oui pictures, and I watched as they searched the audience looking for "the three women." I kept my head down, frightened that my picture in the paper would be seen by my students. I wondered whether I would be able to answer the questions they might ask me about the case, and I feared even more the reactions of their parents. Would their parents call the school and demand that someone touched by scandal—especially scandal of a sexual nature —be removed from her influential relationship with their children?

Finally, I was intimidated by the idea of testifying before this stern-looking group of men—Dr. X's professional colleagues. I wondered how they would receive my complaint. Five psychologists served on the all-male board. Also present were the assistant district attorney, who represented the board, Dr. X, his attorney, two or three women who were to testify on Dr. X's behalf, the first complainant, and Brown and Whitehurst, who were determined not to leave their client open to indiscriminate questioning by Dr. X's lawyer.

The presence of the complainant and her attorneys aggravated Dr. X's attorney. He argued that the case was between Dr. X and the state and that the first complainant was simply not a party to the proceeding. He also declared that he had not been officially notified that she would be involved. He insisted upon his right to depose her prior to any hearing before the board so that he could prepare for the hearing properly. He then made a second motion for continuance. I felt myself growing weary already, wondering whether this would be a drawn-out parade of legal loopholes endlessly delaying the entire process. The board chose to follow custom, allowing the individual who brings a complaint to be recognized as a party, "in order to insure to that person certain constitutional rights of due process, including representation by counsel." I was relieved in the face of our first victory: Brown and Whitehurst could stay.

In Defense of a License

Dr. X's defense was multifaceted. His attorney first challenged the charge that Dr. X had been guilty of "unprofessional conduct as defined by the rules established by the Board." His challenge was not based on a claim that Dr. X had refrained from unethical action; rather, he proposed that the wording of the board's rules regarding unethical behavior were overly vague:

> The Board must look at the acts of intercourse complained of and determine whether or not, in the way Dr. X went about this admittedly foolish behavior, he showed "sensible regard for the social codes and moral expectations of the community." It does not say that violation of the social codes and moral expectations is prohibited. . . . On its face, one could decide that Dr. X was not sensible in what he did and therefore violated principle 3. I would argue that you must go further than that. I would point out that Dr. X did not flaunt his affairs or the fact that he had sexual intercourse with anyone. Also, Dr. X chose to do it in private as much as possible. Neither of these complainants has been able to say that they ever heard of Dr. X bandying about their names or spreading any information about his sexual involvement with them. Also, these two women have had quite extensive sexual experience prior to their involvement with Dr. X.

As I listened to this argument, I was intensely absorbed, and angry. Once again, the stereotype was emerging: Women who are not virgins are less deserving of protection from sexual exploitation, and coercive sexual intercourse with such a woman is not damaging. Fearful again, I wondered, "My God, will they send us all packing now because we weren't virgins?" I found during this proceeding, and during the course of the entire lawsuit, that my faith in the presence and effectiveness of justice would be tested. Sometimes the notion of justice seemed to rest on nothing more than a clever attorney's words. At this moment, however, my faith was buoyed slightly as a member of the board sternly explained that they were not disposed to treating the case in a sexually biased manner.

Dr. X's counsel next challenged the charge that his client was not "of good moral character." Again he asserted that the definition of the term was so broad that no single interpretation of it could be found:

> No person can really determine uniformly whether conduct of any sort evidences "good moral character" . . . and the power delegated to this Board by the Legislature cannot be exercised based on language so broad and vague that psychologists of common intelligence must necessarily guess at its meaning and differ as to its application.

His next point was in response to the complainant's charge that Dr. X had "been guilty of fraud or deceit in connection with his services rendered as a psychologist." He argued:

> Fraud and deceit, to my way of thinking, means that a psychologist somehow indicates to his patients that having sexual intercourse with him would improve their understanding of themselves, their emotional development, or improve their condition in some fashion. Here the Board must determine whether or not it believes the complainants or Dr. X, not in whether or not sexual intercourse occurred, which is admitted, but in how that event actually came about. . . . In each instance, the complaining party knew that sexual intercourse was going to occur, actively participated in bringing about the act of intercourse and much, much later decided that they had something to gain by filing a complaint with this Board and by suing Dr. X for in excess of three quarters of a million dollars.

Dr. X's attorney further argued that sexual intercourse was not even the issue upon which the board should dwell. Although Dr. X had denied the sexual contact when the suits were filed, he now admitted he had been intimate with the two complainants. Nonetheless, he argued, the focus of consideration should be whether or not the doctor–patient relationship temporarily ceased prior to its formal termination. The lawyer contended that during the first complainant's penultimate session, not only was the doctor–patient relationship suspended, but it was replaced with an intimate relationship between two friends.

In his arguments Dr. X's attorney, reiterating the vagueness of the complaints against his client, implied that a forbidden behavior, if it is not well defined, cannot have charges heard against it. He alluded to the division among the psychological community itself regarding the benefits of sexual contact with patients. Couching his argument in a description of the integrity of the man facing the board, he stated:

> Certainly it is my understanding in the past that [the Board] has been faced with no instances whereby a licensed doctor had the temerity and fortitude to admit what the facts were as he conceived them and experienced them at the time. Dr. X is such a man.
>
> And I know that this Board otherwise would have to wrestle with some pretty tough questions. And it is going to have to wrestle with some pretty tough questions anyway, because at the present time in the membership of the American Psychological Association it is fairly new that the APA has specifically prohibited sexual intimacies—which are undefined—between patients and psychologists.
>
> There is a great dispute among the psychiatric community and the psychological community as to whether or not this sort of thing is ever of a benefit to any patient. A small minority in the psychological community and psychiatric community believes that it is at times of benefit as therapy.
>
> You will not be concerned with that issue in this case except if you believe her contention that Dr. X indicated at any time that this had anything to do with therapy, albeit it occurred during the time that a professional relationship existed. If Dr. X is guilty of unprofessional conduct, it may well be that his great mistake was in believing that he could create and control to the benefit of the patient a dual relationship. He knows now that he does not have that ability and that he was wrong. He admits that he was wrong.
>
> He will later present evidence to the Board to indicate that whatever he did that was wrong, he has already to a great extent paid for that wrong. His reputation is gone; his livelihood is virtually destroyed.

Dr. X's attorney challenged the validity of the board's right to hear any complaints against his patient involving sexual misconduct, stating that the board's charter did not actually cover such behavior. This challenge was also overruled, as the board determined unprofessional behavior of any kind sufficient cause for their adjudication. After some time, all Dr. X's excuses for dismissing or postponing the hearing were exhausted.

I felt both relief and heightened anxiety as the hearing proceeded. When the first complainant's testimony was about to be taken, Whitehurst came to remind me to leave, in order to continue to protect the legitimacy of our individual stories. In so doing, he identified me to the photographers. Thus he quickly escorted me out, blocking my face with a manila folder. Left alone in his car, I lay down on the front seat to hide and considered my mixed emotions.

I later learned that throughout the hearing, Dr. X's counsel persistently questioned the complainant about her personal life, in spite of the chairman's repeated objections. The chairman stressed that they were interested only in the corroboration of three facts about the complainant: that she had consulted Dr. X; that the consultation had been part of a professional relationship; and that a sexual relationship or incident had occurred prior to the termination of the professional relationship. Nonetheless, Dr. X's attorney insisted upon his right to question the complainant about her personal and professional life:

> One of the greatest benefits of cross-examination, is that we do not accept what [the plaintiff] says to be true. And in order to judge her testimony, to try to figure out in your own minds, whether or not she is being candid, open and honest, or whether Dr. X is being candid, open and honest, will be aided immeasurably by knowing something about the person you are talking about. . . . We are here seeing the medium rigor of somebody that experienced one wrong thing with this psychologist and wants her pound of flesh.

Dr. X's attorney tried to establish that the absence of an immediate objection to the sexual contact and the delay in terminating treatment was evidence of the plaintiff's acceptance that the doctor–patient relationship had been discarded for a new relationship. He argued that the doctor–patient relationship had been set aside some minutes or seconds before a sexual relationship was established between mutually consenting persons. But the board expressed the opinion that the patient would not have been able to clearly separate the two relationships and would have been unable to change her perception of the psychologist as her therapist with the introduction of sexual contact. Having heard the first complainant's testimony, the board members concluded that they did not wish to hear from me; indeed they had heard enough.

Later that same day, I returned to hear Dr. X testify. During questioning by the district attorney, he confirmed that he had had a professional relationship with the first complainant and had engaged in sexual intercourse with her 2 weeks before he last saw her as her therapist. Under questioning from his attorney, he offered his professional opinion that the doctor–patient relationship was never totally absent but existed concurrently with the intimate sexual relationship. Furthermore, he had believed the sexual contact to be emotionally beneficial to both of them. Under cross-examination, Dr. X further clarified his perception of the replacement of the doctor–patient relationship with an intimate relationship. The professional relationship became a personal one when they moved to the floor.

The actions of the members of the board suggest that they chose to believe the complainant's version of when termination of the doctor–patient relationship occurred: not moments prior to intercourse, but on the day of her final therapy session. They determined that sufficient evidence existed to find Dr. X guilty of unprofessional conduct under Section 23(e) of the state's Psychologist's Certification and Licensing Act, and under Principles 3 and 7 of the APA Ethical Standards. The board temporarily suspended Dr. X's certification and license, effective that day, until a final ruling could be rendered at the following session, 2 months away. Another psychologist appeared before the board and was formally assigned the task of assuming Dr. X's case load.

In the interim, the board notified Dr. X of his privileges at their final session. He would be allowed to provide testimony relevant to three issues: his suffering of any mental illness while treating the complainant, any professional treatment that he entered since that time, and his professional conduct prior to and after his treatment of the plaintiff.

At this final session, Dr. X's attorney offered the board "protective measures" in the form of limiting his practice to couple and family therapy and individual therapy with male patients. In spite of this offer, the board voted unanimously to revoke Dr. X's certificate and license for one year. It further ruled that Dr. X not reapply for certification for 2 years. Underlying this decision was uncertainty of how an appeal might best be handled: The question of rehabilitation remained.

MONITORING ETHICS: 1980

Nearly 2 years later, Dr. X applied for recertification, a prerequisite for regaining his license. In a closed hearing in the late fall of 1980, the licensing board determined that Dr. X had undergone marked changes in his life: He had entered psychotherapy for a period of time and had formulated a plan for further personal and professional rehabilitation. As a result, the board found him eligible for consideration of recertification.

The board presented Dr. X with a series of requirements necessary for his recertification. The purpose of these mandates was doubtless threefold: to allow him the opportunity for further rehabilitation if he possessed the potential for such, to protect the liability of the board in holding him answerable to it, and to uphold the auspicies of a licensing entity that could never unequivocably state that psychological rehabilitation was impossible. He was required to contact the board periodically over the following 2 years. The board agreed to return his certificate upon the adequate completion of the following:

1. That the Board receive a current psychological evaluation from a psychologist chosen by Dr. X from a list of clinical psychologists to be furnished by the Board;

2. That Dr. X work in an exempt agency or as the employee of a licensed psychologist for a minimum of two years. One year is defined as 1500 hours, in not more than two settings, in not less than a twelve month period and not more than a twenty four month period. In either situation the supervision of Dr. X shall be by a psychologist approved by the Board with quarterly reports submitted to the Board for their consideration;

3. That Dr. X be required to take and pass a course in professional ethics under the auspices of a university with an American Psychological Association approved psychology training program. Such course may be by regular class, special problems, or extention to be approved by the Board;

4. That Dr. X enter into a period of psychotherapy to coexist with the period of certification unless terminated earlier by the therapist. The therapist is to provide quarterly reports for the Board's consideration;

5. That, upon satisfaction of the above conditions, the Board consider [his] application for licensure as a psychologist.

But the board did not hold to the original five mandates. The results of the psychological evaluation ordered in the first mandate may not have offered great promise for rehabilitation. The second mandate had to be altered: Dr. X could find no clinical internship program that would admit him. Perhaps the board feared a costly lawsuit from Dr. X for denying him the opportunity to be readmitted to practice; perhaps they wished to hold to the hope of rehabilitation. Whatever the reason, the board would prove more flexible than the complainants and their counsel could understand. They lifted the requirement of a clinical internship. In its place, they set out a requirement that Dr. X practice under the supervision of a licensed psychologist for 2 years, for at least 1500 hours per year.

Both the records of the board and Dr. X's own testimony indicate that he was supervised by at least three different psychologists. The final psychologist was apparently the only individual who would agree to continue supervision for more than a few months. It seemed that Dr. X continuously thwarted his supervisors' attempts to work with him, refusing to cooperate in weekly consultations. Ironically, in his search for a supervisor, Dr. X sought out the minister whom he knew had treated me, who declined the offer. Dr. X also approached a fellow psychologist who, years before, when he first heard of Dr. X's sexual contact with clients, had called Dr. X to express his concern over the ethical breach. Dr. X had immediately threatened the psychologist with a lawsuit if he dared to follow up on his accusations and had had his attorney reinforce that threat with a subsequent phone call. Needless to say, this psychologist, too, refused Dr. X's request to enter into a supervisory contract with him. The psychological community apparently had grown wary of any voluntary professional interaction with this one-time colleague.

It was apparent, therefore, that even the amended version of the second mandate for rehabilitation would suffer from Dr. X's inability to adhere to it. Likewise, Dr. X did not seem to consider that the fourth mandate warranted serious attention. He did not have his therapist submit quarterly reports to the board, nor did he participate in substantial therapy of any kind.

And yet, despite his disregard for the board's stipulations, Dr. X was allowed to treat male and female patients of various ages under the guidance of his last supervisor. He also reestablished his contacts in the medical community and convinced a few local businessmen to help him raise funds for his new organization, the Counseling Centers of America, through which he hoped to found several walk-in mental health clinics throughout the major cities of the state. Before the funds could be gathered, and while Dr. X was still practicing in his supervisor's offices, he wore a white coat and a name tag that included the title "Director." It soon became evident that the Counseling Centers of America would never materialize due to a lack of funds, and Dr. X's supervisor, concerned that patients were believing Dr. X to be the director of what was in fact the supervisor's clinic, requested that he remove the self-designated title from his name tag.

The Self-Declared Impaired Professional

In late 1980, Dr. X gave an interview to a city newspaper to discuss a "nationwide survey" he had completed to study the "impaired professional," specifically, to help those who shared similar problems of acting out sexually with patients. He told the reporter:

> Most of the current aid programs are for drug or alcohol abusers. Hopefully, that will change, because punishing someone has never served to reduce the incidence of the problem. . . . There appears to be a growing interest in helping . . . an impaired professional . . . rather than taking him out behind the woodshed and beating the hell out of him, . . . instead of having professionals thinking they are all super and that if you get rid of the one bad apple the problem will just go away. . . . After all, professionals are people who have the same kinds of money, emotional and sexual problems as anybody else. And the sooner that they and lay people stop perceiving them as heroes or gods, the better.

Although Dr. X claimed to have studied the dilemma of rehabilitating impaired professionals, his insight into his own cases of abusing patients had apparently not changed from the time of his first deposition. He still seemed to perceive himself as a victim of one or two isolated cases that constituted "affairs" or momentary lapses in judgment. He would present this position in his depositons and, years later, in his explanations to future patients. He continued to insinuate that the third complainant was merely along for the money that the lawsuit might produce.

Dr. X applied for and received licensing as a professional counselor from a licensing board set up by the state in 1981. Suzanne Brown suspected that while the professional counselor's board possessed a sentiment against granting him a license, Dr. X had technically complied with the admissions requirements. This board, too, may have feared a lawsuit if it refused to grant him a license. In fact, a consumers' group representing patients claiming to have been abused by therapists threatened the state board with a lawsuit for permitting a known abusive therapist to practice as a counselor. However, Dr. X's lawyer in turn threatened to sue the counseling board if it denied Dr. X's license since their licensing law contained no provisions for denying a license to someone with a record of abusive or unethical behavior in another profession. Unfortunately, the licensing boards were not sufficiently empowered by the state legislature to deal with the ethical infractions of their professionals. Now able to practice as both a licensed professional counselor and a supervised certified psychologist, Dr. X would eventually attempt to use these titles to his advantage.

6

Psychological Recovery: Will I Ever Get Over This?

GETTING OFF THE ROLLER COASTER

U pon quitting my second try at therapy (my sessions with the minister), I declared that I would try living free of treatment for a while. Maybe time and patience were all I needed to overcome depression. I was still seeing Steve, but with decreasing enthusiasm. He rebelled, with predictable timing, against my clinging behavior. Time and again, he condemned our relationship as oppressive. Saying that he felt shackled, he left me for several weeks at a time. Yet he always returned, perhaps as frightened of really ending the relationship as I was. Whenever we reunited, he claimed that we would never be able to love anyone else the way we loved each other. But there was now a hostage-like feeling to his declaration that "we are each others' soul mates."

We had been addicted to one another for so long, both of us

needing the fleeting sense of security that sexual contact provided. Fighting and reconciling was the only way we knew to be intimate. We seemed to confuse emotional intensity with love; there was never a hint of trust between us, and never any peace. Steve's flights of reprieve left me feeling abandoned and jealous—I always assumed he was having affairs with other women. He would confess, more often than not, that he was. But I always accepted him back, afraid to be alone. It never occurred to me that I deserved better treatment from him and from myself.

As time passed, my idealization of Steve began to fade, and I began to loosen my grip on the relationship. Even a lifetime of idealizing men could not help me to endure the burden of Steve's commitment to an uncommitted relationship. Over the years, I had met a few of the women with whom Steve was involved, and I learned that each one of them had fallen in love with him. I began to see that he was not just unable to commit himself to me; he could not commit himself to anyone. His reasons for not seeing me exclusively started to appear less valid. He had told me many times that I did not love him in a way he could understand and accept, because I did not meet his definition of a "Christian wife."

The older I grew, the more distorted and unbalanced his demands seemed. I understood him to want a subservient, worshiping, dollhouse sort of love. I was to mother him and martyr myself, sacrificing my goals for his, and I was to feel fulfilled as a woman by the process. Steve seemed to want more of the behavior I was beginning to balk at. I had always been obedient to men, never questioning what they wanted from me and automatically placing them in a role of authority. Now I saw that I was contributing to my own entrapment in the relationship—and was miserable for it.

I wondered whether our relationship might not be a major source of my continual fatigue. I had hung on too long in a dependent role, hiding from my own strengths and weaknesses. I had tried to make Steve responsible for my feelings, blaming him for going and coming without considering what drove me to reconcile with him each time. Why couldn't I reach inside and grasp some sense of my own authority? Why did I feel as though I had absolutely no power over my life? When Steve wanted to come back, I had always felt helpless to say no. I knew that if I were to be free of him, I would have to be the one to make a separation endure.

Thus I did need to see another therapist, but this time I wanted to see a woman. I realized that since my experience with Dr. X, I was too unsure of myself around men in authority, certainly around male therapists. I was also aware that I needed to feel safe in therapy, and this idea had emerged only when I considered treatment with a woman. My relationship with Suzanne Brown also influenced my decision to see a female therapist, as I had come to see in her a woman with her own sense of authority.

My brother Michael recommended Dr. Evelyn Hammond. On my first meeting with her, I told her of Dr. X's sexual abuse but I did not dwell on it. I just wanted help extricating myself from my relationship with Steve. Yet sometimes in my early talks with Dr. Hammond, my anger with Dr. X broke through. She offered me more than one chance to explore those feelings, but I could not bring myself to do so. I still felt too guilty for being angry with him in the first place.

Inevitably, however, as I tried to find out just who I was, the parallels between my relationships with these two men emerged. The misery I felt with Steve had motivated me to seek therapy from Dr. X, and Dr. X's actions had reinforced what Steve seemed to want; subservient behavior, the subordination of my own needs to his. Having invested so much of myself in pleasing others, I was at a loss to know what to do if I wasn't following Dr. X's implicit suggestions or Steve's explicit demands. I didn't know who I wanted to be, much less what I wanted to do.

My focus on the chaotic relationship with Steve kept me from looking at my own inner emptiness. So I stayed on as Steve's convenient, capricious lover. I struggled with the ambivalence of subjugating myself to both him and Dr. X while wanting to be rid of their hold over my life. Both men had a powerfully engaging presence that left me believing that they not only had all the answers but that they cared more deeply for me than their actions proved. In the absence of my own authority, I had relied on theirs. I came to see how I had not yet given up my childhood belief that men are to be idealized, never questioned, and that subservience to them is necessary to assure their love.

In my relationship with Dr. Hammond, I found myself

facing a woman in a powerful role. Yet she never used her power to exploit me. She did not encourage me to be overly dependent on her, which I was all too ready to do. But neither did she make light of my fear of learning to depend on myself. I started to believe I was worth something alone, apart from the sense of worth I had tried to borrow from the men in my life. I considered giving up the familiar role of victim—I knew I was ready to shed this role when I realized how completely exhausting it was. Within the first 5 months of therapy with Dr. Hammond, I left Steve for good.

My growing feelings of independence from Steve were not all that we explored, however. In one session Dr. Hammond asked me to imagine Dr. X sitting in an empty chair in the corner of her office. Before I could stop myself, I was yelling, "If I had a gun I'd kill him!" I felt tears on my face and was at a loss to stop them. This was my first taste of hatred for Dr. X and the things he had done to me. And then all I felt was grief. The anger was too frightening for me to hold onto, to claim as my own just yet. I did not say anything more for a long while. We talked very little about Dr. X. In spite of my anger, it still felt like a betrayal to tell another person how much his actions had hurt.

Dr. Hammond never pushed me to explore my feelings further than I wanted to. She allowed me to choose the subject and to make the connections I could at the pace I could. This in itself allowed me to experience something totally new: a growing sense of control over myself and my life. But I was not ready to look more deeply at the pain and confusion I felt over Dr. X's betrayal. I had entered therapy in order finally to separate from Steve, and after a few months of treatment, I had garnered the strength to do that. So I left therapy for the third time, pushing aside Dr. Hammond's invitation to return if and when I needed to. I believed I was "all fixed" and would not need to return.

THE GRADUAL EMERGENCE OF POSTTRAUMATIC STRESS

The following year I was happier than I had been since my childhood. I toyed with the idea that I might have the potential for graduate school. I tentatively established a more accepting relationship with my mother. I made a few new friends and tried to reestablish friendships with women who had been significant in my life. I volunteered at a rape crisis center and moved into a house with two other women. I wrecked my car and soon thereafter started dating Ken, the police officer who investigated the accident. And I found Ken attractive in a fundamentally new way: He had no need to control or be controlled. Within 3 months, I began experiencing a deeper, more solid form of love than I had known with other men.

But the happier, more confident moments were often overshadowed by the impending trial. My attorneys warned me of the exposure it promised. No realm of my life would be protected by privacy. I thought I could confront that if I could just manage my anxiety better. But even my best days were undermined by uneasiness. Could I face Dr. X in court? Would people believe me, or would they accuse me of being a seductive, angry patient?

My fears of facing Dr. X publicly and my attempts to ignore the effects of his sexual abuse worsened my anxiety. I was determined never to let another person emotionally malign me again. But to succeed at this unrealistic goal, I needed an infallible judgment of others' sincerity and intent. So, while I waited for this perfect judgment to develop, I resisted trusting people and somehow managed to avoid both closeness and alienation in my friendships. I moved in with Ken and yet often found myself emotionally isolated from him. I was unable to trust my judgment that he was indeed a trustworthy man. I had found someone who was not interested in controlling me, but I expected him to try nonetheless.

My emotional conflict concerning Dr. X increased as new feelings and thoughts about him arose. I alternated between despising him and wanting to forget him. I was plagued with chronic intestinal pain. My moodiness and nervousness began to tax the lives of those around me. Fitful sleeping gave way to night terrors and nightmares that grew more frequent as the months passed. Eventually Ken and I both became alarmed by the number of nights each week I awoke screaming and shaking.

Once again, I had to do something: I was emotionally drained and tired of living with myself. I was reluctant to undertake long-term therapy, to consciously acknowledge the pain and confusion I had been fighting off. But now my body, both in waking and sleeping, was paying costly tribute to my uneasiness. I could not keep ignoring my old problems with separation: the grieving for my father that I had never completed and the inability to face my mother as a woman whose values differed from mine. Nor had I worked through my newer problems: the immense shame I felt over my participation in sexual abuse and anger for having been sexually abused.

The ongoing nightmares were the most impelling incentive to return to Dr. Hammond. Of all my nightmares around that time, one left me feeling especially vulnerable and frightened upon awakening. I recorded this nightmare in my journal:

> I was in a city that was under siege of war. I was walking by a one-story building, reminiscent of the building where Dr. X had maintained his office. He was standing on the walkway calling out to the women who walked by, among the war refugees, telling them that they could find sanctuary there. I grew panicky, alarmed, and tried to keep them from going in, tried to warn them that there was danger there. Then the dream changed. I was living in a huge castle with my parents. There was a man in the house trying to kill me with a knife. He worked there, at the house. I had asked my mother to release him from employment, but she couldn't. He had followed me throughout the house, which was dark, with high ceilings and closed-in walls. I asked him why he wanted to hurt me—but he wouldn't answer. When he began to follow me, I ran to my room, which was a small, dark closet. The heavy wooden door had a feeble latch that couldn't keep him out. He broke through the door, grabbed me, and began stabbing me in my chest, again and again. Then another woman got between us and I began to wake up, frightened, my heart pounding.

Recounting dreams such as this one to Dr. Hammond eventually helped me to uncover my conflict over dealing with the bad father that Dr. X was for me. At first I told myself that I did not need to confront the experience of Dr. X's abuse. I wanted to believe that its effects were behind me, and I struggled to ignore my rage and anguish. I intended instead to fortify myself for the upcoming trial, which was finally set for the following month. Prior to the trial date, Dr. Hammond patiently worked with me on the goal of strengthening my self-concept. We found ways to calm my anxiety over testifying, and I learned to put some distance between myself and my memories. Dr. Hammond did not attempt to force me to look at the emotional melee within me. This was the time to build up, rather than tear down, my abilities to cope.

To my great relief, the case was settled out of court. Whitehurst seemed surprised at my readiness to settle—where was the fighter now? Very tired, from nearly 5 years of pretrial wrangling. Even though the litigation was over I knew I wasn't ready to end my treatment. The emotional trial had not yet begun. I felt a shakiness that had little to do with the relief of settling out of court. I had spent 4 years denying the effects of Dr. X's abuse. The more those effects were manifested, the more adamantly I asserted that they no longer existed. Finally, the nightmares taught me otherwise, and I was ready to confront the issues of the abuse and try to resolve the ugly yet profound meaning it held for me.

TRUSTING MYSELF AND OTHERS

Together Dr. Hammond and I changed the goals of my therapy. She helped me first to realize that I needed to learn how to judge people and trust my own judgment. I could no longer afford to idealize others immediately and thoughtlessly. I had to learn to have a healthy alertness for untrustworthy people. This meant taking risks with understanding, and trusting my own intuition, something I'd seldom done. There was a fine line between learning a healthy discretion of others' characters and fostering distrust, and I was plagued with self-doubt as to the soundness of my judgment. But in my relationship with Dr. Hammond, I experienced a trust that was never compromised. She offered me a safe place in which I could take risks. I realized my judgment could never be infallible, and I would have to risk trusting myself and others or face a life of emotional isolation.

We started talking about the old problems: my unhappiness in an intimate relationship, my depression, my low self-esteem, an utter lack of confidence in myself, and a profound grief for my father's death. And we talked about Dr. X. The more we talked about him, the more frightening my dreams became. At least once a week, I woke myself with my own screaming and stood beside the bed trying to convince Ken that the monstrous spiders I dreamed were indeed real.

I was desperately frightened of being intruded upon, frightened of the vulnerability born of my own naiveté. I had for so long lived a conflict: superficially blaming Dr. X's abuse for all my problems and feeling a blistering anger with myself for my collaboration in it all. One of my dreams recorded in my journal left me aware of my own hatred for myself and my fear that I would never be free of it:

> I dreamed I was staying at a motel, the proprietor being a witch. I had barely gotten settled in before she was attempting to get in to kill me, either by breaking down the door, or "materializing" through the window. She got in, and I beat at her again and again until only her hands could move—but they could stretch to all proportions to reach me. I kept trying to gather my personal belongings together—they were strewn about—while continuing to fight with her hands. I never escaped.

During the course of my sessions with Dr. Hammond, she allowed me to look at myself with a compassion I had not known before. I began to realize some of the ways in which I experienced myself as a victim and ways in which being dependent upon men was a source of power for me. I had resigned myself to Dr. X's sexual intrusion in much the same way that I'd resigned myself to Steve's chronic indecisiveness in our relationship. The greater my dependency on these two men grew, the more vulnerable to abandonment I became, and the more willing I was to sacrifice my own self for the sake of postponing that abandonment. And this was an old dependency. As a child, I had learned—to the point of dangerous imbalance—obedience to and respect for the demands of authority. When I finally reached the age at which many youngsters seriously begin questioning parental authority, my father was dying. I dared not assert myself against him then, as I saw him becoming more helpless. Nor could I distance myself from my grieving mother.

COLLUDING IN MY EXPLOITATION

As therapy progressed, I told Dr. Hammond of my sense of shame that would not ease, shame for having participated in a sexual relationship that was so destructive to me. I also became aware of the guilt I felt for hurting Dr. X by means of the lawsuit. These confessions shed light on one source of conflict within me. Even as I said I blamed Dr. X for his actions, I accepted responsibility for the sexual encounters. After all, weren't women responsible for all that happened to them? And weren't men in authority good and honorable?

Dr. Hammond helped me understand two things: how Dr. X, as my psychologist, held the ethical responsibility for the abuse, and how my needs had rendered me willing to participate in something I did not want. I began to understand how I had become a person who could be exploited. I had neither respected nor valued my misgivings about the sexual encounters. I had, instead, resigned myself to them for the sake of the approval I so intensely needed from Dr. X. They had left me confused because they left me feeling approved of but, simultaneously, contemptuous of both the "approver" and myself.

Clarifying the dilemma of "who was responsible" was one of the most difficult obstacles I faced in therapy. I did not fully understand the unethical nature of the abuse. I never said, "This lousy guy tried to get me to have sex with him in therapy." Instead, I held a muddled picture of Dr. X: the good man who had hurt me. For so long he had been a good father. I could not reconcile that image with his destructive acts. But he *wasn't* the caring father I had perceived him to be. I had idealized him, and he had used me. And then, rather than surrender my idea of him as a loving parent, I had believed that his actions—even sexual intercourse—were intended to help me.

As I tried to reconcile the image of a trustworthy doctor—which I stubbornly retained—with the acts he had committed, I was besieged with questions I could not immediately answer. Would he have done this if he had known how badly it would harm me? Was it possible that he could not believe it to be harmful? Could he not see the consequences of using a patient in so fundamental a way? If he did know, was he so selfish as not to care? The depositions certainly proved that he believed that our sexual intimacy had not been harmful. They also exposed his ignorant belief that the therapist–patient relationship, despite its imbalance of power, could be turned on and off like a light switch. His behavior was inconsistent—sometimes helpful, sometimes hurtful; he was a father figure who seduced his charge. These dual images would not merge.

My anger with Dr. X as a parent to me, even if a malevolent one, was a betrayal to a father long dead. Instead of facing this, I had turned the anger toward myself, for having been so naive. I held it inside, where it was literally consuming me. At first, I couldn't even point to some of my angry feelings toward Dr. X, and Dr. Hammond and I talked about my feelings of guilt when I first brought the lawsuit against him.

At that time—when I first approached Suzanne Brown—I wanted Dr. X to stop hurting his female patients, but I had not wanted to bring him financial ruin. If he could not be rehabilitated, I had wanted him only to cease practicing as a psychologist. My guilt had been strong enough to cause me to vacillate between continuing with the case and dropping it. My indecision came to a head soon after I had filed the suit, when I ran into Dr. X at the airport. He greeted me in the gentle and kind manner he always had and then told me how surprised he had been to see my name involved in litigation against him—this was before he had tried to reach me by phone. My face burned. I felt as I often had around him, like a child caught in the midst of committing a shameful act. I mumbled something about doing what I had to do and walked on, head down and eyes staring at the ground—just as I had walked as a child. By the time I left the airport, I was certain I would drop the lawsuit.

But as I felt my determination waver, as I felt guilt for this man whose professional career I was helping to ruin, I remembered how many patients had talked about his methodical seduction of them. He had sexually objectified patients in a situation that called for caring, support, and therapeutic confrontation. I could not avoid the implications of the other two plaintiffs in the lawsuit or of the many women who had called Brown's office about the case. I still wondered whether Dr. X believed each time he seduced a patient that there was genuine caring on his part and that mutual consent was a given.

By then I was aware of his reputation in the psychology community, and it was not good. It suggested that he had a history of infatuations with patients and with the female staff members of institutions where he had worked. One female social worker had formally complained about his sexual advances. And judging from the phone calls my attorneys received from many of his ex-patients, he showed faulty judgment on more than one occasion. As early as 1974, when working together in our city's primary psychiatric hospital, a colleague had cautioned Dr. X about his behavior, stating, "It would probably help you to be less phallic." During one of his depositions for the case, Dr. X characterized himself during his early years of establishing himself in the city:

A: At the time I had an aura of machoism, and I don't really know how to explain that to you but chauvinistic machoism. Was real proud of myself. It manifested itself in the way I walked through the wards. I think I was cocky. I think I was flirtatious with the staff and manipulative of the staff in terms of getting things done.

Q: This macho thing. I believe you've said that you are over that now.

A: Right.

Talking about these memories with Dr. Hammond brought me face to face with Dr. X's uncaring and using nature. I realized that my sexual relationship with him had been far from a caring one, and I could no longer support the myth that men in paternal roles are necessarily good. Learning about his apparent repetitive seduction of vulnerable patients helped me to begin letting go of my tenacious illusions about him. He had been using me. I found myself knowing in a more certain way that Dr. X was exploitation incarnate. Yet with this recognition, I felt a stinging sense of loss that I could not understand.

The fact that Dr. X had in some ways helped me at the beginning of therapy made it hard for me to make sense of the abuse and to leave my guilt behind. That he encouraged me to keep a journal during the first 6 months, before he began making erotic suggestions, implied that my feelings were important enough to attend to and record. It also made me aware of his interest and concern in what I felt and thought. He suggested to me, early in treatment, that I might be angry with my father for abandoning me by dying.

So, for the first 9 months of therapy with him, I had experienced our relationship as a mutually caring one. But did his caring change when he began taking advantage of my lack of self-esteem and assertiveness? Once the sexual contact began, he never asked me how I felt about it and repeatedly interpreted my ambivalence toward it as resistance to him. In his deposition, he showed no feelings of guilt or remorse for his actions—although I believe with all my heart that he was sorry he got caught. He didn't really believe his actions had caused me any problems. But I did. I was angry and confused, and I continued to engage in destructive relationships. I became convinced that approaching men sexually would give me the approval I needed. Over time, my overly open and trusting approach to people gave way to bruised insulation and circumspection.

When Dr. Hammond and I first started looking at my relationship with Dr. X, I was unable to credit him for any help he'd given me. It was a long time before I understood that the beneficial part of his treatment was separate from his abuse and that no amount of help excused or justified the exploitation.

BALANCING THE POWER DIFFERENTIAL

A turning point in my therapy with Dr. Hammond came about during a session in which we discussed a disturbing dream I had had that week and recorded in my journal:

> I was crouching in the corner of an empty, white room, and Dr. X was leaning against the doorjamb for support, weak and pathetic, unable to enter the room. To my right and a little between us, but not directly blocking our view of each other, Dr. Hammond stood. I felt strength emanating from her, and I felt courageous enough to finally look at him, and see him for what he was. And then I began to stand up, and as I did so, I grew stronger, and he grew more pathetic, more powerless. And then I began to weep as I knew that he truly never had been what I thought him to be.

As I recalled this dream, I grew more and more distressed and finally began sobbing. Dr. Hammond sat with me, waiting for my grieving to subside. As she helped me explore the dream, I found myself relinquishing the last of my illusions of Dr. X as someone who had only good intentions for me. And as I did, I felt profoundly sad. But I was not only experiencing a long-overdue grief for what had actually been done to me; I was also grieving for the loss of my father substitute, my image of Dr. X as a man who would never have considered hurting me. I began to accept the more realistic image of a manipulative Dr. X. And in so doing, I began to attribute to Dr. X his true share of the blame. He had known fully the extent to which I doubted my worth, and he had exploited my doubts to serve his own needs. It did not matter what those needs were—he never should have acted on them. He had encouraged my unhealthy and overwilling dependence on him. His seductions had crushed the paltry self-esteem I had when I entered first therapy. His exploitation brought me shame I never asked for and guilt I never deserved.

Another dream I had during this time in therapy concerned my attempts to take back from Dr. X the immense power I had once attributed to him and the difficulty I faced in doing so, for taking away his power required that I give up needing his approval. From my journal comes the following dream:

> I was a psychoanalyst, sitting on a semi-circular couch with three to four other therapists. We held legal pads on our laps, writing down our observations and opinions of the young woman who was sitting before us, apparently suffering from some severe emotional problems. There were two other women therapists, myself, and two men, one of whom was Dr. X. We were deciding on her treatment, which we all had to agree upon. Dr. X held the only dissenting vote. I argued with him, feeling a sense of urgency and frustration that he would refuse to agree with us. If she were not helped, she would worsen terribly, and we all knew it. I could not see the woman's face, even when she looked at us. I grew both angry at Dr. X and afraid that he wouldn't consent to help the patient. I felt a need for his acceptance of our ideas.

In my conversations with Dr. Hammond, she not only encouraged me to express my anger, she validated its importance to me. I rebelled at the betrayal, I mourned the fact that I had been used as a sexual object. I grieved for the loss of Dr. X as a caring father figure. I grieved that I, even at 20 years, had been more of a naive child than a sophisticated woman and that this naiveté had been used to my detriment. I faced the self-disgust I felt for not having recognized sooner how my need to please Dr. X, and the extent to which I would act to gain his approval, set me up to be used. I faced my anger with myself for having accepted at face value what he had presented as therapy.

It was tremendously difficult for me to let go of my anger at having played the fool. Compassion for myself came slowly and stubbornly. I had been willing to trust Dr. X's authority prematurely, accepting a doctor–god dyad without question. Accepting the reality about my younger self allowed me to experience the first glimmer of self-forgiveness. And when I expressed my anger over the tragedy for which Dr. X was responsible, I started to acknowledge that this should not have happened to me. As I began to forgive myself, I became more enraged with Dr. X. I was, finally, developing the self-love that had been sorely lacking for so many long years.

WHY DID THIS FEEL LIKE INCEST?

In 1979, before I sought treatment with Dr. Hammond for the second time, I went through a training program for volunteers at the local rape crisis center. I chose this work because I wished to understand better the crime of rape. The more I learned about survivors of rape and incest, the more I came to realize that in some ways my experience paralleled many of theirs.

Perhaps the most devastating repercussions of Dr. X's conduct were those relating to the incestuous nature of our relationship. Soon after I entered into therapy with him, I developed a child-like dependency upon him. Underlying the sexualization of our relationship were fear if I did not comply and despair when I did. Clearly, I had problems with separation, for I felt an intense and prohibitive anxiety at the thought of displeasing him. I could not stand up to him. In therapy, my words and actions portrayed the sentiment "Is this what you want me to say? Am I saying what you want to hear?" Instead of challenging me to explore how I dealt with him as an authority figure, Dr. X took it upon himself to benefit from my wish to please.

Our relationship could not help but be imbalanced and harmful to me. Dr. X, however would argue to the contrary, as is shown in the testimony he gave in his last deposition:

Q: When you started having sexual intercourse with Carolyn during the office visits, did it muddy the waters of the therapy with her?

A: It didn't seem to in her case.

Q: So you didn't seem to have any of these problems with the dual relationship or the muddy waters?

A: That's correct. I believe that it does do that but I can't remember it ever doing that with Carolyn. It seemed like everything went along fine with Carolyn and I to me.

Q: When you ceased to function as Dr. X the therapist and started to function as Dr. X the friend, do you not think that constituted a certain kind of abandonment of Carolyn?

A: Not at all.

But I believe that Dr. X and I never possessed an equal ability to consent to a sexual relationship. He was the "expert" and I readily gave him a parental persona, complete with the immense power I bestowed upon men in father roles. I attributed to him a power that greatly exceeded my own. Dr. X's suggestions and ideas carried far more weight than those of other people in my life. My ignorance of what the seemingly mysterious therapeutic process entailed enhanced his power. I wanted for myself what this powerful man wanted for me. I also wanted to avoid what I dreaded above all else—abandonment by another father.

Dr. Hammond explained to me many times the imbalance of personal power inherent to the therapist–patient relationship. Finally I could hear the implicit message: It was all right, even expected and natural, to have bestowed upon Dr. X an inordinate amount of power. It was also understandable that I had been unable to say no to him, just as a child is often afraid to say no to a parent, for fear of risking the parent's disapproval, rejection, and anger.

As I struggled with self-blame, I remembered that I had often had quiet misgivings about the erotic contact—that it was wrong, even destructive. Now I found myself experiencing ongoing embarrassment as I wondered how I could have been so foolish as to distrust my own instincts. What could I have done differently? Feelings of self-contempt surfaced as I insisted that I deserved what happened to me; I was gullible enough to believe him, so it's only right I should hurt like this now. I needed clarification in understanding that I had not been in a position to exercise good judgment. Certainly, with my regret for what happened, I needed a sense of compassion for myself: self-acceptance had to replace self-condemnation.

I had to work through my memories of my own behavior in therapy with Dr. X. Had I in some way enticed this fatherly man to approach me sexually? Not having at that time anything close to a "bigger picture" of Dr. X's mental illness, I listened carefully to him during his depositions, trying to understand whether I had done anything to seduce him. In his last deposition, he presented his perception of my participation in the sexual relationship:

Q: What specific conduct of Carolyn's indicated to you that she had somehow instigated or encouraged you to have intercourse with her?

A: Carolyn was never what you would call an aggressive female sexually or physically toward me. She was instead more softly, passively seductive in posture, mannerisms and particularly in her eyes.

Q: Her eyes. And what would she do with her eyes?

A: In my opinion Carolyn, if she feels it, can look at someone as if they are the only person in the world and make them feel that.

While I had heard there were many other women, I could not yet consider his actions outside the microcosm of our relationship. I had for so long thought about the dynamics of the abuse as unique to him and me, and, therefore, I had considered myself personally responsible in some way. For some time after the abuse, and certainly fueled by the evidence of his words in the depositions I had to attend, I believed what he said and believed myself to be culpable.

In treatment, he had challenged me to relinquish my tomboyish appearance, and I had risen to the challenge. I had started dressing more femininely, wearing skirts rather than the jeans and T-shirts he overtly disapproved of. I engaged in several sexual relationships rather than remaining celibate or monogamous, not only in an attempt to be the open, unguarded individual he encouraged me to be, but to fill the void within me that therapy was not helping me to overcome. And once the intercourse began, I tried to stop it indirectly—getting off birth control, decreasing my weekly appointments to bimonthly, in an indirect appeal that the sex not continue.

Always I felt a sense of collusion. And for months I chose to feel more than my share of guilt. It was one of the most difficult things for me to relinquish because I often thought, "But I agreed; I didn't run from the office." As with incest, as with any situation wherein one individual is dependent upon another, it is difficult for the victim to come to the position of clearly laying the blame where it belongs.

The following dream, recorded in my journal, represented this struggle for me:

> I dreamt I was in a store, where Dr. X was the shopkeeper. The shelves were filled with cheap straw flasks, various sizes, each with long slender necks for holding silk flowers and such. He kept trying to sell me various flowers and flasks, but my eyes fell on a dark brown box I just knew to be of great worth, sitting alone on a top shelf, out of reach. I knew I wanted to buy this box, and felt that it was mine to begin with, and that I had somehow been put in a position to have to buy it back from him. But as he took it down and turned it over, he said, "I don't think you can afford the price," and I knew he was right, for it was far too expensive. I left sadly, walking into the adjoining store, a much newer art shop run by a redheaded woman. The glass shelves were filled with beautiful stones and crystalline art, and I saw a jagged quartz of many colors, and wept because I believed I would never have it either for myself; the price was too high.

Dr. Hammond, whose red hair should be noted here, was a powerful source of support as I undertook the task, of reassigning blame; she was unwavering in communicating to me the proper attribution of responsibility and guilt. One of the most effective ways in which she demonstrated her message was in a story she told of how another of her patients had been sexually abused by a therapist and then consulted a second therapist, who had attempted to excuse the first therapist's behavior, telling her, "Well, he's been having a bad time, going through some tough times in his career; he's trying to rehabilitate himself." In making excuses, the second therapist had only confused the patient. Instead of saying, "What happened to you should *not* have happened to you; you were violated, and there is *no* excuse for it," he attempted to displace the abusive therapist's responsibility for his sexual misconduct.

I believe that Dr. Hammond's timing in approaching my issues of sexual exploitation was crucial to the effectiveness of my treatment. Even though she knew I was experiencing emotional turmoil as a result of the abuse, she first attended to the issues I perceived as problematic. In a recorded interview I had with Dr. Hammond some years later, she recalled:

> I had to wait for a long time before you were ready to deal with the issue of having been sexually exploited. Your emotional energies were tied up in dealing with problems of an ongoing relationship. Even though your relationship with Steve shared so many significant issues of victimization and helplessness, which Dr. X's sexual abuse perpetuated, you could not yet make the connections. Your way of dealing with your relationship with Steve carried with it a lot of reminders—the influence of Dr. X's relationship with you was always present. But it was several months into therapy before you allowed it to become conscious. Not until you were very certain of our own alliance did you attempt to deal with it.

Throughout my therapy with Dr. Hammond, and for many years after, I would wonder if indeed I had done anything to eroticize the transference. With Dr. X's first suggestion of my sexual attraction to him, I was unaware of behaving seductively or flirtatiously toward him, and could not accept his theory. But I can accept the possibility that I saw him as a savior, a conqueror of ills, someone who could be strong for me while I could not be strong for myself. And where there is a conqueror, there is a submissive self, and that also I can accept. And if Dr. X perceived this submissive behavior on my part as seductive, he would have done me such a service to have worked it through with me, bringing it to my awareness, and teaching me that sexual behavior would not help me to meet my needs for belonging in my relationships with men. He might have taught me that sex was not the venue in which self-love is realized. This did not happen, and thus Dr. X not only harmed me by what he did to me, but he failed me by omission, by what he did not help me to understand.

THE PARADOX OF GOING PUBLIC

The decisions to file a public complaint and sue Dr. X were two of the most difficult ones I have had to make thus far in my life. They guaranteed inescapable publicity and emotional pain, yet I made them with little foresight, without considering my own emotional strength or whether I had adequate support. I never judiciously compared the potential benefits and detriments.

There were great costs of going public. It was difficult for me to cope with the stress of the impending hearings before the licensing board and the civil trial. I could not focus beyond such events. But the greatest cost of my choices was the inability to bring to a close all the issues surrounding the exploitation. The ongoing nature of the civil litigation kept alive my relationship with Dr. X. It seemed as if my emotional conflicts would never be resolved as long as these proceedings promised a public confrontation with him.

Thus Dr. Hammond also faced a crucial decision in proceeding with my therapy. Psychological treatment often consists of breaking down ineffectual defenses and establishing more appropriate and effective ways of coping. Dr. Hammond initially faced the need of having to suspend such work with me. In considering the rigors of the lawsuit, she had to help me maintain any defenses available to me—even inappropriate ones—so that I could protect myself in the public confrontation. To do otherwise would have placed me at risk had the case gone to trial. I would have entered an emotionally traumatic situation without sufficient self-protection. Because I could not wait until therapy was completed before starting the complaint and litigation processes, my therapy was retarded. In a sense, my decision to confront Dr. X publicly was countertherapeutic.

In looking back, however, I also see the positive consequences of my decisions. My determination to file suit and make a formal complaint to the licensing board helped me take control of my own life. I had for too long coped with adversity by taking the stance of a victim, and I began to leave this style of behavior and perception of myself behind. I decided not to remain a quiet recipient of abuse. I traded my feelings of helplessness for the experience of taking determined action. I garnered strength from calling Dr. X to account for his misuse of patients under the guise of therapy. I faced my fears of disclosing the long-held secret that I had colluded in by keeping silent.

Therapeutically, I benefited as I was pressed to draw on my reserves of strength. I often found my capacities to be greater than I had previously realized. I discovered substantial sources of support in family members and peers whom I had not believed available to me. I stood up to those family members, friends, and professional colleagues who asked me to leave it all to someone else. I grew up as I shouldered some of the responsibility for making Dr. X less accessible to vulnerable people. Taking such a stance in itself forced me to confront my perception of Dr. X as someone who had had my best interests at heart. I saw my illusions disintegrate as he engaged in muckraking tactics to defend himself against his accusers. Because his defense felt like a smear campaign against my character and behavior outside his office, and because he continually denied the truth, my idealizations of him were undone and replaced with a more realistic assessment.

When Dr. Hammond took me on as a patient, she had to decide whether she was willing to support me through each step along the way. Having me as a patient was at times detrimental to her practice, since she had to reschedule her clients in order to have the time to sit through the various licensing board hearings. She was also willing to have her own credibility questioned in court had she been called to testify to the psychological damages of the abuse. She was further prepared to have her records subpoenaed and to risk a countersuit from Dr. X.

Had I sought therapy with Dr. Hammond prior to making my decision to go public, I suspect we would have explored together the advantages and disadvantages of taking legal action against Dr. X. This truly is not a decision to make alone. And yet ultimately, it must be the abused patient's choice, which the therapist must respect and support. For a therapist to force a patient to push the legal issue when that person is unable to do so is a form of exploitation in itself.

In summarizing what I learned about myself with respect to Dr. X in my therapy with Dr. Hammond, I would say that ultimately my trust in Dr. X as my therapist, my trust in our entire therapeutic relationship, was marred by his sexualizing the relationship. Until I experienced nonjudgmental acceptance from

Dr. Hammond, I did not feel safe to confront my own distorted perceptions of what had happened to me. Until I was secure enough to experience the raw feelings of anger and hurt in reaction to Dr. X's abuse of my trust, I could not work through my tragedy, I could not mourn what had happened, and I could not experience freedom from the psychological trauma I had endured.

7

History Repeats Itself

In the summer of 1984, a young woman who had been in Dr. X's treatment was allegedly seduced by him during several of their therapy sessions. Some months after terminating therapy, she received a request from him that must have struck her as singularly odd: Would she sign a petition he was preparing to present at his upcoming licensing hearing? The petition attested to his high moral conduct and good standing in the community. Disturbed by Dr. X's insistent request, the woman contacted the licensing board. Upon hearing of her complaint, the board's executive secretary referred her to Dr. Hammond, who was by then gaining substantial experience in treating several of Dr. X's previous patients. Through her new therapist, the woman learned of and contacted Suzanne Brown.

The attorney at once recognized the striking similarities

between her last three cases and the situation now described to her, down to the most intricate details, and she accepted the new case. Thus in the summer of 1984, the state licensing board for psychologists once again met to hear a complaint of sexual malpractice against Dr. X.

Just as I had been forbidden to communicate with my two co-plaintiffs, I could not speak to this woman—in order to protect her from the accusation that her testimony was contaminated. Nonetheless, Dr. Hammond suggested I attend the hearing and offer this current victim my quiet moral support. I also needed to attend the hearing for myself, to understand better why it was so difficult to keep this man from practicing therapy.

Three months from then I was to present a paper at the American Psychological Association's annual convention, concerning the effects of sexual exploitation by a therapist. As I considered the remarks I would make, I was confronted with the knowledge that Dr. X was continuing to offer "therapy" while evidently still unable to control his sexual behavior. I was, perhaps, a bit more objective as I sat in the audience at this hearing; but even as I began to fathom the complexities involved in taking and keeping a professional license from a psychologist, I was still distressed, still very angry as I watched an aging Dr. X engage in pathetic attempts at character assassination.

The psychologist's young and attractive third wife sat at his side—courageously, I thought. I wondered whose story she believed and whether she had been influenced by his power of suggestion, believing him to be a victimized soul whose only intent was to help his patients. If she did, she was not alone— many people had believed in Dr. X before.

I watched Dr. X's ex-patient as she sat before the board with her back to the audience. I knew the details of her private life would be made mercilessly and needlessly public. If she had known—really known—in advance how devastating the procedure she faced was going to be, would she have come forward?

The first issue at this hearing concerned the voluntary termination of the contract between Dr. X and his supervising psychologist. The second issue was a request by Dr. X's attorney that the proceedings be delayed. The lawyer complained that he was not prepared to defend his client adequately because the complainant had not cooperated with his request that he be given a photograph of her to circulate at local bars. When asked why he needed to do this, he replied that it was necessary in order to gather information about her social life, which he believed to be relevant to the case. The board refused this request and went on to the third issue: determining, once again, whether Dr. X had been guilty of unethical conduct.

IN DEFENSE OF A CERTIFICATE

Dr. X's first approach to his defense was to challenge the board's jurisdiction over him. He argued that he was now licensed as a professional counselor, seeing some patients as a licensed professional counselor and others as a certified psychologist under supervision. The determination of whether the patient was seen by Dr. X the psychologist or Dr. X the professional counselor was not made arbitrarily. Any patient who was referred to him by one of his current patients received treatment from the licensed professional counselor; anyone referred to him by his supervisor received treatment from the certified psychologist under supervision. Both Dr. X and his supervisor insisted that he had seen the current complainant as a professional counselor. Thus, Dr. X asserted, her complaint was no business of the board's.

The members of the board would not humor him. They found in his testimony clear evidence that the counseling skills he employed in the supposedly different situations were indistinguishable. Nor were the credentials he displayed on his office walls clearly differentiated for the benefit of his patients. Furthermore, throughout the proceedings, he referred to his psychologist–patient relationship, and the petition he had asked the complainant to sign had been intended for presentation to the licensing board for psychologists.

In a strong condemnation of his methodology, one board member charged Dr. X with attempting to confuse the issue in order to frustrate the edicts the board was trying to enforce. Dr. X wanted to claim the ability to take off his psychologist's hat and don his professional counselor's hat when it best suited him. The board found this defense totally unsound and claimed its right to hear the complaint against him.

In the second approach to his defense, Dr. X claimed that he would not have had sex with the complainant because there were too many windows in the office. Furthermore, the office walls were too thin: The act could not have gone unnoticed—he was simply not that stupid. This excuse left me seething with anger. I remembered that he knew how to be quiet and how to tell his patients to be quiet. He knew how to close drapes. He knew how to lock doors, and even without locks he knew that the therapy hour was a time of sanctioned privacy—people do not interrupt a therapist's session with a patient. The waiting room full of people outside his office had made no difference in his actions with me. Nonetheless, the board members spent some time scrutinizing the floor plan of the office and cross-examining the janitor as to whether someone in the hallway outside the office could tell whether Dr. X's office lights were on.

For the third point in his defense, Dr. X claimed he had an injured knee that rendered him unable to kneel on the floor beside the patient, as she alleged he had done. The board members listened patiently to one of Dr. X's golfing buddies and questioned him as to the proper way one kneels to line up a putt. The gentleman demonstrated how Dr. X's alleged inability to kneel interfered significantly with his golf game.

Dr. X's fourth tactic was his claim that the complainant was sexually aggressive. Her alleged seductive behavior during therapy had led Dr. X to decide to cease working with her and refer her to another therapist. His failure to act on either of these decisions did not escape the board's notice. To my dismay, however, the complainant's personal life was laid open in needless and irrelevant detail. Worse yet, over the next three days of the hearing, in their discussions of her relationships with men outside of therapy, the board members occasionally became lax in their discretion. I felt that an unsound bias was creeping into their consideration of the case: Single women are in part to blame for their sexual exploitation during therapy if they are sexually active outside of therapy. The members' occasional failure to refer to the complainant's alleged sexual aggressiveness as "alleged" eventually brought her such painful humiliation that she became tearful and could no longer remain in the room. After some time, I left to find her, and I sat with her, feeling angry and helpless as she wept and told me over and over, "Carolyn, I *don't deserve* this!"

As his fifth point of defense, Dr. X stated that he had been impotent during the time the alleged seduction was supposed to have occurred. This assertion prompted Brown to tell me later a joke about a man who was being sued because his dog bit a jogger. "I keep my dog in the yard," the man stated in defense. When neighbors testified to the contrary, he claimed, "But my dog doesn't bite." When the victim displayed his wound, the man tried once more. "Look," he said, "I don't even have a dog."

The board's attorney refused to accept the claim of impotence. No information regarding the condition was recorded in his personal physician's records. In a man of Dr. X's years, the attorney argued, impotence is frequently a prognostic symptom of serious ailments. Hadn't he been concerned about diabetes or cancer? The attorney doubted that Dr. X, during a thorough physical examination, would have forgotten to mention to his doctor a prolonged period of impotence. I think I would have laughed—or perhaps cried—at this interminable process had I not been so overwhelmed by the tragedy of this entire situation.

In the fall of 1984, the board reconvened and announced its rulings in light of the evidence presented the previous summer: Dr. X was found guilty of violating several of the Ethical Principles of Psychologists. The board determined that their colleague

1. was incompetent in his rendering of therapy—he had demonstrated a greater concern for himself than for his patient
2. had failed to recognize the boundaries of his own competence
3. had not protected the welfare of his patient in both his failure to terminate her as a patient and his failure to seek supervision regarding his patient's alleged sexual aggressiveness
4. had failed to recognize the interference of his own personal problems as they marred his professional effectiveness and resulted in the violation of his patient's trust and dependency upon him

5. had violated the board's order of November 1980, by not having been in psychotherapy at a time coexisting with his supervision-while he had seen two different therapists, the board judged that he had not engaged in therapy with either of them

So ruling, the board stated that neither his license nor his certification would be returned. Nonetheless, Dr. X was still provided recourse: He could ask for a rehearing, and if it were not granted, he could challenge the revocation in district court.

It appears that there is no such thing as a final revocation of a psychologist's license in this state. The board may keep saying no, but a defrocked psychologist may continue to appeal. The legislature has not empowered the licensing board for psychologists to retract irrevocably a certificate or license: It is a form of protection of the public that they do not offer.

After his psychologist's license had first been revoked, Dr. X applied for a professional counselor's license. At that time, there was no statute allowing the board of professional counselors to deny an application based on an applicant's past offenses. This loophole would be closed, however, after the chairman of the professional counselor's board witnessed Dr. X's testimony before the board of examiners for psychologists. The professional counselor's board subsequently empowered itself to deny an applicant's request. A stricter licensing law for one agency alone was, for many concerned, a small consolation but a step in the desired direction. This new requirement, however, was enacted too late to prevent Dr. X from gaining a license from the professional counselor's board.

A DESPAIRING REALITY

I left the administrative hearings with a sense of incredible anger, anger that this man was still allowed to practice, even after a history as blatantly unacceptable and unprofessional as his. And the entire process would have to be repeated: Yet another abused patient would file a complaint against Dr. X. This woman, again with the help of Suzanne Brown and Bill Whitehurst, went on to sue both Dr. X and his supervisor, the latter for failing to provide competent supervision.

Years later, at a meeting of the organization of local psychologists, of which I had become a member, I heard this supervisor describe his apparently frustrating work with Dr. X. He expressed regret at having taken on a task that he came to believe should have been designated to a committee rather than to an individual. As I listened to him, I began to believe that we two had something in common: We were both too easily taken in, both "enablers." Dr. X could manipulate not only patients, but some fellow professionals as well. We had both let Dr. X use us, too willing to believe the best of what the doctor presented in himself. But even as I felt sympathy for the supervisor, I grew angry with him for refusing to accept the responsibility of allowing Dr. X to see patients without comprehensive supervision.

I asked him outright whether he had ever felt intuitively, when supervising Dr. X, that he was working with someone who was beyond rehabilitation. He stated that he had indeed felt this way. But he adamantly declared that his job had been to provide Dr. X with the supervision he had contracted with the board to offer. He held that Dr. X's behavior following his supervision was the board's problem. I left this encounter wondering once again who is left to take responsibility for the professionals who will not take responsibility for themselves.

Dr. X and his supervisor settled their case—the fourth lawsuit against Dr. X—out of court in September of 1986, when the supervisor's insurance company agreed to pay $90,000 to the complainant.

Dr. X attempted to follow through with his promise to the state board of examiners that he would counter their latest revocation of his license with a lawsuit. In January of 1985 he filed a suit against the board, stating that they had denied him ample time before the hearing to procure evidence—such as a list of the complainant's sexual partners since January 1982, her 1983 income tax record, and a picture of her to circulate in local bars in an attempt to find men who had been sexually involved with her. Later in the year Dr. X brought a suit against the board of examiners of professional counselors, charging that their findings about him were "unlawful and improper because they were arbitrary and capricious for they knew of no underlying facts to support [the complainant's] accusations."

The lawsuits would never materialize, however. In February of 1987, the law firm that had represented Dr. X in his 1984 case before the board, sued him for legal fees of more than $15,000, which he had failed to pay.

FINALLY, AN ENDING

The following spring, a newspaper article I read was not so much a surprise as a reminder that no matter what one tries to do to stop a social cancer, it might all be for naught. Dr. X, now 50 years old, had been indicted for sexual assault of a 17-year-old female patient who had been seeing him for marital counseling. Finally someone had opted for a criminal complaint—a second-degree felony charge, with a potential punishment of 20 years in prison and a fine of $10,000. But somehow, with Dr. X, punishment never seems to be fully realized. He was released from custody on his personal recognizance, paying nothing out of pocket besides a $20 processing fee. The newspaper quoted Bill Whitehurst:

> "My concern is that he is still holding himself out to the public as a competent counselor for marriage, divorce, and personal problems. The fact that he is still holding himself out to be a counselor after four cases have been filed against him and settled is a really sad indictment of our policing agencies. . . . [Our firm] has tried every possible way to warn the . . . public about this man."

Suzanne Brown spoke angrily, all too aware of the disturbing reality that continues to allow the victimization of vulnerable patients: "[Dr. X is] not licensed to do anything right now. You can open up a clinic and not say you're licensed and you're not regulated."

It appears that all we have done, from the licensing board hearings to the civil suit and public exposure, has come to nothing: The sanctioning of a fictitious potential for rehabilitation, conflicting licensing procedures, and leniently enforced and easily altered stipulations contributed to the foiling of all we attempted. Suzanne Brown, tenaciously pursuing justice, was overwhelmed by the sense of having failed to realize the primary goal shared by each of her four clients, her co-counsel, and the other women who volunteered to serve as witnesses in 1982. None of us could keep this psychologist from victimizing his patients during the course of therapy: Dr. X continued to practice as a marriage counselor.

In November of 1987, Dr. X appeared in district court with his new attorney. The assistant district attorney had refused to engage in plea bargaining of any kind. I wondered whether Dr. X's attorney had been able to impress upon his client the difference between civil and criminal litigation. Or perhaps Dr. X himself was enough aware of the difference. The assistant district attorney promised that Dr. X's history, from the first complaints in 1978 to the last in 1984, would be brought into the courtroom. This time Dr. X would not fight, much to my surprise. He entered a nonnegotiated and unconditional plea of guilty to the felony charge of sexual assault.

In January of 1988, I walked toward the courtroom with my husband, aware of feeling little more than curiosity as we prepared to hear the judge pronounce Dr. X's sentence. Underneath that curiosity, however, there was a whisper of wanting to bring true closure to this story. I was sitting down in the second row before I realized that Dr. X was in the row in front of me, three seats to my left, his collar turned up in an attempt to cover his face, his hands lifted to his brows. He glanced at me, stood up and went to sit beside an attractive dark-haired woman at the back of the room.

An air of quiet drama seems to run steadily beneath the drone of administrative courtroom procedures. I watched quietly as the witnesses for the state were briefly questioned. There were only two: the psychologist who was the manager of psychological services with the police department, a man determined that criminal procedures succeed where civil efforts had failed to render Dr. X harmless to vulnerable clients; and a diplomate of the American Psychological Association who taught at the university. A past member of the state board of licensing examiners, he had been responsible for referring Dr. X's patients to other psychologists when Dr. X first lost his license in 1979.

The witnesses were called to the stand individually, but the questions asked of them were identical: Given their years in the community and their knowledge of Dr. X, did they have an opinion as to whether his moral character was good or bad? Both answered in the affirmative. "And what is that opinion?" Both stated with an abruptness that left no question as to their personal and professional judgment, "Bad." Dr. X's attorney did not cross-examine nor did he call any witnesses on his client's behalf.

When Dr. X approached the bench, he stood quietly. I wondered whether all the fight had gone out of him, or if he simply realized that fighting in this arena was not in his best interest. He had no questions, denials, or retorts, nothing but a quiet, listening ear for the judge's directives. At that moment, I was keenly aware of my own feelings: There was a surprising absence of resentment and a sense that I had healed, for all I felt for him was pity—not for the punishment meted out, which I thought was less than he deserved, but that he had ever started down the path that would lead to his professional (and, some would argue, personal) destruction.

The probation office and the assistant district attorney had requested "shock probation" for Dr. X, wanting him to spend a brief period of time in prison so that he might get a flavor for what he would encounter should he violate probation. But the local jails had been overcrowded for years and now had reached a crisis point, with the county having to rent space to house prisoners. The judge was not inclined to allow the county to pay $45 a day to hold Dr. X and instead gave him a probated sentence of 10 years and a probated fine of $10,000. The judge promised, however, that if Dr. X broke a single condition of his probation he would be sent to prison for the maximum time of 20 years.

As a convicted sex offender, Dr. X must report to a probation officer once a month for the next 10 years. The district attorney told me that Dr. X had made plans to leave the state but that the conditions of probation would hold; Dr. X had been required to sign a waiver of extradition, so that if and when he broke a condition of probation while out of state, he would be brought back immediately.

The district judge had reviewed numerous letters from the public, as well as findings of fact from the state board of licensing examiners' December 1978 hearings. I suspect there were many letters from the board members, probably many from local psychologists, and perhaps even some communication from the attorneys who had represented Dr. X's victims in the past—all urging the judge to make the one stipulation in the probation statement that flooded me with relief:

> You are not to engage in counseling of any sort. You are not to hold yourself out as a counselor of any sort during the period of probation. You are not to engage in advertising yourself as a counselor. Make no representation about your skills as a counselor.

Someone had done it. Where civil litigation had failed and the hands of the psychology licensing boards had been tied, the criminal justice system demonstrated greater freedom: It had stopped Dr. X, at least for the next decade, from practicing counseling in any form whatsoever. In the face of civil suits, complaints to the licensing board, and even subsequent delicensure, Dr. X had merely sidestepped every attempt to prevent him from practicing as a counselor. But the criminal court could, and did, stop Dr. X.

It is true that if Dr. X is able to keep himself within the boundaries of the law for the next decade, his criminal record as a felon will be removed. Some of us who have known him do not expect him to be successful. His victims—and I cannot help but believe there will be some—must be found in some other context.

Periodically now I see him on television, where he has attempted to gain a foothold as an actor in commercials. At 51 years of age, he remains a person whose false sincerity can skillfully deceive. To the people who will inevitably come to trust Dr. X, I wish them luck and safety and an ability to forgive themselves for being taken in. I believe they may need it.

Epilogue

This book has been 7 years in the writing. The process has been at times both cathartic and grounding, and at times a great and unappreciated burden. But I would have had it no other way, for the process of telling this story has also provided me with a way to integrate into the realm of assimilated experience both Dr. X's betrayal and my role as victim. I have gained through writing, therapy, and simple self-reflection a greater understanding not only of the subtleties of my own experience, but also the impact of Dr. X's mental illness on other women and on the entire profession of psychology. Most important of all, I have let go of the sense of shame I once felt in knowing that this was part of my history.

From the time I was 12 years old I had anticipated that I would include graduate school in my educational training. By the time I was in high school, I was considering psychology as a future profession. Although my experience with Dr. X certainly soured me on pursuing a career in this profession for many years, with time and subsequent therapy, I realized that Dr. X was hardly representative of the entire profession of psychology, nor the best it had to offer people. Two years after the lawsuit was settled, I followed through with my original goal. At the time of this writing I am completing my professional training in a doctoral level counseling psychology program in the Southwest. I am also enjoying my seventh year of companionship with my husband Ken, and have learned much about the joys and trials of being a stepmother to his son and daughter.

On April 20th of 1988, 2 days after my 33rd birthday, I sat in my dining room alone, holding in my hand a birthday card from my mother with a picture of a small child of 5 on it. In blue dress and apron, she was stretching wide both her arms with the wonderment, innocence, and irrevocable trust that youth can know. I realized that I had been a child in whose eyes my mother had seen these things. And then I felt for myself the desire to protect such innocence, a feeling I believe she must have had for me as her young child, and must have for me now. I know I have written of things that have caused her grief—things she would have preferred left between the two of us, as a matter of family privacy. But I believed that even those details that were uncomfortable to relate were necessary for portraying what I could of the complex tapestry of my life and circumstances. It is my hope that my mother can understand and accept this, as she has accepted that her fierce protectiveness could not save me from taking the emotionally troubling path that was mine to walk.

That same evening I found myself studying a photograph of my father that hangs in my dining room. The door on the opposite wall was reflected on its glass, making it seem as if he were looking at me out of a doorway lit from behind. I was struck by the fact that my father did not live to see my graduation from high school, college, and now from a graduate program where I have learned more about myself than I ever imagined I could know, even though the journey of self-understanding is only just underway. I have lived more than half of my lifetime now without my father, and I cannot know how he would have felt or what he would have thought about all of this—an irrefutable reality that sits more easily with me as time goes by, but is not yet without its discomfort. I can only hope that he would have consoled me as he could; that he would have supported me in my fight to compensate a wrong and in my attempt to prevent further wrongs through the frustrating and sometimes inadequate means of seeking legal accountability, and through the telling of the story. And although I now know that I am all right even without the certainty of his approval, I still pause to wonder if he would have understood.

II

DR. BRODSKY'S ANALYSIS

8

A Professional's Analysis of Sex between Therapist and Patient: The Perspective of the Expert Witness

AN INTRODUCTION TO THE EXPERT WITNESS

Carolyn's story has been presented to you, the reader. If you were on a jury charged with determining the damages that resulted from her encounter with Dr. X, you would be entitled to hear the opinions of expert witnesses who are qualified to judge the extent of damages already sustained and to project the possibilities of future damage. Before a potential witness is accepted or stipulated as an expert by the court, questions are asked of him or her to determine parameters of expertise. The standard questions regard name, degrees, credentials, current and past positions, honors, publications, work of relevance to the specific area of expertise, and any potential conflicts of interest. So that you may know as much about me as a jury would have had Carolyn Bates's case gone to trial, I will introduce myself here as the potential expert witness.

My name is Annette M. Brodsky. I received a bachelor of arts degree in psychology from the University of Miami in 1960 and a master's and doctorate in clinical psychology from the University of Florida in 1962 and 1970, respectively. I interned in clinical psychology at Walter Reed Army Hospital (1963–1964). I have been licensed as a psychologist in Illinois, Alabama, and California. My past employment as a psychologist includes positions held with the United States Disciplinary Barracks and Munson Army Hospital, Fort Leavenworth, Kansas; the Counseling Center and Department of Psychology, Southern Illinois University; the Department of Psychology and Psychological Clinic, University of Alabama; and the Forensic Unit at Bryce State Hospital, Tuscaloosa, Alabama. I am currently chief psychologist and director of training at Harbor–UCLA Medical Center. I am also a professor of medical psychology in the Department of Psychiatry and Biobehavioral Sciences of the UCLA School of Medicine. During most of my professional career, I have also been engaged in the part-time private practice of clinical psychology.

Of interest to the case of Carolyn Bates versus Dr. X, I have written about women's treatment in psychology and have co-edited a book on research in psychotherapy (Brodsky & Hare-Mustin, 1980). I have served on state and national ethics committees and have done survey research on sex between patient and therapist. My curriculum vitae includes over 50 publications and a lengthy list of offices held in state and national psychology organizations, including that of president of the American Psychological Association's Division on the Psychology of Women. I am familiar with forensic issues, having testified in cases wherein the defendant's plea was not guilty by reason of insanity and/or incompetent to stand trial, as well as in cases of malpractice. Sex between therapist and patient is an area in which I have researched, written, made presentations, participated in workshops, and acted as a consultant to licensing boards and ethics committees.

Thus the court and the jury know me. They have a right to know the qualifications of the professional who renders an expert opinion. They, as well as the judge who accepts the expert as qualified to make a professional opinion on the matter at hand, must come to their own conclusions as to the credibility of the testimony. The opposing side may also hire experts to counterbalance points of view that may not be clearly established by the state of the art of the profession. In cases of sexual intimacy, it is difficult to find experts who would be willing to testify that sex between a patient and therapist is not generally damaging. More specifically, it would be difficult to find any expert who would be willing to testify that Carolyn Bates was not damaged by Dr. X. This difficulty is increasing as we amass more knowledge about the phenomenon of sexual intimacy. My own history of involvement in this field parallels the development of the knowledge that we have and the events that prompted the research in the last 2 decades.

A HISTORY OF SEX BETWEEN THERAPIST AND PATIENT

Early references to the issue of sex between therapist and patient go back to the Hippocratic oath of the ancient Greeks, which warns physicians not to have sex with patients under their care. It has also been stated to me that the code of Nigerian medicine men includes advice against "sexing the patient." The relationship between doctor and patient is considered a sacred trust. In the early days of psychoanalysis, Freud, in a letter to Sándor Ferenczi, suggested that analysts who do not stop before a kiss might encourage other colleagues to go further: "There is no revolutionary who is not driven out of the field by a still more radical one." Freud was concerned that younger colleagues "will find it hard to stop at the point intended" (cited by Jones, 1957, pp. 163–165). But getting caught or being reprimanded for going too far was not the order of the day. Helene Deutsch, an analyst of great stature in Freud's Vienna circle, and an author of a book on the psychology of women, unwittingly offered the standard alibi for a therapist's misconduct. She wrote of women patients' "far fetched allegations" and "wish fulfilling fantasies" (Deutsch, 1944).

In the 1950s and 1960s, some psychologists were aware of colleagues who were known to have had sexual relationships with their patients. But these shady events were not easily reported, nor were they considered the proper subject of survey research. In 1955, Bruno Klopfer shared survey data with participants in a workshop, but never published it (Gluck, 1988). Forer did not present his data, collected in the 1960s, until 1980. Dahlberg, a psychiatrist who also collected data on the subject in the 1960s, reported in an article published in 1970 that he failed to gain a forum for his views in a "larger organization" because of the controversy of the topic.

During the late 1960s and early 1970s, two professionals published accounts of their own positive consequences of patient-therapist sex, recommending that such treatment might benefit certain patients. James McCartney, a psychiatrist, wrote about "overt transference" as "a visible, audible, or tangible muscular or glandular reaction" to an inner feeling of a patient that represents a need to do more than talk (1966). His patients and their families supposedly consented in advance. Martin Shepard, another psychiatrist, suggested in his book *The Love Treatment* (1971) that there are potential beneficial effects of therapist–patient sex. These authors were cited by those who wanted to justify their own sexualized behaviors with their patients. Eventually, both authors were negatively sanctioned by professional entities, although in neither case was it due to a patient's complaint.

It was during the controversial climate surrounding the emergence of the women's movement in the profession of psychology in the late 1960s and early 1970s that I became involved with these issues. In 1969, at the first American Psychological Association convention meeting of a group that developed into the Association for Women in Psychology, clinical psychologists voiced their concerns about abuses of women in psychotherapy and sought a way to identify therapists for the benefit of women who would be vulnerable to sexist practices, including being seduced by the therapist. The next year, I produced the first national roster of feminist therapists—a listing of credentials and services by therapists who stated their own definitions of their feminist philosophy.

That same year, Phyllis Chesler, a New York psychologist, stunned her APA colleagues with a presentation of interviews with women patients who had had sex with their therapists (Chesler, 1972a). She encouraged them to sue their therapists for malpractice. Later, she published *Women and Madness* (1972b), a best-seller, in which she addressed the issue of sexual abuse in psychotherapy and protested the treatment of women who are mentally ill. The case of Roy vs. Hartogs, in which a psychiatrist who had sex with his patient was successfully sued, became widely publicized as a result of a book, entitled *Betrayal* (1976), written by Lucy Freeman and the patient, Julie Roy, which was then made into a movie for television. Other civil court suits also emerged during this period, further motivating the feminist movement in psychology to demand action by their professional establishments.

I was working in a university counseling center at the time and receiving referrals from women who were being sexually harassed by their professors and/or therapists. The problem was becoming more apparent to me. My APA colleagues had approached the governance of the association with grave concerns about the issue. In 1973, APA appointed me, along with seven other psychologists across the country, to serve on a task force on sex bias and sex role stereotyping in psychotherapeutic practices (Brodsky *et al.*, 1975). Sex between patient and therapist was only one of our charges, but it was obvious to some of us that that issue was the primary cause for our existence. We had discovered that between 1970 and 1974, only four cases of therapist–patient sexual intimacy were investigated by the ethics committee of the association. Of these, three were dismissed. In only one case was the psychologist negatively sanctioned. His membership in APA was dropped for nonpayment of dues.

The task force had already sent out its own survey of psychologists in APA regarding information about sexist practices so that it could develop guidelines for the treatment of women. One of these guidelines dealt with the seduction of female patients. But because of one negative vote, the task force could not obtain a unanimous agreement that having sex with a patient was sexist. The guideline could only encourage therapists to avoid seducing patients or treating them as sex objects.

Upon completion of the task force, Jean Holroyd and myself, the co-chairs, agreed to pursue the sexual seduction issue. In its survey, the task force had discovered that most respondents reported cases of male therapists as perpetrators and female patients as the victims of seduction. Based on this feedback and on a survey of Los Angeles physicians in which 10% admitted (anonymously) that they engaged in sexual intimacy with their patients (Kardener, Fuller, & Mensh, 1973), we surveyed licensed psychologists in the 50 states to study the extent of erotic practices in psychotherapy (Holroyd & Brodsky, 1977). This self-report survey explicitly requested respondents to answer questions regarding the number of patients they had ever kissed, hugged, or touched with erotic intent and the number of patients with whom they had had sexual intercourse. Questionnaires were returned by 70% of the 1,000 randomly sampled licensed psychologists. Approximately 10% of the male respondents admitted that they had engaged in some form of erotic behavior with at least one patient, but only one female respondent admitted any erotic contact. Many of the men who reported that they had had erotic contact with patients also noted that the experience was not positive for either their patients or themselves, but 80% of them were so involved more than once.

Other surveys supported similar statistics with male therapists (Pope, Levenson, & Schover, 1979; Bouhoutsos, Holroyd, Lerman, Forer, & Greenberg, 1983). Women therapists were dramatically different in their incidence of sexual intimacies with patients. Perry reported that of 156 respondents to her survey of women physicians, none had sexual intercourse with patients, but many engaged in nonerotic touching (1976). Holroyd and I found that among the practitioners in our earlier survey, less than 1% of the women engaged in sexual intimacies; and in another analysis of the data, those practitioners who used nonerotic touching were at more risk for sexual intimacies only if the practice of touching patients was restricted to one sex (Holroyd & Brodsky, 1980).

Other studies using small samples tended to corroborate these results. In addition, they provided more insights on the nature of sexual relationships in therapy. Butler and Zelen found the therapists to be vulnerable and needy (1977). The sex was not planned and, in retrospect, was not considered beneficial for the patient or the therapist. The therapists were not discouraged from having further relationships with patients by their professions, nor did they voluntarily seek help for their behavior.

In the 1980s, the data on incidence rates and almost exclusively male perpetrators indicated some changes. Pope, Tabachnick, and Keith-Spiegel (1987) found respondents reporting considerably less sexual contact with patients (1.9%). Cases of same-sex therapist–patient contact were becoming more commonly known by ethics committees and licensing boards. The American Psychological Association Insurance Trust (Bennett, 1987) noted that sexual misconduct represented their greatest cost. They accounted for one fifth of total claims reported in the last 10 years (Murray, 1986). Sexual misconduct cases comprised the category most frequently reported by the APA Ethics Committee (1987). Complaints were escalating in all the mental health professions, and negative sanctions were becoming more frequent and more severe. Sex between therapists and their former patients was becoming a controversial issue as expatients began to trace their problems to coercion based on therapeutic transferences that originated in therapy. In a study of the handling of therapist–patient sexual intimacies by psychology ethics committees and licensing boards, Sell, Gottlieb, and Schoenfeld (1986) found that those therapists who claimed, as a defense, that the patient was no longer in therapy were given more severe sanctions than those who did not make such a claim.

Although the media have reported, and even sensationalized, the more dramatic cases of patients' suing their therapists for huge sums of money in damage awards, it is interesting to note that about half of the patients in the study by Sell *et al.* who had sex with their therapists were not aware that it was unacceptable, either ethically or legally. An even more interesting statistic found by Pope and Bajt (in press) is that a persistent 4%–5% of psychologists still believe that sexual conduct between patient and therapist is not unethical, and 9% knowingly engage in the practice although they are aware that it is unethical. They justify their behavior with the belief that there is potential benefit to the patient or to themselves.

In fact, since the mid-1970s, the mental health professions have stated explicitly that sexual intimacy between therapist and patient is unethical. Both the American Psychiatric Association and the American Psychological Association voted to include statements in their ethical and professional standards specifically prohibiting sex between therapist and patient. Many states throughout the country have begun to include sex between therapist and patient as cause for the revocation of an independent practitioner's professional license. One state, Minnesota, has gone so far as to mandate that knowledge of a therapist's having sexual intercourse with a patient be reported by professionals; and at least two states, Wisconsin and Minnesota, have legislated that a therapist who has sex with a patient is guilty of a criminal offense.

Today the issue is not whether sex between therapist and patient is appropriate. Clearly, it is not. The issues involve the parameters of the behavior. Some of the questions being addressed in the literature include: What constitutes sexual intimacy? When is a patient no longer in therapy? (see Brodsky, 1985); Is it ever appropriate to have a relationship with a former patient? (see Sell et al., 1986); Can interventions be helpful once a relationship has developed? (see Bouhoutsos & Brodsky, 1985; Pope, 1987); Is there rehabilitation after such intimacies? (see Gonsiorek, 1987; Schoener, 1988).

The following chapters address these issues in the context of Carolyn Bates's relationship with Dr. X. Carolyn's case is illustrative because she represents many of the typical, rather than the extreme, situations in which sexual intimacies are problematic. Carolyn was intelligent but vulnerable and naive about therapy. She was not severely disturbed either before, during, or after therapy with Dr. X. Nevertheless, she was exploited, damaged, and devastated as a result of the experience. The relationship with Dr. X and the resulting lawsuit had an impact on her life, her dreams, her physical functioning, her relationships, and her self-esteem. She was able to recover and progress significantly through further therapy over the years, but flashbacks and remnants of the impact on her self-esteem and of the insecurity about her judgment remained. Her case also illustrates the difficulties of a profession in trying to screen out, train, monitor, or stop a dangerous colleague who would use his role as a father figure to seduce his vulnerable, dependent patients into destructive incestuous relationships.

9

The Phenomenon of Sexual Intimacies in Therapy: Who's Doing What to Whom?

In coming to an understanding of what happened to Carolyn and the other women in this case, I have attempted to answer one basic question: How do these women fit the pattern that emerges from the research literature and the previous legal cases? My findings are of concern to both the psychologist and the patient involved in a sexually intimate situation. I have examined the boundaries of sexual intimacies, the kinds of psychologists and patients who are vulnerable to engaging in intimate relationships in therapy, the kind of remediation that

Adapted from A. M. Brodsky (1986). Sexual exploitation of patients and students. In R. Kilburg, R. Thoreson, & P. Nathan (Eds.), *Professionals in distress: Issues, syndromes and solutions in psychology* (pp. 153–171). Washington DC: American Psychological Association. Copyright 1986 by the American Psychological Association. Adapted by permission of the publisher.

makes sense, the instances when remediation does not make sense, and what one can do to prevent the behaviors that inevitably lead to sexual exploitation.

DEFINITION OF SEXUAL INTIMACY

The American Psychological Association states under principle 6A of its ethical principles for psychologists (American Psychological Association, 1981) that sexual intimacies between therapist and patient are unethical. "Sexual intimacies," however, are not defined. Almost anyone with a cursory knowledge of the issues might understand that it is unethical to have sexual intercourse with one's patients or even with one's students. But what other behavior might constitute intimacy or sexual exploitation? This question presents the first difficulty in defining sexual intimacy. Varying perceptions of intimacy pose another difficulty. Surveys of professionals indicate a persistent minority belief that there may be a positive aspect to sexual intimacy between patients and therapists (Bouhoutsos et al., 1983; Gartrell, Herman, Olarte, Feldstein, & Localio, 1986; Holroyd & Brodsky, 1977; Kardener et al., 1973). Several other issues involving the intent and the judgment of the therapists also influence the definition of intimacy.

It may seem clear that the intention to arouse one's patient sexually or to satisfy one's own needs is a violation of an ethical code; the word *intent*, however, has a variety of parameters. First, one must consider whose intent. With regard to the intent of the therapist, is it acceptable for the patient to become sexually aroused by something the therapist does as long as the therapist disclaims the intention to arouse sexually? Courts have engaged in skirmishes over this issue in cases where the patient has maintained that the actions of the therapist were clearly intended sexually whereas the therapist maintained that the patient may have been aroused without cause or intention. One can imagine that the therapist who engages in physical touching of patients to demonstrate affectionate support or to acknowledge caring might be inadvertently behaving in ways that a patient could misinterpret as erotic or sexual. Thus kissing, hugging, affectionate touching, or stroking could easily have more than one meaning for either of the parties involved (Holroyd & Brodsky, 1980).

There is a distinct difference, however, between the kind of touching that occurs when a therapist is himself or herself aroused and has an intention to elicit a reciprocal reaction from the patient and the nonerotic touching and holding by a therapist with benign, caring intentions. A patient is frequently aware of the subtle difference, even when the therapist does not consciously intend that the patient recognize the erotic feelings of his or her countertransference. Thus a female patient can distinguish the intent of eroticism when a male therapist rubs his hand up and down her arm from the intent to console when he puts his arm around her shoulder when she is distraught and crying. Therapists who are accused of sexual intimacies often deny such refinements of intent (Brodsky, 1985). In Carolyn's case, she did not perceive a sexual intent in the first hugs; she accepted them as fatherly concern. Increasingly, however, she became aware that the touches were erotic, but her great need to feel that Dr. X was a trustworthy father figure compelled her to ignore the cues.

Those of us working with patients who have complained of therapists' being sexually intimate are inclined to extend the definition of sexual intimacy from intention to arouse to the effect of arousing. That is, if a therapist is so naive as to be unaware that the physical touching or seductive statements made in therapy are arousing the patient sexually, then the therapist is in great need of further sensitivity training. If the behaviors have the effect of sexually arousing the patient, one might conclude that sexual intimacy has occurred (Brodsky, 1985).

I know of at least one legal case in which this issue became central because the patient produced evidence, corroborated by the therapist's own notes, that she had told him explicitly that his physical touching—stroking of her arms, hugging, and rocking her back and forth—were sexually arousing to her and that she had sexual feelings toward him. Thus when he continued these behaviors, she could only assume that he was encouraging her sexual arousal, which extended her own belief that he was interested in having a sexual alliance with her. His defense—that he was mothering her rather than being sexual—was hard to accept given that he had acknowledged her direct comments that his particular behaviors were sexually arousing to her. Dr. X's rubbing the exposed abdomen of his female patients could readily be arousing even if he maintained that *he* was not aroused.

A second factor in defining sexual intimacy in therapy involves the judgment of the therapist. Is the therapist truly competent if he or she is not aware of a client's or patient's major emotional states? Can a competent therapist possibly miss the signs of sexual arousal in a patient with whom he or she has engaged in physical touching or in the intimate discussion of sexual details? This is not to suggest that a therapist and a patient should not discuss the patient's sexual feelings and sexual fantasies; rather, the therapist needs to know where discussion ends and arousal and action may begin. A confounding factor is that some therapists believe that although the unusual, innovative approaches they use may violate the more traditional boundaries of touching in therapy, these innovations are beneficial to the patient and therefore justify violation of traditional personal boundaries (Holroyd & Brodsky, 1977). Thus the therapist who engages in intense physical touching, such as rocking a patient back and forth, holding or hugging for several seconds, or more than momentary stroking, may consider himself or herself a brave pioneer in uncharted territory. Such techniques, however, are not really innovative; if they were, they would have been adopted more widely decades ago when previous therapists experimented with them.

In the 1960s, Masters and Johnson became aware of the need to eliminate any actual sexual behavior by the therapist or a surrogate during the treatment of sexual dysfunction. Masters and Johnson no longer provide sexual surrogates in therapy, let alone permit the therapist to engage in any sexual acts with the patient (Masters & Johnson, 1976). Other so-called innovators promoting physical touch that might intimate sexual behavior, such as McCartney (1966) with his overt transference or Shepard (1971) with his love treatment, found to their dismay that the initial interest in their proposals was temporary at best and resulted in dismissal from their respective professional organizations. Modern-day reinventors of erotic psychotherapeutic techniques are even less likely to be considered purveyors of a brave new cure (Keith-Spiegel, 1979). Dr. X's use of a rubbing technique as a way to relax his patients goes beyond the boundaries of normal and customary practice. But this "technique" was not being researched or monitored. Nor was he taught to behave in such a manner by any established person or theory.

Dual relationships are a third aspect of the definition of sexual intimacies. An instance of sexual intimacy between therapist and patient is one example of a dual relationship. In such relationships, there is more than one purpose. A therapy relationship, however, is meant to be exclusive and one-dimensional. The therapist is the expert; the patient, the consumer of the expertise. Once a patient accepts an individual as a therapist, that individual cannot, without undue influence, relate to the patient in any other role. Relating to the patient as an employer, business partner, lover, spouse, relative, professor, or student would contaminate the therapeutic goal. This contamination is much more intense in a psychotherapy relationship than in the relationship between a client and a professional in any other field, for example between a client and an internist, a dentist, a lawyer, or an accountant.

Acting upon a sexual feeling or developing a personal relationship beyond the professional one would not have consequences nearly as serious for nonpsychotherapeutic dyads: in the psychotherapy relationship, the relationship is part of the service owed the patient, whereas in other professional dyads, it is not. Almost all psychotherapies, except perhaps a few technical behavioral programs, involve the development of a relationship between the therapist and the patient. This relationship is not egalitarian; the therapist comes into the relationship with all the power and authority of an expert who has something to sell. In the case of therapy, what is being sold is a promise that the relationship will help the patient improve his or her personal life. Indeed, it is the mismanagement of love relationships in a patient's life that is so frequently the impetus to enter therapy. For the therapist to contaminate and de-objectify his or her role in helping to resolve the patient's problems is unforgivable. Therapy is not the selling of friendship, the selling of one's body, a mating game, or a place for lovers to meet. In fact, such misuses of therapy clearly would be ethical and moral violations (American Psychological Association, 1981). Dr. X could not ethically consider Carolyn or his other patients as friends as well as patients. They were not psychologically free to be his friends; they were involved on another, more intense level of interaction that prohibits the aspect of free choice inherent in a mutual friend-ship.

Nonsexual dual relationships between therapists and patients are also unethical but probably less damaging. Bartering goods for therapy, a practice that was more common and more acceptable in the past, is now recognized as potentially problem-atic, and individual situations involving such relationships have resulted in negative sanctions by ethics committees (Hare-Mustin & Hall, 1983). The therapist who hires a patient to mow a lawn, paint a portrait, babysit, or sell a house creates a dangerous situation that may be as damaging to the therapist as to the patient. Business deals that fail, investments that lose money, and contracts, services, or products that do not meet expectations can affect the transference and countertransference in the therapeutic relationship.

None of these consequences matches the humiliation and the devastation to one's self-esteem that result from the patient's discovery that the promise of a sexual or romantic relationship that had been awakened in therapy was only exploitation (Free-man & Roy, 1976). It is an interesting finding that patients who have sexual relationships with their therapists also tend to have intimate knowledge of their therapist's personal life and to have other types of dual relationships with their therapist. The thera-pist who crosses the boundary of the professional relationship tends to do so in more ways than one and tends to be at high risk for being involved with a patient sexually (Belote, 1977; Bouhoutsos et al., 1983; D'Addario, 1978). This clearly was a phenomenon of Dr. X's therapy with Carolyn—he used her to convey his own problems. He used other patients for their busi-ness skills.

A fourth, and final, aspect to consider in defining sexual intimacy involves the therapist's selectivity. Those therapists most likely to be involved with their patients sexually, treat patients differentially on the basis of age, sex, and attractiveness. Thus the male therapist who touches, holds, kisses, or hugs female patients but not male patients is at higher risk for sexually exploiting his patients (Holroyd & Brodsky, 1980). All four of Dr. X's patients who filed civil lawsuits were younger, attractive women. No males came forward at any time.

PSYCHOLOGISTS AT RISK

When I receive a call from a lawyer whose client is a patient wanting to sue a therapist for damages resulting from sexual intimacy, I can often describe the therapist before the lawyer says a word. The therapist is male, middle-aged, involved in unsatisfactory love relationships in his own life, and perhaps going through a divorce. His caseload is primarily female. He becomes sexually involved with more than one patient, and his victims are, on average, 16 years younger than he. He confides his personal life to the patient, implying that he needs her, and he spends their therapy sessions soliciting her help with his personal problems. He is a lonely man, and even if he works in group practice, he is somewhat isolated professionally, not in close consultation with his peers. He may have a good reputation in the psychological or psychiatric community and have been in practice for many years. He tends to take cases only through referral. He is not necessarily physically attractive, but there is an aura of power or charisma about him. Although his lovemaking often leaves much to be desired, he convinces the patient that he, above all others, is the one with whom she needs to be making love (Butler & Zelen, 1977; Chesler, 1972; Freeman & Roy, 1976; Smith, 1982; Taylor & Wagner, 1976). Dr. X fits this prototype closely.

There are several variations on the prototype of the sexually abusive therapist. First are therapists in love. They are more likely to be younger, inexperienced in therapy, and genuinely involved with only one patient emotionally. They have difficulties with professional boundaries, particularly with the sanction against dual relationships. They do not recognize, or have not been adequately trained to realize, that a therapy patient is not free enough of the influence of the therapeutic relationship to make an informed, voluntary, consenting decision about an extratherapeutic relationship with the therapist. Should they realize that their feelings toward a patient are more than that of a caring parent figure or of a professional treating a vulnerable, needy patient, they may recognize their poor judgment and genuinely wish to remedy the situation or at least clarify what has happened. Being inexperienced, however, they may think that the solution is to give up the therapy sessions and enter a full-fledged affair, which they believe to have long-term potential, including marriage.

When the therapist and patient end therapy and become lovers or spouses, the ending is what counts. That is, when they live happily ever after, the fact that the therapist originally courted his or her love in the therapy hour does not seem to be a problem. But if the love relationship sours, the former patient will be able to appreciate that it developed as a result of the therapist's taking advantage of the patient's transference in the therapeutic situation.

Second are therapists with a personality disorder, which may be classified as antisocial personality. They abuse their power by playing the role of expert. Their line is "trust me." Unfortunately, they are the last people in the world whom patients should trust; they have only their own needs in mind. They sometimes engage in sexual intimacies with many patients no matter what a patient's presenting complaint is. They may be unable to form meaningful relationships, and their alliances with patients rely heavily on persuasive power, dishonesty, and charm. They are often likely to do the greatest damage. They may encourage patients to act in ways that are diametrically opposed to therapeutic behavior. For example, a male therapist may encourage an inhibited female patient to become sexually promiscuous or tell her that incest is all right and that she should look to him as a father. They may also engage patients in other kinds of dual relationships, bilking them of their money, using them as cheap labor, and otherwise exploiting them. They will not be interested in resolving any issue a patient might bring up related to the poor treatment, and they will deny intent to arouse or seduce. Such therapists can be very dangerous and may lie when confronted, but they may be supported by colleagues who, unaware of the extent of the behavior, overidentify with their claims of being victimized. Dr. X exhibits many of the features of this type of offender.

Third are the falsely accused professionals. False accusations are rarer than valid ones, but they do occur. The false accusation may result from a perceptual problem between therapist and patient. For example, a therapist's behavior may encourage or permit a patient to misinterpret; a therapist may not be aware that a patient is sexually aroused; or a therapist may misinterpret a patient's romantic comments, hoping that they are just affectionate and caring rather than sexually related. Thus therapists who feel complimented when a patient says "you are special to me," "I am in love with you," or "I dreamed I went to bed with you last night" must recognize that such pronouncements may well be direct sexual confrontations. Therapists who interpret such comments as merely evidence of a need for a nurturing relationship or of a normally developing therapeutic alliance may be surprised later. Therapists who pat or stroke a patient who has just verbalized very positive feelings toward them may stimulate the patient's sexual desires rather than reassure the patient of the mutuality of the caring. Although their intent may be innocent, the patient's interpretation may not be. It is the therapist's responsibility to evaluate the situation and keep the boundaries of the relationship and the limits of the behavior in that relationship clear (Brodsky, 1985). Those therapists who have difficulty maintaining boundaries in the professional relationship are frequently guilty of other instances of poor judgment.

We can only speculate as to whether Dr. X was merely a naive therapist who crossed the boundary and only later in his career took an active aggressive stance, exploiting the techniques that enabled sexual alliances with patients earlier in his career. There is little question of his having engaged in sexual intimacies with two of the three women in this case. Although he later admitted that he did have sex with Carolyn and another patient in the case, he presented himself as falsely accused until the evidence was produced.

PATIENTS AT RISK

If psychologists can be identified as being at risk of engaging in intimate relationships by virtue of certain characteristics, then patients can also be so identified. Data from cases presented to state ethics committees, licensing boards, and insurance trusts suggest that female patients of male therapists are most at risk of becoming sexually intimate with their therapists. The next most frequent group at risk are patients of either sex with a same-sex therapist. The patient is frequently reasonably attractive, young, naive, dependent, and in need of working on relationships, particularly love relationships. Most patients who become sexually involved with their therapists do not enter therapy with an initial complaint about their sexuality. Sexual difficulties are often interpreted first by the therapist.

Most patients who become involved with their therapists are especially trusting of the therapist. They do not question whether the doctor really does know best. Though they may feel that the sexual innuendos or overtures during therapy are improper, they repress or submerge these feelings and try to live up to the therapist's expectations of them. They may or may not be sexually attracted to the therapist; if they are so attracted, it may be because they already confuse their respect and awe of the therapist with sexual desire and love. By the time a sexual relationship is imminent, they are so entangled in the therapeutic relationship that their sexual participation is far less important to them than are the doctor's approval and the continuation of the initial relationship.

Instead of questioning the therapist's judgment, they question their own judgment when it conflicts with the therapist's. If they are not sexually aroused, they may hide their lack of response. When the therapist's behavior is later identified as unethical and exploitive, they feel devastated by their inability to have recognized it sooner (Brodsky, 1985). Carolyn is not atypical of victims generally described. Patients with a genius-level IQ, in an extremely responsible position, in a supposedly happy marriage, or suspicious to the point of paranoia in other situations may be unwittingly exploited sexually in a therapeutic situation.

A patient who commonly becomes sexually involved with his or her therapist is the one who has been physically or sexually abused as a child by his or her own parents. These patients tend to play out the role of abused child with the therapist and become extremely vulnerable to the therapist's demands, however subtle. Thus they do not question statements by the therapist such as "What we are going to do is secret; don't tell anyone" or "I know best that this is what you need to do." They understand these statements as "Your role is not to question me but to please me, and if you do not please me, I might leave."

For example, a woman incest victim is usually not very surprised if a father figure such as her therapist is interested in a sexual relationship. In fact, she may have already given cues that she expects to give something of her body or self to the therapist in exchange for his attention. She has learned to relate to men in authority in ways that are readily sexualized. It may be the discussion of confusion about previous sexual relationships with an incestuous father that encourages a therapist to begin to fantasize a sexual relationship with her (Bouhoutsos & Brodsky, 1985).

In the case of the physically abused patient, the sexuality may not necessarily be there, but the same dynamics appear to play a part in her looking to the therapist as someone who must be obeyed in order for her to receive care and love. Such patients frequently report that during the sexual episodes they have out-of-body experiences or use other related dissociative coping mechanisms. They attempt to isolate the sexual experience, disown it, and then treat the rest of the therapy hour for what it is (Brodsky, 1985). While Carolyn was neither physically nor sexually abused, she was raised in a family that administered corporal punishment for any attempt to challenge parental authority. She related to Dr. X as her father and indeed played out a role similar to the incest victim who dissociates an experience that does not fit with the reality she wants to believe. She would not complain or tell the "secret" for fear of abandonment.

Patients who have not been abused and may be extremely naive about abuse by anyone are also vulnerable to sexual intimacies with their therapist. For example, women who have led sheltered lives in which their ministers, uncles, fathers, and brothers have been honest and caring may be ill-prepared to enter relationships with men outside the family. Thus Carolyn, whose strict but caring father died when she was 15 years old, later started dating men who did not treat her in the trusted, protective way that she knew. She entered therapy to work on her difficulties with a boyfriend. The therapist exploited her trusting nature by encouraging her to become intimate with him. She was convinced that she had been overprotected in the past and would therefore be naive now if she did not go along with the solutions the doctor offered. If the trusted doctor said that having a sexual relationship with him would help her learn to deal with the men in her life, then the doctor knew best, and, as a good patient, she should comply even if it felt wrong.

This particular type of patient is most likely to be misunderstood by others and faulted for having complied with the therapist's suggestions. In fact, such patients may be fairly well integrated otherwise, very intelligent, and easy prey only in this type of situation. For them, the experience may be devastating when they realize that again they have been naive and overly trusting and cannot differentiate between a potentially harmful person and one who is genuine. They may develop posttraumatic stress disorders, complete with nightmares, somatic complaints, and confusion, long after the relationship with the sexually abusing therapist has ended (Brodsky, 1985). Carolyn's posttraumatic stress disorder was classic—nightmares, physical symptoms, numbing, and confusion.

Another patient vulnerable to sexual intimacies with a therapist is the woman with a personality disorder who is demanding and acting out. Such a patient becomes involved sexually with her therapist by confronting him with the full force of her personality, daring him to follow through. The therapist succumbs to her manipulations and complies with the demanding, flirtatious, seductive pattern she has developed as a way of interacting with others to get her way. What she needs from the therapist is limits on, not collusion with, the behavior. How can such a patient learn the limits and reality related to her demands when she finds that even the exalted therapist is putty in her hands? Therapists who fall for the demands of such a patient, whether she is diagnosed as antisocial, borderline, or having other personality disorders, are essentially incompetent. Therapists are trained to be sensitive to the needs, dynamics, and diagnostic categories of their patients. A therapist may find a patient's sexual overture ego-inflating but to give in to this overture, even tentatively, only reinforces the patient's belief that such techniques will always work. Especially in the case of women, they may learn that sex is all that men want.

Carolyn was unlike such demanding, aggressive patients. She did not know what men wanted of her and was ready to do whatever the authoritative Dr. X expected of her. Instead of helping her define limits to sexual behavior, he encouraged her to remove existing limits and sexualize all relationships with men.

It is important to note that while there are no absolute predictors of clients who will be abused, some types are more vulnerable than others. All types have been exploited sexually by therapists, and most clients who fit the preceding descriptions are not sexually exploited by their therapists. The best single predictor of exploitation in therapy is a therapist who has exploited another patient in the past. Dr. X was such a therapist.

SITUATIONS AND CIRCUMSTANCES AT RISK

Patients at risk and psychologists at risk may often get together in situations at risk. Just as there are boundaries in relationships between professional and patient or student, so there are boundaries for professional settings. The environment in which a patient is seen communicates the degree to which the relationship can be expected to remain strictly professional. Most patients expect to be seen in an office with typical office furniture, such as desks and chairs. They expect the therapist to be fully clothed and in business attire. They expect a waiting room or secretary and consistency in office hours, length of sessions, and payment schedules. Patients who become intimate with their therapist are more likely to see the therapist during evening or weekend hours. There may be no other personnel in the building, or therapy may be conducted in a house, coffee shop, or other casual place. There may be unusual furnishings, like pillows on the floor, soft or unusual lighting, or closed drapes. To the extent that the setting in which the patient is seen varies from the traditional office, the risk for sexual intimacies is higher (Brodsky, 1985). Other than closing drapes and locking the door, Dr. X was strictly conventional. In fact, he was so much so that he refused to change his billing statements to accommodate the patient who "blew the whistle" after he refused her demand for the return of money she paid for her therapy.

Therapist's verbalizations can also be conducive to sexual intimacy. Therapists are trained in verbal techniques to make patients comfortable, emotional, open, truthful, and talkative.

The therapeutic jargon that they learn can also be handy for the sexual seduction of patients. It includes statements that give certain messages, such as telling a woman "you need to trust men, and this is a safe place for you to learn that"; "I hear what you're saying; only I understand"; "others may be awful, but I really care for you"; "you can do anything you want here—it's safe"; or "it's okay to talk about anything; you can trust me." All such "psychologese" may be aimed at relaxing patients and drawing them out therapeutically but can also be misused to encourage the patient to agree to sexual intimacies. Some therapists are not even aware that their techniques can be misapplied in this way. They delude themselves into believing that patients are really head over heels in love with them because of their own personal magic rather than because of the fluent verbalizations in which they have been trained and the power of the setting in which the verbalizations are used. Dr. X had a well-developed psychological "line" that was usable no matter what the personalities of his patients. His message was "Trust me; you must demonstrate responsiveness in relating to me if you want to improve relationships with other men."

Seduction may involve the gradual relaxation of a patient, be it formalized relaxation therapy, hypnosis, or something quite informal. Some of the Gestalt techniques of referring to body language and other nonverbal cues can be extremely seductive, and certainly any physical touching can be construed as an invitation to be intimate.

Frequently women who have been involved with their therapists report that prior to the sexual intimacy there was a personal intimacy in which the therapist began to disclose more and more about his own life. It can be very seductive, particularly to women who want to feel needed, to hear of the therapist's problems with his wife, children, office mates, academic rivals, or bosses. Although self-disclosure by the therapist may indeed be therapeutic when used judiciously to help a patient realize that she is not alone in having problems, in being humiliated, or in feeling like a failure, it is not helpful to a patient when the disclosure reveals the therapist's personal relationships, particularly with other women in his life. Dr. X's use of self-disclosure is a classic example of this. He used Carolyn to work out his own problems.

The stage was set for Carolyn's seduction by Dr. X. She was vulnerable by virtue of her neediness, her naiveté, and her overprotected background. Dr. X was prepared by his professional training and his intimate knowledge of her specific vulnerabilities. It was easy for Dr. X to convince Carolyn that his judgment was better than hers and for her to trust him rather than her own feelings. Also in his favor was the assurance that, should a problem arise with a complaint, his colleagues would be more likely to believe him than his patient. The scam was highly developed and apparently frequently used.

10_____

A Profession in a Dilemma:
What Are We Supposed
to Do?

When the victim of a therapist's sexual abuse decides
to seek redress by taking the case to the state ethics committee
and licensing board and through the civil courts, the community
of professional psychologists must face the issue from another
perspective. That is, the large majority of highly ethical, caring,
and competent therapists have to deal with their errant colleagues, such as Dr. X. The poorly trained, marginally ethical
(PTME) therapists are also the bane of insurance companies that
cover the profession and of the profession's governing and
sanctioning bodies whose function is, in part, to monitor and
screen out the PTME therapist. In order to appreciate the di-
lemmas of the community of psychologists, one must understand
the structure of the profession with regard to the levels of sanctions that can be used against one of its members.

PROCEDURES OF ETHICS COMMITTEES

In American psychology, ethics committees exist at the local level. Even in large cities, they can be very small, their members are often relatively inexperienced in dealing with ethics issues, and they may have scanty funds with which to investigate a case. Thus they often serve merely as a conduit for receiving information and passing it on to a committee at the state level or through other channels. They may also serve an educational function, by presenting issues to the profession in a newsletter.

In most states, it is the state psychological association's ethics committee that represents the first practical level for investigating complaints of ethics violations. These committees are composed of senior members of the profession who serve on a rotating basis; they are appointed or elected to terms of about 3 years. The complainant may have to follow a particular procedure of bringing a charge against a member of the state association. Such a procedure is meant to assure due process to both the complainant and the psychologist. If the psychologist is not a member of the state association (and membership in one's state association is not required in any state), the state association can do nothing. If membership is ascertained, however, then the state ethics committee can receive materials and proceed with an investigation that may include *in vivo* hearings, those in which the involved parties present their views.

Most state organizations do not possess the resources to conduct fact-finding investigations that involve site visits or detective work. If the committee, through its own due process procedures, is convinced that there is sufficient evidence to sanction a psychologist, it can close the case with recommendations ranging from a reprimand to dropping the person from membership. Obviously, the committee's power is not very strong. For greater sanctions, it can proceed in other directions. It can recommend that the case be brought to the APA Ethics Committee in Washington, D.C., or that the case be pursued within the state by the state licensing board.

The ethics committee of the national organization is a much more powerful group whose members are chosen from a national slate and have much more broadly based expertise. The national organization may be appropriate for an initial complaint when the therapist has membership at the national level but not at the state level. This committee also has greater resources in that it has better access to legal advice, the latest literature, and consultants culled from the national organization. On the other hand, it has more problems getting the data on a particular case since it operates from the nation's capital and does not have the capacity to request *in vivo* contact with both parties. The APA Ethics Committee provides for the possibility of face-to-face confrontation as an appeal procedure on an ethics case when its recommendations based on written materials are not accepted by the offending psychologist. Such an appeal could bring the psychologist to Washington, D.C., to plead his or her case in person before the committee.

If the complainant, like Carolyn, is a patient rather than another psychologist, he or she is not involved directly. An ethics complaint is an issue for the profession to decide. The profession must monitor its own members, and the matter is between the committee and the defendant. The offending psychologist is brought before the committee to answer to peers regarding a charge that violates professional ethics. Until a few years ago, complainants did not even have access to an ethics committee's final decisions regarding the case. A complainant would receive only a "thank you for cooperating in the case" and notification that the investigation had been completed. At this time, APA bylaws have been changed to the extent that an individual is now informed, generally, about the nature of the sanction.

The severest sanction from the national ethics committee is being dropped from membership. Fortunately, the impact of this sanction is not as superficial as it may seem. Communication about the revocation of membership may be released "confidentially" to all 68,000 members of the organization and may also be sent to state licensing boards, professional boards for advanced status (such as the American Board of Professional Psychology), and insurance companies who can—and often do—drop the individual's liability insurance. The psychologist also now has a record of having been convicted of an ethics charge that is reportable in many contexts, such as when questions are asked by prospective employers or licensing boards. In the case of Dr. X, revocation of his APA membership prohibited his being allowed to chair a symposium at the national convention; unfortunately, it did not keep him from formally presenting his views as a participant at that same symposium, since members can sponsor nonmembers to present papers. Few in attendance at that symposium knew that Dr. X had received the severest sanction that APA could give to one of its members. His views on the "impaired psychologist" were not known to be in the context of someone who sexually abused his patients.

Sex between Therapist and Patient from an Ethics Committee Point of View

In some states, sex between patient and therapist is illegal, and in two states (Wisconsin and Minnesota) it is a criminal offense, a felony. Sex with minors who are clients has been prosecuted as statutory rape or child abuse, as has sex with clients who are mentally retarded. In most other states, because it falls under an APA ethics principle that explicitly states that sexual intimacies between patient and therapist are unethical, it is considered only under broader categories of gross negligence or unprofessional conduct in the professional code of the practice of psychology. Even prior to the adoption of that principle— including the time when Dr. X was treating Carolyn—sexual intercourse with a patient was still considered unethical; it was implied in the principle regarding the prohibition of dual relationships.

Over the years, the APA Ethics Committee has spent considerable time discussing the issue of the boundaries of a therapeutic relationship. For example, during economic recessions some therapists wanted to barter for their services. With products that have a clear monetary value, such as chickens or computer supplies or a lawn mower, both parties can agree readily on a market price to be applied toward the price of the therapy sessions, and the barter should not affect the relationship. In contrast, the proscription of a dual relationship appears to prohibit exchanging services for psychotherapy, since doing so puts the therapist in the additional role of employer. If a patient offers to baby-sit for the therapist's children or mow the therapist's lawn or paint a portrait or fix the therapist's teeth, there could be a serious problem. While services may have a monetary value that can be clearly determined in advance, the quality of any service may result in disappointment based on unfulfilled expectations. Thus if a therapist is unhappy with an ugly portrait, how does that influence his or her feelings toward the patient? Also, a therapist ordinarily does not wish a patient to know very much about his or her family affairs, as the patient might be influenced positively or negatively and/or intimidated by such knowledge. As a baby-sitter, the patient would be in the therapist's home and have access to knowledge of the kinds of books the therapist reads, the cleanliness of the house, the type of food eaten, the children's attitudes toward their parents, and many other aspects of the therapist's personal life that would have an impact on the way the patient perceives the therapist. This knowledge may or may not damage the relationship, but it is very likely to do so and thus is considered inappropriate in the context of developing the kind of therapeutic relationship in which the patient is expected to transfer general feelings toward others to his or her own therapist. The objective stance that the therapist represents is destroyed by the amount of detailed personal information available.

In Carolyn's case, Dr. X's sexual exploitation clearly brought them into the realm of a dual relationship. Although there was no relationship outside the office and Dr. X did not offer a personal friendship or love relationship to Carolyn (something that does happen frequently when patients and therapists become sexually involved), Carolyn did listen to Dr. X's own problems. Had he understood the guideline for separating other relationships from the therapeutic one, he might have realized that talking about his personal problems with Carolyn would complicate the transference relationship. In addition, there is evidence that other patients did engage in extrasexual, extratherapeutic relationships with Dr. X. Suzanne Brown learned that some of the women who approached her about the case talked of being involved in business transactions and may have worked for Dr. X.

As Carolyn has reported, in the licensing board hearing Dr. X's attorney stated that Dr. X had demonstrated "sensible regard" for the social codes and moral expectations of the community in that he was discreet in his sexual relationships with his patients. Of course, it was to Dr. X's advantage not to be "bandying about their names," as that would only cause him more damage. But the real issue is that it is not the social code of the community that was most at stake. If Dr. X were a lover of Carolyn's, then he might have been acting appropriately discreet, but he was not her lover. He was her therapist, and the ethical principle governing this situation is concerned not with the social appropriateness of lovers being discreet about an illicit affair but with the community's expectation that psychologists show respect for the moral values of the community by not having sex with their patients. The judgment of what is reasonable and customary for a professional in a community is usually considered by ethics committees, as well as state boards, to be determined by experts in the field based on what the typical professional would normally do in the given situation.

The "community," incidentally, is not necessarily defined as the local metropolitan or rural area. The community, in psychology, usually applies to psychologists in any area of the country. Thus in most incidents California psychologists do not have a more liberal code of ethics or community standards than do Mississippi psychologists. Most of the time, as far as the practice of psychology is concerned, all psychologists are in the same community.

COMPLAINTS TO STATE LICENSING BOARDS

If a psychologist is not a member of the state or national psychological association, then another option available to a patient seeking redress of grievances is the state licensing board. All states require licensing for the practice of psychology, and most states have adopted common criteria for granting licenses, including adherence to the APA ethics code, either specifically or generally. Unlike sanctions by ethics committees, sanctions by state licensing boards can be devastating to a psychologist. Losing one's license is tantamount to losing one's livelihood. But state licensing boards do not readily revoke a license; they consider this sanction very severe. Less severe sanctions might include a confidential reprimand, public censure, suspension of the license with probation, a period of required professional supervision, or a specific plan of rehabilitation in which the psychologist may take steps that serve to reassure the board that he or she is ready to regain or maintain the license.

Licensing boards, in general, may become more closely involved in a case than ethics committees do, as they often have an investigative team that can discover further information from collaterals. But licensing boards are limited by lack of funds, restrictive state laws, and the fear of litigation by defendants displeased with negative sanctions. Also, the licensing board cannot deal with an individual who is not licensed. Therapists who are not licensed as psychologists but permit themselves to be recognized as such can be sanctioned by the board licensing psychologists for misrepresenting themselves. If the therapist has never implied membership in the profession of psychology but was merely working as a "counselor," there may not be a case of misrepresentation unless there is also a state law licensing counselors, in which case the complaint would be filed with the latter professional board. Many states are working toward licensing all mental health practitioners in order to monitor their behavior. Some states still do not license social workers.

MALPRACTICE LITIGATION

The last alternative in seeking redress for professional wrongs committed by one's therapist is to file a lawsuit, charging malpractice. In a civil suit, as in Carolyn's case, the complainant requests a judgment against the therapist for damages as a result of the malpractice. This process raises many issues that psychology and the other mental health professions do not wish to confront. As I shall discuss in Chapter 11, suing presumes that a price can be put on psychological damage and that such damage can be clearly documented. Civil litigation is less involved with the therapist's unprofessional behavior than with the effect of that behavior on the patient. Thus in Carolyn's case the licensing board cared more about what Dr. X did as a professional and how his treatment differed from that of the average reasonable psychologist both in competency and in moral behavior toward his patients, while the civil court was more concerned with Carolyn's claim that she was hurt by Dr. X because of his inappropriate deviation from normal practice. Thus in civil court Carolyn needed to prove that the therapy with Dr. X resulted in psychological distress, or damage, and how much that distress or damage is worth in dollars.

Issues of Ethics, Licensure, and Malpractice

As Carolyn's story reveals, some of the issues regarding complaints before ethics committees, licensing boards, and civil courts have not been resolved. Psychology as a profession does not have a long history. Before World War II, psychologists were researchers and theoreticians. The practice of using psychological principles to treat individuals by means of psychotherapy evolved from both psychoanalysis, which had its roots in medicine, and the experimental analysis of behavior—the application of experimental psychology. The diverse forms of therapies that are used today have proliferated without much restraint because of the acceptance of both scientific and clinically based treatments. Those concerned with the ethics of psychology have tried to tie a scientifically based rationale to any treatment of individuals, but the criteria for such a basis of treatment cannot be more refined than the state of the art of current therapy practiced by the psychotherapeutic community. Thus it is very difficult for the mental health professions to challenge practitioners who deviate from the norm in the name of innovation. The standard of care for psychotherapists is much more difficult to define than the standard of care for most medical specialities (such as surgery). Unethical therapists often take advantage of such ambiguities to rationalize their actions and threaten counteractions against their accusers.

While sexual relations in therapy are explicitly unethical, sexual intimacy with a patient who is not currently in therapy is less clear. Dr. X's attorney raised the question of whether the patients of Dr. X were in therapy at the time he had sexual intercourse with them. At first Dr. X claimed that the doctor–patient relationship was suspended and replaced with an intimate relationship between two mutual friends. The period of "mutual friendship" then disappeared when they returned to therapy. As mentioned in Chapter 8, research evidence from state licensing boards and ethics committees indicates that when a psychologist's defense includes a statement that the acknowledged intercourse did not occur during therapy but at an extraneous time or even after the therapy relationship ended, then the sanctioning boards and committees were less likely to exonerate the psychologist (Sell et al., 1986). That is, psychologists who tried to excuse their behavior by manipulating the factor of when the sex occurred were more likely to receive severe sanctions than were psychologists who conceded that the sex occurred during the therapeutic relationship. Apparently, not only is this defense not believed by licensing boards and ethics committees, but they react negatively to it.

It is interesting that the APA is currently considering including in its ethics code a direct statement that sex between therapists and their *former* patients is unethical. If this revision passes, it will clarify any remaining ambiguity as to how long after termination of therapy a patient is considered to be influenced by a therapeutic relationship.

In Minnesota, a therapist who has sex with a client after termination can still be charged criminally if the therapist used "therapeutic deception," leading the client to believe that the sex was a part of or consistent with therapy. The therapist can also be charged criminally if the client was sufficiently "emotionally dependent" on the therapist to be unable to withhold consent. If the sex occurs within two years of termination, the client can also sue. In Florida, it is illegal for a therapist to have sex with a former patient no matter how long it has been since the therapy was officially terminated. Other states and the professional associations are considering extending sanctions against therapists' relationships with former clients.

Another issue raised by Dr. X's attorney was that a minority of psychologists feel that therapist–patient sex might be beneficial. In the survey of psychologists discussed in Chapter 8, Holroyd and I asked those who admitted having sex with their patients whether they perceived any benefit to either themselves or the patients (Holroyd & Brodsky, 1977). Among the few respondents who reported believing that sexual intimacy could be beneficial, various contradictory circumstances were mentioned: The patient was particularly inexperienced and therefore needy of sex, or, conversely, the patient was very experienced and therefore needy of sex. Some believed sex might be appropriate only if it was related to the patient's problems or, conversely, only if it had nothing to do with the patient's problems. There was no consensus as to situations under which a patient might benefit.

The article reporting these findings tapped professional opinions from the early 1970s, when articles were still published in the professional literature proposing the possible benefit of sex between patient and therapist. The later literature clearly proscribed such behavior. There does remain, however, a small minority of psychologists, psychiatrists, and other mental health professionals who believe that sexual intercourse with a patient may be beneficial (Gartrell et al., 1986). This hard-core minority may well include those who do not like to eliminate any potential benefit from the wide range of therapeutic techniques currently available to patients. Perhaps it is also from this same minority that the new cases of sexual intimacy between patients and therapists come, and that the belief is really just a rationale that has emerged from a retrospective examination of their behavior.

Smith (1982) has written about the psychodynamics of a few of these therapists, proposing that they are unaware of the severity of the negative effects of their sexual behavior toward patients and that they exhibit a concurrent masochism that includes a need to experience danger—the danger of getting caught; thus the behavior may show less stupidity than a sense of excitement generated by daring to see whether one can get away with it. Such psychologists could be considered "impaired" or "distressed"—that is, by virtue of drug or alcohol abuse or some other distress or illness in their lives, they have performed below professional standards and come to the attention of their colleagues as a result of their behavior.

SEX BETWEEN PATIENT AND THERAPIST AS A CRIMINAL OFFENSE

As I have mentioned, in two states, Wisconsin and Minnesota, sexual intercourse between doctor and patient is, for the doctor, a felonious offense punishable by various sanctions, depending on the degree of the assault. In other states, patients have been known to bring sexually abusive therapists to criminal court on charges of assault and battery or rape. If the patient is a minor, statutory rape may be charged. Some states have considered the possibility of enacting legislation to enforce mandatory reporting if a therapist has knowledge that a previous therapist had sex with a patient. Such laws would provide that the anonymity of the patient be maintained. Thus no action would occur immediately, but evidence would be accumulated to enable the investigation of a therapist should his or her name be linked to more than one patient.

One of the issues here is safeguarding the confidentiality of those patients who do not want to file charges and who ask their therapists to hold such information in confidence. Fear of mandatory reporting could result in patients' withholding the information from their therapists or, alternatively, dropping out of very much needed therapy. Thus it is difficult to ensure the protection of all parties, and any legislation must be worded extremely carefully.

But without the ability to discover repeated abusive behavior by therapists from an accumulation of reports by their patients or former patients, the isolated individuals who do present cases will have difficulty amassing sufficient evidence to convince a jury. This was precisely the need that Brown and Whitehurst felt when they presented the state supreme court with a request to contact Dr. X's patients for additional corroboration of his behavior. They reasoned that unsolicited reports from 12 ex-patients might be the tip of a very large iceberg comprised of dozens of patients who were not aware of the publicity in the local newspapers.

CONSEQUENCES FOR THE THERAPIST

The attorney for Dr. X argued that even though Dr. X may have committed a misdeed, he had already paid for it by virtue of the loss of his reputation and livelihood. To some extent, there can be a great loss for a therapist just from a patient's public accusation of sexual intercourse in therapy. In 1979, Keith-Spiegel presented a list of ten reasons why it is stupid for a therapist to consider getting involved in sexual intimacy. Most of the reasons relate to the social, professional, and legal consequences of getting caught.

When Dr. X admitted his behavior, his reputation was ruined but, unfortunately, only among those who heard about him in the media and then believed he was at fault. As with many an underdog—whether right or wrong—there were those who believed that he was victimized by Carolyn and the other patients who sued him. And he continued to see patients who apparently did not know of his reputation.

Carolyn's case occurred in the early years of the struggle that licensing boards and ethics committees faced with the issue of sex between therapist and patient. Since the case was heard, a huge number of complaints have been brought before state boards and ethics committees and have gone to civil litigation. Surveys show that in recent years the largest single number of ethics complaints and complaints to licensing boards in psychology throughout the 50 states have been specifically for sexual intimacies between patient and therapist (American Psychological Association, 1987; Sell *et al.*, 1986).

MALPRACTICE INSURANCE

Currently some insurance companies will not indemnify against damages a psychologist or other mental health professional who has had sex with his or her patients. Sex is not considered part of the practice of psychology; therefore, insurance companies do not consider that they have to cover the behavior. If a therapist knows that sex with a patient is prohibited, he or she does not need insurance to cover it. Yet the insurance companies often will *defend* the psychologist against a sexual intimacy claim, but only up to a limit of $25,000 (American Psychological Association Insurance Trust, 1986), and no judgment is likely to be paid if the psychologist is found guilty.

Consumer advocates note that this is a problem for the victims, since there is no way to claim damages from an insurance company for sexual misconduct in therapy. The professionals' answer is that insurance is for the coverage of the professional, not to provide victims with large sums of money. Successful malpractice claims would then have to focus on the related incompetencies of a therapist who permitted sex to enter into the therapy relationship. Thus criminal prosecution is often a more appropriate means of redress.

INCOMPETENCE AS MALPRACTICE

Frequently there is a relationship between unethical behavior and incompetence. Issues of incompetence were raised in the lawsuits against Dr. X. For example, negligence may be an interpretation of his failure as a psychologist to understand his impact on a patient or, more simply, his failure to understand his patient's needs. Thus when Carolyn and the other patients acquiesced to the sexual intercourse, he rationalized that during sex with them he felt that they knew that he was not engaging in therapy, that they believed that this was an act between friends, that they did not see him as a therapist at that point, that the desire for sex was mutual, that they enjoyed it, and that they were not confused. It is possible that if indeed he was truthful in reporting his "understandings," some of them may have been the result of his incompetence. It is highly unlikely that Dr. X would have misread *all* of these insights about his patients if he were not grossly incompetent.

One of Dr. X's points of defense was his claim that he was mentally distressed at the time the sexual relationships took place and, therefore, should be exonerated from some of his misbehaviors. This claim should be considered in light of a principle of the APA code of ethics that implies that a therapist who is suffering emotional difficulties should stop seeing patients who might be affected by any interaction with that disability. Thus if a therapist is very depressed, treating depressed patients objectively and helpfully may be beyond his or her capacity. A male therapist having extreme difficulty with women in his personal life should seriously consider not seeing any female patients having problems with their love lives. An appropriate procedure for a therapist to follow in a personal crisis is to consult with a colleague and/or go into therapy. Dr. X did not consult another professional about his cases. If he were indeed suffering from a mental illness at the time that he was having sex with his patients, he did not recognize his own problems as having an impact on his patients. In his deposition, he admitted to being in therapy, being hospitalized, and receiving psychotropic medication for a mental illness during periods of his professional career, but during the periods of illness that were known to him he continued to see patients.

CONSEQUENCES FOR THE PATIENT

When patients bring a suit against a therapist for malpractice, they publicly reveal details about the therapy and about their personal life. For Carolyn, this meant the possibility that, like a rape victim, she would be asked marginally relevant, or even irrelevant, questions about every detail of her sexual life, about her most personal thoughts, fantasies, and reactions. A public trial would have meant that her mother, her boyfriends, anyone with whom she had a relationship could be brought to the trial and exposed to the public. Carolyn's decision to go forward with the case did not involve only herself; it affected many people in her life.

Thus, while there is the potential of ruining the reputation of the therapist, any malpractice lawsuit brought by a psychotherapy patient can also ruin the reputations of the patient and/or people in the patient's life who otherwise would have been innocent bystanders.

11

Evaluating the Damages: How Much Is This Worth?

One of the tasks required to document the damages in Dr. X's patients was searching for an expert witness. Brown and Whitehurst initially employed a local psychologist, who met their immediate need for someone who could administer psychological tests that might give them something tangible upon which to base their case that the complainants had been maltreated in therapy. Subsequently, however, they decided against using anyone in the immediate area because the local psychological community was just small enough and cohesive enough to complicate matters with regard to peer pressure or intimidation. They also decided against using a psychiatrist, believing that the standard of care under consideration needed to be scrutinized by a person whose education and license was similar to Dr. X's. ("Standard of care" is a concept legally determined by what an expert convinces the court is the minimum level of competent practice of any professional in a given situation.) Early in the litigation proceedings, Brown began compiling a list of those psychologists who had published works on the subject.

In 1978, there were few individuals recognized as experts on the issue of sex between therapists and patient. And among those, there were even fewer who had had experience testifying in court. Most of the forensic work by psychologists and other mental health personnel did not encompass this issue; perhaps the closest parallels were rape, incest, and malpractice cases against therapists for incompetence or the betrayal of confidentiality. Brown wrote to and/or spoke with several psychologists. She later confided that she chose me because she was impressed with my credentials, my publications on the subject, and high recommendations by several colleagues.

Brown and Whitehurst entertained great concern in their choice of a woman as an expert witness. Particularly in the early 1970s, experts on sex between therapist and patient were women, and they tended to identify strongly with feminism or the women's movement because, after all, they were involved with the issue of the exploitation of female patients. Brown and Whitehurst did not wish to promote the image of a battle over women's issues fought by feminist soldiers. They warned me that when my deposition was taken, attempts would be made to present me as a radical feminist supporting her cause. Indeed, such attempts were made:

Q: Okay. Do you, yourself, just from a personal standpoint, Dr. Brodsky, dislike men?

A: No.

Q: You get along with men all right?

A: Yes. Some of my best friends are men.

Thus the greatest test for me, as an expert witness, would be of my own integrity.

Brown and Whitehurst appreciated my sincere interest in working for the case. For me, it offered a new opportunity to integrate into the arena of civil litigation my therapeutic practice and research as well as my interest in forensics, ethics, and women's issues. I was not a hired gun whose career was enhanced by testifying on behalf of disgruntled complainants.

Brown and Whitehurst sent me copies of the original MMPIs that Dr. X had given the three women who were complainants in the lawsuit, along with the subsequent diagnostic evaluations administered by the local psychologist, Dr. X's deposition, and the original pleadings. At my request the complainants were given additional MMPI tests, which were scored in the state in which they resided and then mailed to me for interpretation. In Carolyn's case, there was also an MMPI taken in 1975, just after she entered therapy with Dr. X. Some months after receiving all of this, I flew to the state to reevaluate the three plaintiffs. From this and one further visit with the women, I gathered sufficient data to provide a fairly comprehensive view of the historical progression of psychological effects that resulted from Dr. X's actions toward the plaintiffs.

MAPPING OUT A STRATEGY

Aware that licensing boards, professional codes for psychologists, and, thus, the criteria for civil suits differed from state to state, I needed to know the boundaries and limits within which I could frame my statements. Brown and Whitehurst reminded me that the issue in the civil litigation primarily involved documenting psychological damage as a result of malpractice by the psychologist. All the evaluations and all of the information to be conveyed were to address only this issue. I was not to treat the women involved, even though I expected to feel their pain and would want to advise them. I would have to let them know carefully that my role was that of an evaluator. They were supposed to be completely open and honest with me, yet they knew that anything they said to me at any time could be discovered by Dr. X's attorneys and revealed in court. I was also aware that they knew it would be to their benefit to appear damaged. They could slant their answers in their own favor, even unconsciously. My role was to determine what had actually happened, how it had affected them, and what it would cost—in a marketable figure, that is dollars—to correct through further treatment or to compensate for pain and suffering.

I was also aware that anything I said in court, be it about testing, evaluation, therapy, or diagnosis would have to be backed up by valid evidence and would have to be of the highest standards of the profession. I could be challenged mercilessly by opposing counsel for any minute error or inconsistency. Thus, even though a very strong impression or interpretation might be prominent in my mind, I would have to hold back statements about it unless I felt I could document it with an explanation clear enough for a lawyer and, more important, for a lay person on a jury to understand.

Because I was evaluating the women in the case specifically for the damages that resulted from Dr. X's misbehavior, I needed to look at any patterns he demonstrated in the treatment of all women in his therapeutic practice and to come to some conclusion about their appropriateness. I would be appraising his professional behavior in light of the standards of all psychologists. In so doing, I would have to be very careful not to personalize the therapist's behaviors in therapy by rendering them as an evaluation of him as a human being. I was not to judge his mental health or personal life, nor was I permitted to interview him. My interpretations of his motives were not relevant to my testimony. Yet on this point, too, I was tested in my deposition:

Q: Have you expressed an opinion to [Brown and Whitehurst] about how you feel about [Dr. X]? In other words, do you hate his guts? Do you dislike him? Do you think he's a swell fellow, or what?

A: I don't know him personally. I have never met him. I've tried to concentrate very clearly on what his behavior has been, what he has done, and what the result of that behavior has been.

While I had access to details from the patients' depositions that related to the sexual and other treatment issues in therapy, I did not have the kind of psychiatric histories and data I needed for a thorough evaluation of the specific issues of sexual abuse, so I drafted a structured interview for each patient. This interview comprised specific essential questions that were asked in such a way as to minimize leading the patients to answers they might think would help their case.

For example, I wanted to know why Carolyn entered therapy when she did, how she got to Dr. X rather than to someone else, what she felt about him on very first contact, what her expectations for therapy were, what Dr. X presented therapy to be, what he asked in that first session, and what that meant to her. I wanted to know how Carolyn experienced the development of the sexuality—when she first recognized that anything sexual might occur between them; whether this was a sudden or a gradual revelation; how she felt about it; how she felt about Dr. X; whether she perceived him sexually before, during, or after the incidents; how she thought the sexual part of the relationship related to therapy as a whole; how much power or control she felt in the relationship; whom she told about what had happened in therapy and why; what actions she took as a result of the therapy and as a result of consulting others; how she justified her role in the relationship; and whom she blamed or credited for what happened between herself and Dr. X. I also wanted to know how she felt about Dr. X's therapy beyond the sexual relationship—how the therapy benefited her, if it did; how much the therapy hurt her, if it did; and how competent she felt Dr. X had been, both at the time and in retrospect. Finally, I wanted to know how she had changed during therapy and after and what she perceived as her needs now and for the future.

THE INTERVIEW

When I met Carolyn, I was unprepared for my initial impression. She presented herself as a poised, secure, relaxed individual. At first sight, it would be very hard for an observer to believe that she had been very depressed and very anxious, that she had colitis and nightmares, that she had been sexually promiscuous, and that she had been in a therapeutic relationship with a therapist who had sex with her. Indeed, she did not look like an individual in trouble, who was suffering, who had been harmed. My first thought was: How would a lay person believe that this woman was involved in such an incident?

My first contact with Carolyn was for the formal evaluation, a session that would provide the material that could be used in court. I immediately informed her of the restrictions regarding our relationship and the limits on the confidentiality of my evaluation. At times I was concerned about this because, though she acknowledged the statement, she apparently treated the situation as if she could trust me implicitly and assumed that I would use the material with discretion. Though I discovered that she had very grave difficulties trusting men in personal relationships, Carolyn had not lost her almost naive trust of people in authority who were supposed to be helpful to her. She perceived me as such an authority because I was hired by her attorneys, whom she trusted.

The information I received from Carolyn about her childhood that might have had significance in her relationship with Dr. X included the following. Carolyn was the youngest child in a family of five children in which the oldest is a brother 19 years older and the next youngest a sister 4 years older. She described her childhood as secure but not especially happy. She was a tomboy and a loner as a young girl and was somewhat withdrawn. She spent many of her days after school in the company of a Mexican man who worked for her father. Her parents had a relatively good marriage, and the family was fairly private. She remembers herself as always having a temper and perceived herself as having some problems in the relationship with her mother, who was often somewhat distanced from her. She always enjoyed writing and, even at the age of 6, wrote about girl orphans making it on their own as astronauts and pioneers. She had little social life as a teenager and was very distressed while her father was dying.

She met her first boyfriend at age 15, in church. She dated him for a year, broke up, and dated one other boy steadily for a year. She engaged in her first exploration of a sexual relationship with him in the form of mild necking, which gradually advanced to heavy petting. Her only previous sexual experiences were two unwanted approaches, one, at the age of 9, when in a swimming pool someone grabbed her, pushed his hands under her bathing suit, and felt her. When she was 13 a man exposed himself to her. She essentially learned about sex after asking her mother questions about a Walter Cronkite news report of a rape. She also learned from reading novels and "dirty" books she found when she was 13.

Her first experience of sexual intercourse was with her

fourth boyfriend, Steve, whom she met in college at age 18. She was involved with Steve for 5½ years. During the time she saw Dr. X, she dated several young men in addition to Steve. Her difficult and conflicted relationship with Steve was one of her reasons for going into therapy. She couldn't cope with Steve's infidelity and felt insecure in the relationship.

Carolyn was referred to Dr. X by a girlfriend who had heard about him from a co-worker in a hospital. Carolyn remembered very clearly Dr. X's stating his initial assumption that her problem was a relationship with a man. His direct and confident questions about both her and Steve embarrassed her and impressed upon her his powerful omniscience. The loss of her father was a major, if initially unstated, reason for Carolyn's entering therapy. Treatment included working on depression, relationships with men, and, much of the time at the beginning, crying.

I asked Carolyn about her first impressions of Dr. X. She recalled that he was an older man whom she readily perceived as a father figure. She believed that he would help her and that she could confide in him and depend on him. She felt very good about paying for therapy with money from her own savings, and she felt that Dr. X really liked her as a human being. For the first 9 months of therapy, he was very professional. The only physical contact was their shaking hands. One isolated time in those early months of therapy, he gave her a hug, which seemed spontaneous, affectionate, and nonsexual.

The first indication of anything being wrong was a feeling of "walls coming up" when Dr. X began to suggest that she was avoiding looking at what he believed was her attraction for him. She found it hard to say anything. She became confused by several sessions of "relaxation" techniques that involved his sitting beside her and massaging her abdomen as she lay on the floor. She found herself very passive, "like a rag doll." She did not see Dr. X as sexually attractive. When she talked with him about a relationship she was currently having with a boyfriend with whom she had "zero chemistry," Dr. X considered that an emotional problem.

Two or three months before sexual intercourse took place between Carolyn and Dr. X, he talked of his sexual attraction to her and asked her, "How do you feel about *me?*" Carolyn told him she did not think she had sexual feelings toward him, but he challenged this. He told her a story in which a patient who wore skirts and no underwear was trying to seduce him, and he interpreted her actions as breaking through one of her barriers. This story implied to Carolyn that she should acknowledge her alleged attraction to Dr. X, and she believed that taking off all her clothes would help prove that she, too, wanted to overcome barriers. She complied. He would frequently comment on her body and looked at her breasts often. She did not react to his ideas or demands. In retrospect, she felt that Dr. X might have thought her passive compliance represented a green light for him to proceed sexually, but she was taken aback when, during his deposition, he accused her of being seductive in therapy, saying, "Your eyes are telling me."

Carolyn rarely questioned the physical aspect of the therapy relationship, and when she did it was tentatively and indirectly. Dr. X replied, "You're putting up walls between us. How will you learn to have relationships outside if you can't have a trusting, open relationship in here?" She felt that he was so important to her in helping her overcome her depression that she must accept his sexual advances. She never perceived him as a lover and felt guilty that she couldn't, believing that she was supposed to. Upon reflection, Carolyn felt that his having sex with her was selfish; but because she had such low self-esteem at the time, she never considered questioning his motives. He never asked what she liked about sex. There was never any foreplay, just the rubbing of her stomach. She never had orgasms. She recalls lying on the floor, putting her arm over her face, being scared, and making no movements; she felt exposed and humiliated. She would try to think of other things during that time. The intercourse was brief, never more than 5 minutes. Afterward, he would often talk about something completely unrelated, like school. They never talked about the sex.

It did not make sense to Carolyn that, as perceptive as she had known him to be, he did not see that she was not receptive to the experience and that she didn't want to be there. But he did not mention this, and her passivity did not cause him to hesitate.

As she has described, Carolyn once called Dr. X at home because she was distressed over a breakup with Steve. Dr. X told her to come to his house to talk. He met her at the door, led her to his bedroom, and took off her clothes. They had intercourse, but he never asked her about the problem with Steve. About 2 weeks later, he again asked her to come to his house, but she refused and they never talked about it.

Her impressions of Dr. X's philosophy about sex were that he believed in multiple affairs and that in a good relationship there are "no strings"; there was no reason not to have sex with someone with whom you simply wanted to have sex. Sex was like a handshake.

After a while, Carolyn tried to stop the sexual episodes with slightly more assertive protests. Dr. X would consistently accuse her of setting up more barriers between them. Once when she suggested that she might like to quit therapy, he discouraged her, telling her it was too soon. Finally, after a year and 10 months of weekly sessions, she stated that she wanted to stop, and he agreed, with no argument whatever. She never told him the real reasons she was leaving.

During her last few months in therapy, Carolyn saw Dr. X only once every other week, and she started attending his group therapy sessions. She remembered thinking that he was using the group members to feed his ego, and she began to feel as though the group sessions were more for him than for the members and that he never worked with the patients to temper their perception of him as a highly powerful person to whom each member looked for approval. She began to realize that she was doing better with only two sessions a month; and with other aspects of her life going well, she began to believe that it might not have been the therapy that was helping her move forward.

Carolyn entered therapy fully trusting the process and wanting to learn about herself. She never questioned the assumption that Dr. X was highly competent, knew what he was doing, and had her best interests at heart. She was more concerned with what she might find out about herself in therapy than with what she might reveal about herself to the therapist. Carolyn experienced therapy as proceeding slowly at first, but she was grateful to Dr. X for working with her. Anything she was asked to do, such as write a diary or think about something, she willingly agreed to and worked hard to do it well. That was her style. She was a compulsively hard worker and a very dutiful, compliant patient.

The fact that Dr. X talked about himself, his divorce, and his problems seemed to her an appropriate aspect of therapy. She did not appreciate the potential confusion of patient–therapist roles that personal knowledge of Dr. X's homelife would foster; she initially felt good that he was sharing those intimate aspects of his life with her. After a while, however, she began to feel that therapy wasn't going anywhere. That is, while she was learning to trust Dr. X and feel good about him and take journal notes and talk about things that happened in her life, her interactions outside the office were no different. She continued to be mired in a destructive relationship with Steve.

Although she had not initially questioned the appropriateness of the sexual intercourse when it became part of therapy, she slowly began to wonder about it. She felt that something was wrong, that it was somehow not good therapy, but she did not know *what* was wrong. If Dr. X said do it, she did it because she believed he would never ask her to do anything inappropriate. It felt to her like a very gentle persuasion.

Carolyn thought that Dr. X's requests and actions were unusual, but she didn't think they were unusual as therapy. It never dawned on her to differentiate between what was and what was not therapy in the therapy hour. She said:

> I had spent 9 months in there trying to trust him. He had been helping me to try to trust him, and he had been trying to gain my trust. I also went in there with a very naive idea of, you know, he's a professional, he's a doctor, he's a healer, he's an older man. You're supposed to trust people that fit into that slot. I have never met anyone who fit into that slot before who wasn't trustworthy, and a lot of the trust just came with his position. I never assumed that that's what he had in mind or that even if he had had that in mind that he would take that step. And when it happened I didn't have the ability to question his motives. I could not do that.

I asked Carolyn what she got out of therapy that might be beneficial. She responded that she was getting better for a while, but she later attributed this to her new role as a student teacher. Some things were going better for her just by virtue of the passage of time and her maturation.

She began to have a lot of ambivalence about continuing therapy because she was wondering what the therapy was doing for her. Her "confrontation" with this was very mild. It came out as a question to Dr. X, "Are you sure this is all right?" It was a "very tiny little attempt" to question the method of therapy. The answer she got was "You can't get anywhere on the outside until you get somewhere in here." Yet her memory was that she "felt dead a lot in the last few months of therapy."

Her reaction during the sexual intercourse was to dissociate: "I literally went up and watched us from the corner of the room. . . . That's eerie." Of this experience, she said, "I think there was something within me that was realizing that [the out-of-body experience] was going to take care of me in spite of . . . [Dr. X's] influence—which was incredibly strong—which is incredibly strong." So the dissociation served the purpose of allowing her to function as an independent person; the "other" person in her could go ahead and have the sexual relationship that Dr. X wanted from her.

She never told him about the dissociation experiences. When she quit therapy, she did not tell him why. By then she knew that there was something wrong, but, as she stated, "I still loved him." While she sensed that his techniques must be wrong because she wasn't improving, even at the end of therapy she did not perceive that they were wrong because he was unethical or immoral. She had no way to compare his behavior with that of any other therapist. She did not know what therapists were supposed to do. The therapist she loved was "the figment that he was in my mind, who I thought he was. That was the person I cared for."

Toward the end of her therapy, as she observed the other women in the group therapy sessions, Carolyn became aware that Dr. X was probably having sex with some of his other female patients as well. She did not feel that she was either special or different from the others. Nonetheless, she believed that Dr. X had her interests at heart, no matter what he did with his other patients. Before leaving therapy, she wanted to communicate to him that he was wrong about the way he was treating her, but she couldn't do that. To reject his treatment was tantamount to rejecting him, and she felt guilty even considering that. She couldn't challenge him, so instead she simply said good-bye.

Carolyn's realization that she was angry with Dr. X for what he did emerged later, during her therapy with the minister she saw within a year after leaving therapy with Dr. X:

> The way it happened was that [the minister] was egging me on, and he got me very angry. He wasn't letting me play a game in therapy, and I just yelled at him and said "That's not the way it is, Dr. X." He looked at me and said, "I'm not Dr. X," and I fell apart. I just lost it. I lost it all. And when I told him what had happened, he told me I wasn't the first client he had heard complain about Dr. X's sexual advances. He told me there was nothing I could do, but later as I began to talk with him he said, "Carolyn, some day someone is going to get Dr. X, but I don't think there's anything you can do legally."

But the seed had been planted. After that incident, Carolyn realized how angry and how hurt she was and how she had not been allowing herself to feel it until then. So it was the second therapist who helped bring out Carolyn's anger with Dr. X, even though it had not been the minister/therapist's intention to do so, as he was not previously aware of the occurrence or its impact on Carolyn.

Carolyn became aware that she had been exploited, that Dr. X had indeed done something inappropriate, when a 16-year-old student told her about seeing a counselor whom Carolyn knew had an office across from Dr. X's. This was a year after Carolyn's therapy with Dr. X, and she was concerned for the student when she realized that the girl might have seen Dr. X instead and he might have treated her as he had Carolyn. The student was, she said, "symbolic" of all the other 16-year-olds who would walk into that office, "and that's when I started feeling like the only choice I had was to act on it."

Even at this point, when the feelings of anger and the feelings of having been abused surfaced, there were also feelings of self-blame. As Carolyn said, "He did not put a gun to my head." She was angry with herself for not realizing sooner that the sexual intercourse was inappropriate. She saw herself as naive and weak and she realized that others were going to have feelings about her role in the situation. She wondered how she could convince anyone that someone as intelligent as she was supposed to be didn't know what was going on and couldn't see that sex was sex and not therapy?

She was very worried about how her family would take it, for among them it was

> a cardinal sin to admit that you couldn't handle your own problems and needed some kind of help . . . and then to have the help turn on you in such a way or allow something like that to happen. . . . I came from a family where whatever happens to you, if you're female, you have essentially done something to bring it upon yourself, and so you're responsible for it. I was very worried about how it would be received, especially by my mother.

When I asked Carolyn whether she ever thought about what her mother would say if she knew that Carolyn was having sexual intercourse in therapy, she responded:

> Yes . . . I thought she would be shocked just as she was shocked that I was having intercourse with men outside of therapy. She would be shocked both at the intercourse in therapy and outside of therapy, but then she would be shocked that I was having therapy anyway. . . . At that time I was operating from leftover teenage beliefs that mothers don't know anything, and I was writing off her reactions with, "Well, she doesn't know what goes on in therapy and she doesn't trust Dr. X like I trust him."

Based on this interview of Carolyn's perspective of what happened to her in therapy and her recalled conscious reactions to it, I was ready to proceed with some standard psychological tests that might help tap some of Carolyn's less consciously available perceptions, attitudes, personality traits, and psychological states.

12

Plotting the Stress of Litigation: Carolyn's Progress as Recorded by Psychological Test Data

P art of Carolyn's original petition was given to me so that I could see what her lawyers concluded had happened to her psychologically. The claims were (1) that Carolyn had previously existing psychological problems that were severely aggravated and that she was permanently psychologically scarred by Dr. X's conduct; (2) that Carolyn had a sense of fear and a distrust of males both emotionally and sexually that had been severely aggravated, creating new, deeper, and more pervasive distrust and an inability to relate both emotionally and sexually and that her ability to enter into or sustain an emotionally rewarding and trusting relationship with anyone in her personal or professional life had been damaged by Dr. X's betrayal of the dependence and trust nurtured in her; and (3) that Carolyn now has permanent feelings of shame, guilt, anxiety, and depression as a result of Dr.

X's conduct and as a result of his encouragement of her to become promiscuous.

As a psychologist, I was uncomfortable with the wording of the complaints. For example, mental health professionals do not conceptualize psychological feelings as permanent, and *scar* is a term that implies visibility. Inability to relate sexually or emotionally did not describe Carolyn's status at the time, or her potential for the future. In my deposition, I was able to soften the extremes of the legal complaint to my own level of comfort with the extent of damages:

Q: What do you envision that the future holds for Carolyn?

A: I think she's going to need a lot of therapy. She's going to have physical problems. She's going to have relationship problems. I think she's going to have flashbacks about this even after she has been through therapy.

Q: Well, will she ever be back to almost normal, which is where she was when she came in to see Dr. X, do you think?

A: . . . I don't know if she will be back to almost normal. She can never return to where she was before because things have happened to her. I think there is a permanent impact that this will have. I think she can improve, and I think she can do better over a period of time, but I think she will never forget this and it will always come back at some point. . . .

Q: Well I realize she probably won't forget it. I mean people remember a lot of things until they die. What I mean is do you think she will be able to get over it and go on and function in life as an ordinary individual would.

A: She will be able to function in life as an ordinary individual. She will always have, I think, some residual of this. It will not go away completely. She will not return to what I believe she could have been had she not seen Dr. X, had she received competent care.

EVALUATION

I had difficulty sorting out Carolyn's previous psychological problems and how they would have been aggravated by her interactions with Dr. X. I needed to look for indications that she now showed the distrust and inability to relate to men, the fear, the difficulty in entering rewarding and trusting relationships, and any other feelings that I could relate to her having been in a dependent and trusting relationship that, when exploited, left feelings of betrayal, shame, guilt, anxiety, and depression.

I had access to the raw data on Carolyn's responses to the psychological tests she took when she first presented her case to the lawyers as well as the local psychologist's evaluation. Thus I knew that Carolyn was very bright, with a tested quotient of 135 on the Wechsler Adult Intelligence Scale, which puts her in a very superior category of intelligence. From personality testing, the psychologist had detected anxiety and concerns about control. He had also noted that Carolyn's profile was that of a highly competitive person who suppressed hostility, experienced family discord, and could have impulse problems. She showed significant self-blame and distrust of males. She was confused sexually and showed evidence of depression.

In my own testing, I used drawings as the first task; this is often a good warm-up exercise in that it allows individuals to talk about themselves in relation to their drawings. Carolyn's drawing of a house was very tiny and placed up in the extreme top left-hand corner of the paper (see Figure 1). It was a bilevel house hidden in a hill. In discussing it, she remarked that much of it was underground, but it was in a very rocky place. She saw herself living in it with her fiancé, Ken, and she pictured it as a sunny, breezy, cool, open, and serene place. Her greatest need was for "good interior decorating," which she believed it would have. This drawing provided a somewhat transparent view of Carolyn's environment in the sense that she felt she needed to work on internal aspects of her life and that she was doing this with her fiancé but that much of her feelings were still in the rocky place where she was emotionally.

Her second drawing was a tree (see Figure 2). A tree often represents a person's feelings about himself or herself developmentally. She described the tree as an oak on her property, very old and partially dead. The upper trunk on one side was damaged from a split in the middle. Thus it was growing up wrong. No one had shaped or pruned it. Its best feature was that the living parts could be saved, and its worst feature was that by trying to save it, one might kill it because huge chunks would have to be cut off and the entire tree might go into shock. The solution was that perhaps one should take off one large limb and wait a few years before taking off the other. What it needed most

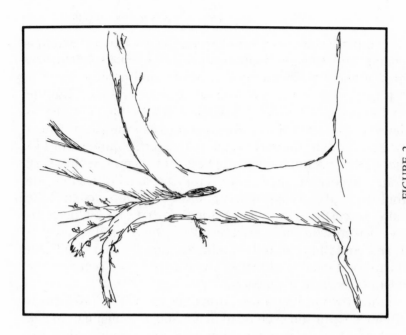

FIGURE 2
Carolyn's rendering of a tree.

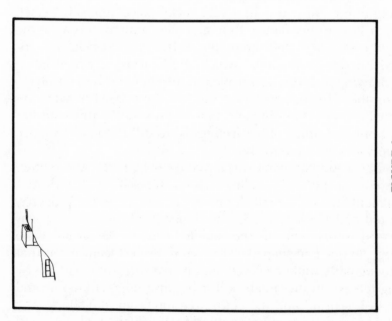

FIGURE 1
Carolyn's rendering of a house.

to become healthier was proper attention, and Carolyn hoped that it would receive this attention. Again, although Carolyn may not have realized how obviously the tree represented herself and her fears for the future, her tree and its story can easily be taken as a metaphor for the damage that she experienced and her feeling of vulnerability in terms of trying to repair that damage.

Next I requested that she draw a person. A drawing of a person usually represents one's presentation of self to the world. Women more often than men draw figures of the opposite sex, partly as a response to the generic request for a person being perceived as a request for a male. Carolyn's figure was a male, not very well defined in terms of clothing and with a lot of sketchiness in the face and body (see Figure 3). She described him as a 23-year-old student at the university posing for a camera. He was a person with a good mind but not very good looking and needing someone to understand him. Carolyn feared that no one would look beyond his appearance, but she hoped he would find someone who would look within him, someone who would be a regular, caring person. She did not provide a detailed description of the man, but from the drawing and the related discussion her self-identity issues as a college student who needed understanding surfaced.

Afterward, I asked her to draw a person of the opposite sex, and she drew a woman wearing shorts and a casual shirt (see Figure 4). She described this person as looking like a friend of hers. She then said that the woman in the drawing was a forest ranger or a biologist working with the environment. She was in the woods collecting data, a confident woman who knew who she was. Carolyn explained that her short arms were the result of her having had polio, but this deformity didn't hold her back. Her greatest need was for companionship, and she was torn between striking out by herself and having to change her life style in order to accommodate a companion. The positive ending was that this woman would find someone to love. So again, Carolyn presented herself as an individual facing conflicts between what she wants to be and her sense of wanting to overcome having been damaged or disabled. It was encouraging that her figures resolve their problems and turn out well.

Carolyn's second task was to take the Rorschach Inkblot Test. In this she demonstrated a high form level, indicating that her intellect was not disturbed by cognitive dysfunction. She did

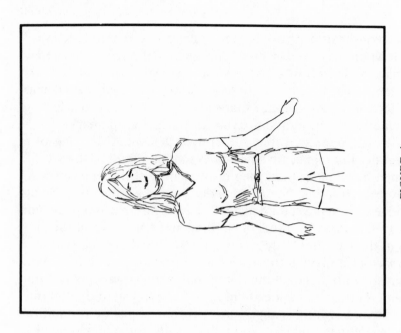

FIGURE 4
Carolyn's rendering of a female.

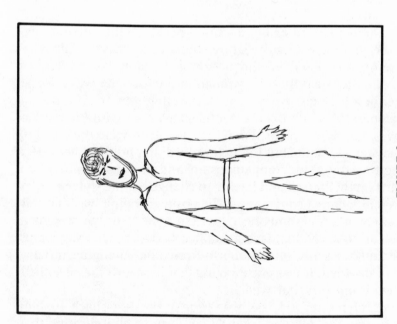

FIGURE 3
Carolyn's rendering of a person.

not show severe depression but in the content and form level of her responses gave some hints that she was preoccupied with frightening, occasionally bizarre thoughts and had a high degree of emotionality. Her sex role confusion was apparent in her reactions to the Rorschach cards. Her most disturbed percepts included the pelvis of an ox that has been slaughtered and a crazy old woman whose legs have been cut off and is playing patty-cake with herself in a mirror. Right after reporting the latter percept, Carolyn spontaneously talked of having had some violent dreams in which she killed people and they killed her. These people were strangers, but somehow she knew them. She did not know who they actually were in real life. Her killing was in self-defense and always with a legitimate reason.

While one could see that almost all her percepts were drawn from the form of the stimulus provided by the cards, they all showed an unusual quality that would not be considered popular or average—such as seeing "Bullwinkle without his horns," "the back view of a bat in flight as it flies away from you," "a black queen in the looking glass looking back at herself in the mirror." Here again she made a spontaneous comment—"The farther you run, the faster you don't get anywhere" (a reminder of Alice in *Through the Looking Glass*). She also saw animals from prehistoric times, little wizards, humans falling into hell, and a rabbit. The Rorschach certainly indicated a deep level of emotionality: Carolyn did not distort the world in the sense of having a thought disorder, but she distorted it in the sense of taking a commonly seen percept—such as a rabbit, a bat, or a figure looking in the mirror—and perceiving it from an unusual perspective—one that is more threatening or frightening, or dangerous for the unreal creatures from cartoons and fairy tales.

Next, I showed Carolyn some Thematic Apperception Test (TAT) cards (pictures from a set of cards selected to raise issues in areas of suspected conflict or importance in one's life). The pictures I chose were scenes of introspection or of males and females interacting. I was looking for specific things—issues that might be related to Carolyn's therapy with Dr. X.

Carolyn's responses to making a story of these scenes played out as follows. To a picture of an individual leaning over a vague object—a picture that often elicits a depressed or thoughtful reaction—Carolyn responded, "A severe conflict. A young German girl thinking about committing suicide. She's lying there exhausted trying to determine, but she has no idea what to do. People in her life . . . she'll live through it, but she won't be happy unless she gets into another environment altogether." To a picture that shows a woman looking into a room, Carolyn responded, "The woman is the housekeeper of the family that is well-to-do in the early 1900s. She walked in to see something out of the ordinary, but it doesn't surprise her what's going on. I can't imagine what it is." When asked how the character felt, Carolyn responded that the woman would have been disturbed and would deal with the emotion inside of herself. She would not talk to anyone; she would feel burdened, but the sense of burden would fade with time. Thus Carolyn's TAT stories also produced a sense of damage, depression, and hope.

Carolyn's MMPI, an objective personality inventory, revealed a profile often found in a person who has experienced a posttraumatic stress disorder. That is, her profile showed elevations on scales having to do with a great deal of body concerns, such as Carolyn experienced with her nightmares, colitis, and other stress-related problems. It was also raised on a scale indicating confusion, alienation, and difficulty perceiving things the way others do. Finally, she also showed evidence of repression or denial of her fears and ubiquitous depression. Her confusion over sexual interactions and sex role identification was also apparent from the MMPI, a finding that was corroborated by the confusion in identity issues evident in her drawings of persons and by the quality of male–female interactions evident in the TAT.

My evaluation of Carolyn's test data and interview in 1981, 3 years after her therapy with Dr. X, was that she was still experiencing the stress in a way that may be likened to a chronic postraumatic stress disorder. She still experienced nightmares and night terrors, intestinal problems, and repression of the impact of the anxiety and the depression on her interactions. She alternated between being hopeful that it would all work out and being fearful that she was severely damaged in a way that would not allow her to recover fully. She still harbored a sense of confusion about her identity as a woman and as an independent adult capable of judging others and her own reactions to them. Her nightmares were still very real at this point. She was anticipating a long legal battle, which would entail public exposure of herself and her loved ones.

Combining the data from the previous psychological tests, my interview with Carolyn, and the psychological testing I conducted in 1981 gave me sufficient evidence to conclude that Carolyn had indeed been damaged by Dr. X's treatment of her. Much of her history showed that she had reason to be confused by and to misunderstand male–female relationships, that she had a sense of needing affection and approval, and that she could not trust her own judgment of authority figures. She could be impulsive and adventurous but lacked direction. Evidence suggested that her condition was exacerbated by some kind of major emotional trauma. Thus her perceptions of damage and emotional crippling; her experiences of physical stress and body reaction; her dissociation from the sexual intercourse in therapy; her anger with and confusion about Dr. X, including the ambivalence demonstrated by her still having a sense of loving him; and her inability to trust her own judgment, including her inability to decide who she would see for treatment, what she would do with her life, and how she would confront her relationships with men—all of these were apparent at the time of my evaluations and easily related to her experience with Dr. X and her attempts to justify and rectify that experience.

While it is impossible to make a perfect analysis of an event in someone's life, clearly connecting it to the individual's behavior in other situations, in Carolyn's case the association was quite apparent. Between 1976 and 1981, there were no other major traumatic events in Carolyn's life. Her perception of the treatment was traumatic. Her reactions to the therapy—her promiscuous behavior, her distrust of men, her indecisiveness regarding personal and career plans and her relationships with others are all behaviors commonly seen in women who have experienced sexual abuse in therapy. Dissociation is frequently seen in rape and incest victims during the abusive episodes. Nightmares and physical stress disorders such as stomachaches, indigestion, and chronic intestinal distress appear in individuals who have been in traumatic situations, such as war, imprisonment, or incest. Anxiety and depression are seen in individuals who have a poor self-concept because they blame themselves for behaviors they later realize were the result of poor judgment in trusting or believing others.

The pattern of Carolyn's behaviors and reactions fit psychologically with the experience she had as she described it and as we know it from all of the depositions in the case. Carolyn would indeed need therapy for a long period of time to resolve the issues. She would be expected to suffer long-term effects from her experience with Dr. X. She would be expected to have flashbacks, to experience painful reminders, and to have recurring feelings of depression and self-doubt. The hope lies in her strengths. Carolyn is extremely bright, she had a basically good background, and she is a fighter.

REEVALUATION

A year after my initial interview and evaluation of Carolyn, I was called back to give a deposition, which would allow Dr. X's attorneys to discover what I would say about Carolyn before a jury. Since so much time had passed, I requested a short reinterview and additional data. For this update, I had Carolyn take another MMPI. Her profile showed that the stress level was elevated as before, the scale indicating confusion and alienation was slightly lower, the energy level was considerably lower. Carolyn was becoming increasingly immobilized.

She was now in therapy with Dr. Hammond and was intensively preparing for the trial. She was preoccupied with the trial and the effects of the publicity upon herself, her family, and her job. Her nightmares and physical symptoms had exacerbated. She had entered graduate school to study engineering. She was feeling much anxiety and helplessness, and her nightmares were about her father; a boyfriend's father, who had been the same age as her father when he died; and people being raised from the dead. In one dream, she was looking for help from the confusion and was very frightened. The father of her boyfriend was trying to climb a mountain and was not able to trust the rotting wood of some wooden walkways. He was afraid of losing his balance, and he looked weakened by cancer; but in spite of his fear, he helped Carolyn to solid ground, and she was very surprised that he could do this in his weakened condition. He didn't make her climb up, and she was relieved that he could help her. Her own conflicts about her ability to go through with the lawsuit and her ambivalence toward Dr. X for having been helpful in spite of his "weakness" are possible interpretations of this dream.

In another dream, she was chased by a man who wanted to kill her. He had a knife and he wouldn't listen to reason. She didn't know where she was, but she got lost in a big house. Her sister arrived and murdered the man with a gun. This particular dream surprised Carolyn, since her sister is a very peaceful person. I wondered whether the dream was a way of distancing the part of her that was trying to murder Dr. X by means of the lawsuit from the part of her that she considered very passive in relation to Dr. X.

Carolyn also dreamed that she was going to a police station to gather up her clothes. She picked up her underwear even though she was fully dressed, but she kept dropping it and was frantic that she wouldn't get it all and would be late. At the time of this dream, Carolyn was engaged to Ken, who was a police officer. I wondered whether this showed her fear of exposing herself and her sexual relationships and what that exposure might mean to her family, friends, and fiancé.

In a fourth dream, Carolyn was staying at a hotel owned by a witch. She was putting together her underwear, scarves, and T-shirts and was getting ready to leave, but she couldn't. The witch had claws, and her thin hands were scratching Carolyn. Carolyn beat the witch, but the witch still reached her. This is another dream in which there is some sense of sexual exposure and an attempt to flee from a noxious person, perhaps a mother (or therapist?) or a part of herself. When she tried to attack her adversary, she got hurt even more.

In a fifth dream, Carolyn was in the water, and people were trying to kill her. Her boyfriend's deceased father could send high-voltage electricity through the water to kill her enemies, and he tried to rescue Carolyn and her friends by this method. Carolyn told him that he is dead and should leave. Perhaps in this dream Carolyn realized that Dr. X as a father figure and friend is dead and that she can't be helped by him and might even be killed by him.

From the updated MMPI and interview, it was apparent that Carolyn's stress level was at its highest and that she viewed the imminent trial as a major trauma. She was concerned about what people would think of her, about exposing herself, about having to recall in vivid detail scenes that were most unpleasant. She was somewhat repressive and liked to put things out of mind. She was having difficulty doing that since the anticipation of the trial was keeping the whole episode alive.

A FINAL ANALYSIS

In 1986, as Carolyn and I were writing this book, I asked her to take one last MMPI so that I might compare it with the previous four. Armed with Carolyn's five MMPIs, I consulted Dr. Alex Caldwell, a preeminent MMPI expert. I wanted to get a "blind" analysis of these tests to counteract any biases I may have accumulated in my five years of contact with Carolyn. I told Dr.

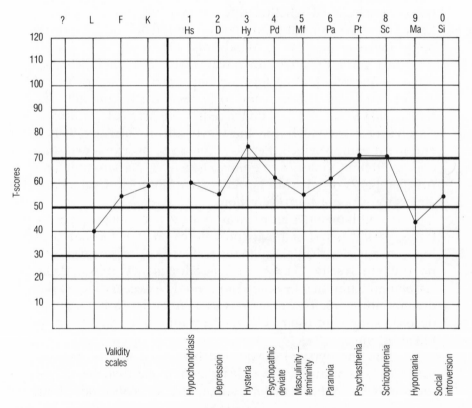

FIGURE 5

Carolyn's MMPI, October 1975, after her first meeting with Dr. X.

Caldwell only her sex and age, the dates on which the profiles were taken, and that they were all taken by the same patient. I asked him to tell me what the profiles said about the patient, without knowing anything about her.

The first MMPI was taken 6 months after Carolyn's 20th birthday, 5 months after she had returned home from a small college where she had become sexually involved with a young man but had not completely separated from Steve (see Figure 5). For the first time in her life, she was involved with more than one boyfriend at once and was miserably guilt-stricken. At home, she found her relationship with her mother strained and so she moved to a small apartment. She was confused about her college goals and changed her major from nursing to education. It was at this point that she entered psychotherapy with Dr. X.

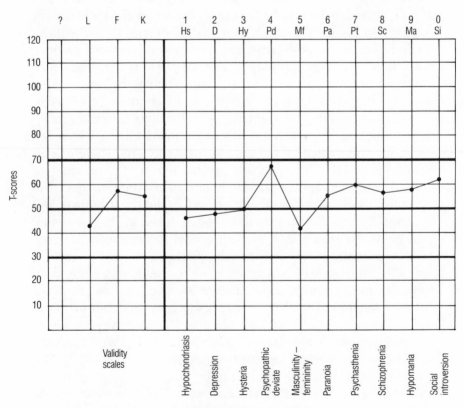

FIGURE 6
Carolyn's MMPI, July 1978, after her decision to sue Dr. X.

At this point Dr. Caldwell found Carolyn inhibited and anxious. Something was confusing her—she was ambitious but confused about her goals and her energy level. She was having trouble with personal closeness and needed assurance that she was okay. The profile shows tenseness and physical concerns, but she was bland (not excitable) about them. She was not very stable at this point but as an adolescent is not considered particularly disturbed.

Carolyn took the second MMPI when her attorneys believed her case would go to trial within 6 months and wanted psychological evidence to help determine whether Dr. X's actions had been damaging to her (see Figure 6). Although two of her brothers had contacted her immediately upon hearing about the lawsuit, offering support and encouragement, other family members and some of her acquaintances wanted her to drop the proceedings. Steve, who was still in and out of her life, was among them. Five months before, she had terminated therapy with the minister. She had begun to date different men without having intercourse with them but was feeling pressured to sleep with them. She was applying to various physician assistant programs in order to get out of town, and she had begun wearing makeup and more feminine clothes in an effort to find herself.

In this profile, Dr. Caldwell saw Carolyn exhibiting reactions to having been treated coldly or let down. She may have felt used. She was turned off by someone or something. There was an indication of rebellion, perhaps against her family, or ambivalence toward telling off someone in authority. The tenseness and nervousness of the last profile remained, as did the trouble delaying gratification. There may have been some ill-judged sexual acting out. There is a large shift in gender balance to femininity, and the somatic problems have disappeared.

The third MMPI was taken while Carolyn was living with Ken, her future husband (see Figure 7). The trial was to occur within a few months, and her attorneys again wanted psychological evidence to determine how she had changed over the years. At this point, she knew that what happened to her was unethical and that other women had been similarly treated by Dr. X. She had just quit teaching and entered a graduate program in engineering, in which she was unhappy. She was experiencing nightmares and physical symptoms. Her sexual drive diminished, and—since she had a few female friends who were bisexual or

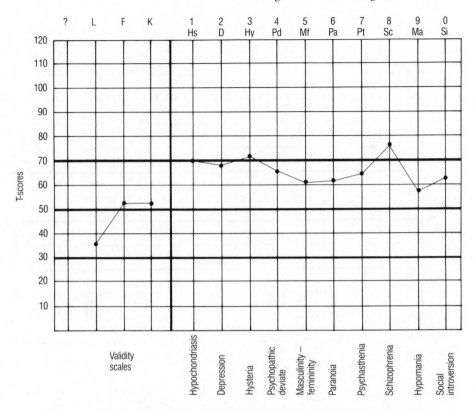

FIGURE 7

Carolyn's MMPI, September 1981, shortly before the trial was to take place.

lesbian—she wondered whether Dr. X was correct in his suggestion that she was a lesbian. She felt guilty for living with Ken out of marriage, something that was in contrast to her upbringing.

In the third profile, Dr. Caldwell detected something wrong with Carolyn's self-esteem. The profile indicates a struggle with her sexual identity and difficulty with sexual involvement. She may have been wondering whether she was a lesbian. She was again plagued by somatic problems and may have been settling into a particular physical problem. This is the first profile showing significant depression. She may have been struggling against it and be spaced out about it. Her thinking showed odd shifts, moving off in tangents. Her struggle over her life's goals was more acute. She needed help from others to develop structure in her life. She was having trouble setting goals by herself and was feeling ambivalence toward family or authority. There is a sense

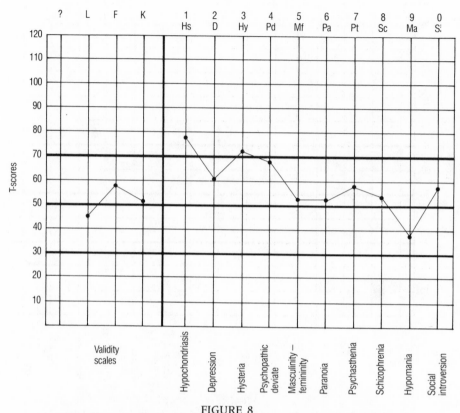

FIGURE 8

Carolyn's MMPI, October 1982, 3 weeks before the trial date.

of loss—that something that she had hoped for and expected has disappointed her.

At the time Carolyn took the fourth MMPI, the case was set to go to trial within 3 weeks. There was a question about settling out of court, but Carolyn had to be prepared to confront Dr. X at a trial. The nightmares and stomach disturbances had peaked. She had withdrawn from graduate school for a semester in order to decide whether or not to continue. She found the course work difficult. She was exhausted by teaching and refused to return to that field. She had been married to Ken for six months and had been faithful to him but was having difficulty enjoying the sexual aspect of marriage.

Dr. Caldwell found the fourth MMPI the most concerned with somatic symptoms, but it also showed a lessening of depres-

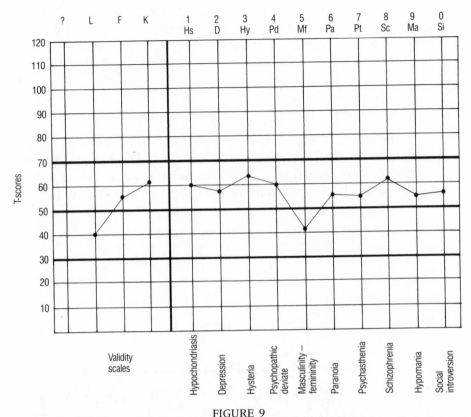

FIGURE 9
Carolyn's MMPI, October 1986, while writing this book.

sion and sense of loss. At this point, Carolyn was less tense but still confused about her goals and sex role. Dr. Caldwell noted an unusual amount of variation in energy level across the profiles. On this one, she has a collapse of energy. She couldn't get things done and was treading water with life. She was not achieving well and needed motivation and direction.

When Carolyn took the fifth MMPI, the case was 4 years behind her, and she was writing this book. She had been married for 4 years, very happily, and had been functioning successfully for 2 years in a doctoral program in counseling psychology.

Dr. Caldwell called this the best profile of the bunch. He noted that Carolyn's energy had returned and that there is only subtle evidence of her attention wandering. She was more controlled, and her rough edges were more polished. Yet a vulnerability to somatic problems remained. She was more feminine again, although there was an unevenness in the issue of sexuality. In the context of goals, she was functioning well. This profile is in the normal range.

SUMMARY

This series of MMPI profiles plots Carolyn's psychological reactions to the treatment by Dr. X, the filing and litigation of the malpractice case, her therapy, and her relationships. Figure 10 superimposes the five separate profiles, demonstrating how her

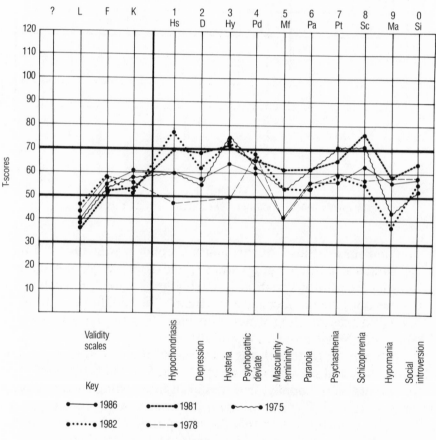

FIGURE 10
Carolyn's composite MMPIs, 1975–1986.

perceptions and reactions changed as events in her life had an impact on her basic personality style.

1975. Carolyn starts therapy with Dr. X. She is an inhibited, anxious, confused, late-adolescent who internalizes conflicts into physical symptoms, which she then denies. She also tends to be impulsive and somewhat rebellious and misunderstands the subtleties of close relationships.

1978. By the time she has discovered, through others, that Dr. X has misled her, she has become more confused, angry, and rebellious, sexually acting out through promiscuity. Yet she is ambivalent toward Dr. X, so that the tension and nervousness that earlier resulted in somatic symptoms are now channeled into more direct actions. In some ways, she is stronger than before; in other ways, she is more conflicted and confused.

1981. The legal process of preparing for the trial has been the greatest source of stress. Physical symptoms and nightmares reappear as she relives the abuse, her ambivalence toward Dr. X, and the prospect of public exposure. Her confusion has interfered with her life's goals and sexual relationships. She is least sure of herself during this period.

1982. As the trial becomes imminent, Carolyn's physical stress becomes most acute. Yet she is more sure of what she is doing and is developing a better sense of herself as a worthwhile person.

1986. Ten years after her therapy with Dr. X, Carolyn has progressed through a recovery aided by therapy, a good marriage, a fulfilling career goal, and a sense of purpose in documenting her experiences in this book.

If I were to put Dr. X's contribution to Carolyn's life in perspective, I would blame him most for the confusion surrounding her sexual identity, the exacerbation of interpersonal problems with men, and the insecurity in focusing on a career goal. To the litigation process I would attribute blame for the crisis period of greatest stress and confusion. I would credit both Dr. X and the lawsuit with the traumatic life crisis that enabled Carolyn to move forward in her career plans, perhaps farther than she would have if she had not experienced the trauma. The vulnerability of Carolyn's well-being and self-esteem are likely to be the most enduring, recurring, and damaging effects of the exploitation in therapy with Dr. X.

13

The Training and Rehabilitation of Mental Health Professionals: Can We Screen Out, Change, or Stop Dr. X?

This chapter is concerned with the education and training of mental health professionals in a way that may prevent sexual intimacies in therapy. How did Dr. X survive the screening process to become a psychotherapist, and at what points along the way of his training and obtaining credentials could his vulnerability have been discovered and his behavior prevented? First, one needs to look at the options that exist for entrance into a mental health profession as a psychotherapist. Second, one needs to consider the realities of those options and how they work in a system that permits poorly trained, marginally ethical (PTME) therapists to proceed to licensure and become the bane of the mental health professions.

OPTIONS IN PROFESSIONAL
MENTAL HEALTH TRAINING

There are several entries into the mental health profession. Psychiatry is the most prestigious and best remunerated mental health profession that produces psychotherapists. To become a psychiatrist one first needs to become a medical doctor. After a 4-year medical curriculum and 1-year internship, a 3-year full-time residency program in psychiatry prepares a physician to become a board certified psychiatrist. During the 3-year residency, the individual is exposed to a large number of mentally ill patients in a variety of settings. However, the training involved may not require more than the equivalent of 10% of one year practicing psychotherapy. The rest of the time may be occupied with assessment and medication of individuals in crisis, in-patient diagnosis and treatment, and so on. So the psychiatrist with 4 years of medical school, 1 year of internship, and an additional 3 years of a psychiatry residency may complete the entire curriculum and enter an independent practice of psychiatry having seen less than a dozen patients in psychotherapy. The great majority of psychiatrists, having completed their training, will go directly into private practice in which psychotherapy may be a main activity.

Another option for the mental health professional who wants to practice as a psychotherapist is in professional psychology. The doctoral-level psychologist can be licensed to engage in the independent practice of psychology after completing a graduate school professional training program, which may require four years of course work and a research dissertation. Of this training for the doctoral degree, 1 full year in an internship program and 2 years of part-time practicum is a typical requirement for "clinical" activities, most of which is psychotherapy. The graduate student in psychology, by the time he or she receives the doctorate may have seen fewer than a dozen psychotherapy cases, as few as a certified psychiatrist. Most states now require that psychologists have an additional full year of clinical training beyond the doctoral degree, although a few states still license psychologists who have master's degrees. Many psychology trainees work full-time with therapy patients during the postdoctoral year, but one could complete the entire year practicing no psychotherapy at all.

The social worker, usually after receiving a bachelor's degree, will go on to a master's level program, which takes an average of 2 years to complete. Most of the work during these 2 years is clinical in nature, and much of it focuses on psychotherapy. The licensing of social workers varies among the states, and additional requirements, such as practice hours under supervision, are diverse. Licensed clinical social workers are permitted to practice independently in most states; but some states still do not license social workers, and others permit social workers in less-qualified categories to practice independently.

Counselors of various kinds (marriage, family, child, sex, school, and pastoral) are now also being licensed in some states, and this newly credentialed profession is struggling to incorporate criteria for the training of its mental health professionals to work with individuals who have less severe pathology, or "problems in living." At this point, however, most counselors will have completed fewer than 2 years of academic course work and clinically oriented training combined, and they are less likely to have been exposed to the mentally ill during their training.

Other mental health professionals may also receive some amount of supervised training with individuals in a therapeutic relationship (i.e., medical caseworkers; nurse practitioners; art, dance, and occupational therapists; and clergy). But in none of these professions is psychotherapy considered central to the professional training, and the training may not be particularly focused.

There are also paraprofessionals working in limited roles who are briefly trained to do crisis or peer counseling—suicide or rape hot-line workers or support- or recovery-group facilitators working in the areas of alcohol and drug abuse, weight control, infertility, and so on. These individuals are not trained in any of the mental health or related professions and are considered to have very restricted areas of expertise narrowly focused in a specific crisis or addiction behavior.

Finally, there are some counselors who are not controlled at all by a license, and we do not have the ability to sanction them regarding psychotherapeutic treatment. Thus members of the clergy may engage in pastoral counseling with no formal training, or they may take courses in pastoral counseling and have supervised experience with parishioners. Yet there are no formal criteria and no licensing to control their practice. Likewise, individuals who have learned hypnosis can be registered in some states as hypnotists and may be able to offer themselves to the public as providing "treatment" for mental health problems such as eating disorders, low self-esteem, and addictions although they have had no counseling training at all.

THE REALITIES OF MENTAL HEALTH PROFESSIONALISM

With some notable exceptions, mechanisms are generally in place to screen individuals who wish to offer psychotherapy. One might even assume that by ascending the informal hierarchy of professional prestige (which is roughly related to the length, type, and intensity of training and the degree of difficulty that one encounters in obtaining credentials), one could be more assured that a therapist will be well trained, competent, and ethical. That assurance may be ill-placed, however, if one considers some unfortunate realities. First, the most prestigious psychiatry and psychology programs may provide less supervised psychotherapy training than some of the academically weakest unaccredited counseling programs. Thus quality and quantity of training are not necessarily highly correlated. Second, while students selected to attend the most prestigious schools are generally superior in all professional qualities, it is possible for unempathic, nonpsychologically minded, and marginally ethical individuals to be selected, their inadequacies tolerated (if they are discovered) and to graduate and become licensed with full privileges. And third, some of the less well known institutions provide closer supervision and monitoring and are more willing to deny course credit or a diploma to marginal students.

The problem of marginal students exists for several reasons. It is very difficult, for example, for any professional program to inform a student that he or she is not appropriate for that specialty and ought to leave the field. This is the stuff of lawsuits, unless some tangible evidence can be documented. The therapy skills of psychiatry residents, in particular, because they already have their medical degree and work with a certain amount of independence, may not even be well known by their immediate supervisors and training directors.

In psychology, to meet the demand of individuals who want to be private practitioners in lucrative urban areas but are unable to get into highly competitive APA-accredited graduate programs, a flood of new programs has arisen. These accept lower test scores and a less rigorous academic background and require less time in which to earn a degree. Entrepeneurs discovered that they could start private programs in psychology to prepare students to sit for licensing exams in the various states. Many students are willing to pay dearly for their graduate education, going into debt for many years to pay off loans in order that they might enter the private practice of psychology alongside psychiatrists and psychologists and be able to command prestigious or lucrative positions.

Some of these programs are laudable. They train selected individuals to be fine psychotherapists—a psychotherapist does not need to have the intensive medical training of a medical doctor or the scientific background of a psychologist with a doctoral degree. But with money as the object, and lowered standards for admission, some of the new programs have admitted individuals who do not possess either the intellectual potential, the interpersonal sensitivity, or the moral character to become a psychotherapist. Licensing examinations do not always ferret out these individuals, particularly when most states permit an individual to retake the examination an unlimited number of times. Licensing examinations are not very accurate in measuring moral character or therapeutic sensitivity.

A similar problem exists when one considers the other mental health professions. Social work is struggling with its own criteria for licensure, and the profession is beginning to move toward granting higher-level degrees, such as that of doctor of social work. Nursing has developed a doctoral program in order to attract more highly qualified individuals to the profession. Counselors are just beginning to set standards, and in some ways the flood of individuals wanting to be counselors supports a market for programs that offer degrees to those who can spend weekends and/or evenings in classes for a year or two while doing other work full-time. For example, a group of lawyers decided that they could earn more money from their divorce clients by also counseling them, so they hired some supervisors to teach them counseling at the minimal level for licensure, and in their spare time they are earning credit toward a counseling certificate.

In some states, a counseling license occupies the role that a real estate license has held for the last couple of decades: as a way for middle-class women who wish to enter the workplace at midlife to assume a professional career with short-term preparation. One can go to school part-time or on weekends and evenings, not do the more intensive graduate work of researching and writing theses and dissertations, and not be bothered spending all of one's time in an accredited program. The problem is not that individuals who complete abbreviated programs will be incompetent and/or unethical because they have found an easier route to becoming therapists. The problem is that there is such a wide range of individuals accepted into these programs that few effective means exist by which to screen out those who are inappropriate as counselors either intellectually, personally, or morally. And it is also possible for the training to be so lax that individuals are not even aware of their deficiencies in training or inadequacies in practice.

THE TRAINING OF DR. X

From his depositions and other material used in Carolyn's court case, I have some knowledge of Dr. X's training. His first mental health experience was during a military tour, where, he stated, he screened soldiers brought from their Marine units in crisis to determine whether they should be discharged. He talked about seeing as many as 30 recruits a day for evaluation, spending less than 10 minutes with each. His training to make major decisions regarding whether to reject individuals on psychological grounds was gained from watching other mental health professionals perform in these 5-to-10-minute interviews. He was then permitted to do this screening himself without individual course work or training.

By his own testimony, it is known that Dr. X had difficulty getting into a program in psychology. He was rejected by 16 programs before finally being accepted into an unaccredited program in educational psychology. This program was relatively new when he was accepted. One can surmise that his body was needed to increase enrollment, and that the administration did not bother to screen him carefully, personally or academically. When asked about his training in this program and the courses he took dealing with psychotherapy, his recollection was that most of these courses consisted of "encounter groups" in which the classmates themselves were participants. In effect, the students received course credit for talking about themselves in a therapeutic group. His predoctoral internship was in a hospital setting, where there was some question about his working with the female staff, but he successfully completed the internship and successfully passed his licensing examination. After this, he entered full-time private practice.

The question arises: Would Dr. X have been discovered earlier in his career as incompetent or unethical had he been trained in a more rigorous program or had the licensing criteria been tougher? I would like to answer with a resounding yes, but I can't. Many offenders of sexual intimacies in therapy and of other incompetencies in practice are graduates of the very best programs in all of the mental health fields. There have been criminal felonies, malpractice judgments, ethics censures, and delicensures involving chairs of ethics committees, directors of professional training programs, members of credentialing boards, and presidents of local and state professional associations. On the other hand, some of the most moral, competent, sensitive practitioners are graduates of the least difficult programs. But I do believe that there is a correlation such that the higher criteria and the more intense screening that exist in the better programs lead to the lesser likelihood of a Dr. X slipping through. Unfortunately, no data exist to support this impression. Some states will begin publishing the rates of passage of licensing examination by students at educational institutions. This is one step toward public awareness. Another might be the publication of educational programs by the number of graduates found guilty of licensing board infractions, state ethics committees violations and malpractice.

SCREENING OUT INCOMPETENCE

Three areas in which we can make improvements to help screen out or avoid incompetence are (1) the selection of candidates into the mental health professions, (2) the psychotherapy-related training of students in mental health programs, and (3) the prevention of unethical behavior after training. To determine the cues that might allow us to recognize a potential Dr. X, I shall trace some experiences of professional psychology students from selection by a graduate program to licensure as independent practitioners.

The Selection of Candidates

Applicants to professional programs in psychology are usually requested to submit test scores, transcripts of college courses and grades, letters of recommendations, and personal interviews. Almost all schools require the Graduate Record Examination (GRE) as either the only, or the major, test. Scores on the GRE correlate with success in graduate school and thus help screen out applicants who might fail academically. Students with marginal GRE scores may be expected to have difficulty expressing themselves in writing, understanding complex, theoretical material, or interpreting quantitative procedures necessary to produce research or evaluate scientific articles. But GRE scores do not help administrators to differentiate between competent and incompetent psychotherapists. The "psychological mindedness" necessary to understand and empathetically treat disturbed patients cannot be evaluated *a priori* from any paper-and-pencil test.

College grades can provide some subtle clues. Those who consistently do very well are not only bright enough to understand the material taught but also have shown their application to hard work and the ability to follow rules over a period of several years under the tutelage of many professors. But undergraduate grades are complicated by the fact that some professors and some schools give inflated grades to all students, while other schools and other professors demand much stiffer requirements for the same high grades. Moreover, some courses have much more relevance to psychotherapy. Thus courses requiring practical experience with patients or other populations requiring assistance contribute more in terms of predicting therapeutic technique than do courses focused on statistical analysis or the memorization of facts.

Letters of recommendation provide other clues. Not only does a professor or supervisor gain a sense of an individual's competence in the course work or techniques that are monitored, but he or she also has access to the individual's personality and ability to work with others—peers, superiors, staff, and patients or clients. These are matters close to the heart of the psychotherapy experience. Unfortunately, there are problems in trusting letters of recommendation. In most states, an applicant is permitted by law to read any letter of recommendation written about him or her. This is meant to ensure that an applicant can defend against negative comments. But the effect of such a law is to inhibit the writers of recommendations from conveying their concerns and negative opinions. In a litigious society it is easier to refuse to write a letter for an applicant who requests one or to leave out the critical statements than to risk an honest appraisal that is negative.

Some applicants have learned that they can shop for the best letters by demanding to see what will be written and throwing out all but those letters that treat them very favorably. Some applicants have been known to threaten supervisors with lawsuits for slander if they are rated as personally inadequate. Although such threats probably cannot achieve legal success, professors are reluctant to get involved and simply suggest that the applicant find someone else to write a letter. Finally, writers of recommendations may not be aware of critical instances of incompetence, poor judgment, or unethical behavior. For example, a student might establish "good rapport" with the children he or she has to test by surreptitiously bribing them with candy and other favors.

Personal interviews are used by many programs to help screen candidates who wish to be psychotherapists. In a face-to-face interview, a candidate can be probed about motivations for entering the profession, attitudes toward psychotherapy, and so forth. Interviewers might be alerted to the individual who is hostile to women, callous about others' comforts, or unable to pick up cues about feelings. Spontaneous conversations, interactions in groups at dinner, an ability to arrange and manage a visit to the prospective program site—these are other aspects of the personal interview that provide data about a person's ability to interpret social situations and interact with others. Some applicants reveal their deficiencies in judgment in their reactions to secretaries, their preoccupation with themselves, their provocativeness with opposite-sex peers, and so on. Given Dr. X's continuing problems with the women in his life, it is possible that a sharp interviewer would have had reservations about his candidacy at the time of a personal interview.

But personal interviews can also lend themselves to discrimination against certain candidates. Biases against race, sex, unattractiveness, regional accents, and other characteristics may influence how a candidate is viewed. Also, the stress of competition may work against candidates who are anxious during interviews. And, of course, the more sociopathic candidates, like Dr. X, may already be masters at charm and superficial concerns.

Thus a balance in weighing the various methods of screening candidates for admission to a graduate program in psychology is not easily achieved.

Training in Psychotherapy

Once accepted into a training program, a prospective psychotherapist is taught the skills to enable him or her to be effective in a psychotherapeutic relationship. These skills include ways of gaining a patient's trust, methods of encouraging a patient to talk more freely and reveal material that may have been repressed for years, and techniques for overcoming resistances to revelations or problems of trust. These therapeutic tools are powerful. The assumption is that the therapist will use them appropriately, for the welfare of the patient. The American Psychological Association now requires that ethics be taught as part of the formal course work in its accredited programs. When Dr. X was in graduate school, many programs did not require ethics courses, and Dr. X himself stated that he had never had an ethics course.

Recognizing one's vulnerabilities to sexual intimacies is not specifically mentioned as a necessary part of the training curriculum in most programs in any of the mental health disciplines, even though the opportunities to address this subject arise frequently. In a study by Pope, Keith-Spiegel, and Tabachnick, 90% of psychologists admitted being sexually attracted to one or more of their patients (1986). Such attraction is a common feature of a relationship between two individuals who meet privately and regularly to discuss the personal matters of one of them. The warmth and caring that enable the transference relationship to facilitate a therapeutic alliance between patient and therapist also can arouse erotic feelings, which complicate the therapeutic alliance.

This important training feature may be ignored because it strikes a sensitive chord in supervisors, who may not have resolved their own discomfort in handling such situations. In fact, supervisor–trainee sexual relationships have been a problem in the psychotherapeutic professions. Pope *et al.* report that 25% of female students in psychology have had a sexual relationship with a male professor during their training (1979). Dr. X may have noted this behavior in his program and felt free to model himself after his male professors in his later work with female patients and colleagues. There appears to be some evidence that professors who engage in sexual intimacies with patients may spawn students who do likewise with their patients (Pope *et al.*, 1979; Glazer & Thorpe, 1986).

In preparing a paper on countertransference issues in psychotherapy, I queried students about the sexuality of their supervisory relationships (Brodsky, 1977). One female psychotherapy student explained how the pressure of a supervisor trying to promote a sexual relationship with her discouraged her from discussing with him the sexual difficulties of her patient since she wanted to avoid sexual references in the supervisor's presence. The therapy suffered, as did her ability to learn how to handle sexual matters in psychotherapy. The supervisor never knew the impact of his trying to sexualize the supervisory relationship. Likewise, it is possible that Dr. X could have been unaware of his impact on patients with whom he had sexual intimacies. He denied that his sexual intimacies with Carolyn had affected her, but we may never know how much of his denial was a result of his lack of knowledge, sensitivity, or adherence to the truth.

Case conferences are another means of learning about transference relationships. To the extent that there is tension about such learning situations due either to sexual relationships between supervisors and students and/or a critical atmosphere when presenters reveal weaknesses or vulnerabilities, this source loses its effectiveness. A student who admits sexual feelings toward a patient to a supervisor in a one-on-one training session may be honest and open, but a student who would discuss his or her sexual feelings toward a patient for the scrutiny of a room full of peers and superiors is truly courageous (Brodsky, 1980). Perhaps if Dr. X had been monitored more closely by his trainers and peers and had observed others struggling with the issues, he would have had some appreciation of the deviancy of his behavior, and his supervisors would have found some clues to suggest his future problems as a sexually abusive therapist.

Because sex between therapist and patient has become so predominant as a specific area of ethical and therapeutic concern, training materials have become an issue. In the mid-1970s, I began to present workshops at various training programs and mental health centers on how to handle sexualized relationships in psychotherapy. From those early experiences, I developed videotapes of some of the situations that most caused concern or fear among the participants. A set of vignettes were produced and made available for trainers (Brodsky, 1979).

I have used these vignettes in over 35 workshops since then, and they are still relevant today, with the same concerns being raised. Women trainees express the most concern over how to handle aggressive male patients who refuse to take no for an answer to their wishes to sexualize the relationship. Male trainees are more concerned with how to handle the dilemma of a female patient who misinterprets a nonerotic caring for a sexual interest, leaving them with the delicate task of setting firm limits without implying a rejection of the patient's love.

The feedback from such training sessions has been encouraging. Participants gain awareness of their unpreparedness to handle sensitive situations that may not yet have occurred to them but which they can envision. They benefit from discussion with others at their level of training, learning that sexual attraction for patients may be unavoidable, but that such feelings can be acknowledged to themselves without ever acting on them. Unfortunately, there is no mandatory training in this area for either trainees or licensed practitioners, and voluntary workshops at conventions tend to attract only those practitioners already aware of the problem and willing to address it. In the last few years, there has been an increasing interest in learning about sex between therapist and patient. The audiences for convention presentations has now expanded to ethics committee and state licensing board members, as well as supervisors in training institutions and internships. One can wonder about the supervisors in Dr. X's program: Had they had training, they may have been alerted to the need to train their own students in this area.

Materials for trainers are also becoming more abundant. The American Psychiatric Association has videotapes on the subject (1987), the Minnesota Walk-In Counseling Center provides guidelines for therapists (Schoener, Milgrom, & Gonsiorek, 1983), and the Committee on Women of the American Psychological Association has released a brochure for patients, which is included in the appendix to this book.

The Prevention of Unethical Behavior in Psychotherapists

If students and independent practitioners are not specifically trained in primary techniques for appropriately handling erotic transference in psychotherapy, what can we do to at the next stage of prevention, which arises when the situation is imminent?

The answer depends on the reasons for the therapist's involvement. The abusive therapist types mentioned in Chapter 9 would require different approaches to rehabilitation and different sanctions. Schoener describes other types one might add to the list, such as those who engage in an isolated instance of bad judgment or loss of control and those who are overtly psychotic, both relatively rare (1988). Also, Pope and Bouhoutsos discuss finer separations of the types mentioned already (1986), which would lead to even more variability in individual approaches to preventing further episodes by known offenders.

The easiest preventive measures for therapists who identify themselves as being at risk are education and consultation. Books and articles (such as this one) can teach a therapist what is wrong and why, and state and national organizations can put individual therapists in touch with expert consultants who might advise them on how to manage an impending problematic situation. Pope has written a how-to article for therapists that is meant to enable them to identify a problem in sexual intimacy arising in psychotherapy (1987). The therapist who is aware and feels in danger of losing control has the resources for help. The bigger concern is with the therapist who is unaware of his or her risk, overly self-assured as to the mastery of a sexualized situation, or callous about the possibility of hurting a patient.

Many indications from Dr. X's deposition are predictive of his unawareness, incompetence, and disregard for the recipients of his sexual advances. Some examples follow.

In giving his opinion of what kinds of problems might occur as a result of a dual relationship, he stated, "If you have a dual relationship, it probably takes away from the scientific endeavor of therapy, and makes it more of a nondirective or multidirective relationship rather than just the process of psychotherapy."

When Carolyn's lawyer questioned him about hypothetical potential damage to clients arising from his having dual relationships with them, he responded, "It hasn't . . . in these cases . . . in my opinion. . . . I've heard of cases across the country where people have alleged damage. But as far as did it hurt someone? I don't know."

Asked whether sexual intercourse could be harmful to patients, he responded, "I've never witnessed it being harmful in my experience. . . . I know that there are an awful lot of people who allege—you know, in known court cases that I've read that they've alleged that it caused them to be depressed. But it certainly hasn't happened to anybody in this room. That's the extent of my experience."

In response to the question "And you think just having this sexual intercourse with you was helping her?" (referring to Carolyn), Dr. X responded, "I can answer that by saying it did not appear to be not helping her."

In discussing his view of the "perfect termination," he noted:

> Ideally, it's a thorough discussing of all the issues that have been taken up and worked through in the psychotherapeutic process, and then an agreement to terminate, and to end the visitation session in that the patient—well, Carolyn is a perfect example of a perfect termination, where we agreed to no longer meet as doctor–patient in that she had benefited and I felt she had benefited and we parted ways.

Dr. X was not a good candidate for rehabilitation at any point. He did not appear to learn from his experiences, other than that he was capable of avoiding punishment through denial, lies, and legal assistance. His testing of the limits of an ethics committee, the state licensing board, and professional psychology organizations all left him in a position to continue his exploitation of unsuspecting female patients/clients. It took criminal action to mandate a stop to his professional practice. We do not yet know whether the criminal court has been effective in stopping him. His probational status leaves open another chance for his rehabilitation. It also leaves open the additional risk that Dr. X will continue to abuse women. His opportunity to prove his ability to adhere to the conditions of probation are provided at the expense of the public and the professions.

The frustrations of victims and sanctioning bodies in trying to stop the various Dr. X's of the therapeutic professions arise in part from a desire of the courts and other professionals to be compassionate with the "impaired" professionals who "in momentary lapses of judgment" are tempted to behave in ways that are contrary to their usual nature. However, sexual intimacy with a patient is not a trivial transgression unlikely to have a major impact. It is much more likely to be a serious offense, known by the perpetrator to be unethical and damaging. The therapist who in a personally needy, vulnerable moment hugs or kisses a patient and then apologizes, or the therapist who confuses boundaries between therapy and personal life out of ignorance and for which he or she is later remorseful and willing to receive remedial education or rehabilitation is not the therapist who is likely to be delicensed or sued for malpractice. In a reference to sociopathic offenders considered for probation in California, the executive officers of the licensure boards for all mental health professionals noted that

> sexual misconduct merits revocation of the license. In those few cases in the past where revocation has been stayed and probation ordered, we found that the staff time required to monitor compliance with the terms of probation is substantial and the public protection minimal. It is not inconceivable that a probation order can go unenforced as result of human error. Additionally, it is not inconceivable that even after a probation order is effective, the respondent, as a result of differences in interpretation, may tie up the boards' funds and staff time in lengthy legal petitions . . . In

any case, prospects for rehabilitation are minimal and it is doubtful that they should be given the opportunity to ever practice psychotherapy again. (Callanan & O'Connor, 1988)

Even though Dr. X may have been mentally ill at times during his life, even though he may have been poorly trained, even though he may have been unable to maintain professional boundaries, he was still responsible for the consequences of his unprofessional actions during the therapeutic relationship. Just as we have become aware that there is a prior volitional aspect to the behavior of drunk drivers who kill or physically maim someone when they are out of control on the road, so we have become aware that the sexually abusive therapist has advance warning that sexual intimacy in therapy is a dangerous and illegal practice that must be avoided. We restrict the option of driving when drunk, and we should restrict the option of sexual relationships when providing therapy. A defense of impaired judgment is an *ad hoc* excuse. Judgment was not impaired before the individual entered the situation. Professionals who are experiencing mental problems know that they need to be in treatment, and their ethical codes clearly require that they restrict their practice when they are impaired by personal problems (American Psychological Association, 1981).

Testimony from my deposition relates to this issue:

Q: Do you make any allowance in your judgment of Dr. X for the fact that he, himself, might have been having problems at the time this took place?

A: No, I don't make any allowances because I am not really looking at him as a person, either positively or negatively, and I'm not really concerned, in this evaluation [of Carolyn], with his needs. I'm concerned with what he has done and how that responds to his competency. His reasons for it do not seem to be relevant.

Q: I mean, you wouldn't recognize as an excuse for, say, his conduct the fact that he may have been under a lot of strain himself at the time, or was having personal problems himself?

A: No, because again, there are many guidelines for what a therapist should do when under stress—about dropping their patient load, about referring patients who are connected with their own kind of problems.

Gonsiorek (1987), who works with the Minnesota Walk-In Counseling Center, which has seen over 300 victims of sexually abusive therapists and has worked with the rehabilitation of many male offenders, reports an opinion that I and most experts in the field would endorse. "Sanctioning bodies need to separate the illegal and administrative aspects of the offense from the rehabilitation of the offender. If we are to consider sex between therapists and patients as the serious act that it is, we should not enter into the equation the factor of the therapist's motivation." I would add that should the offense become a criminal act, as it is now in two states, then the offender could plead a defense of insanity. Such a defense would have to meet the state's criteria for insanity in the commission of any crime. Having poor relationships with women in one's life, or being under "mental strain," would not qualify in most courtrooms.

CODA

The story of Carolyn's relationship with Dr. X is not over. It is not over in her mind, in her dreams, or in its impact on her life and relationships. It is not over for Dr. X. He is under court orders to desist from counseling relationships of any kind with any women, but history would predict that he should have difficulty adhering to the conditions of probation. It is not over for the professions as they continue to move to tighten sanctions for sexual abuses in therapy. It is not over for those of us who work in this field, trying to find solutions to the dilemma of dealing with our colleagues who harm their patients in the name of the profession. The incestuous father was once a hurt child; the cycle of abuse will not be broken if he is permitted to continue to abuse his children. Above all, we must first address the best interests of the child—in this case, the vulnerable adult/child who enters a sexual relationship in therapy with a father figure who exploits his position of trust and power.

Appendix 1: Chronology

1975

October 28   Carolyn enters therapy with Dr. X.

1976

March 25   Carolyn begins group therapy concurrent with in-
              dividual therapy. Dr. X reduces his fee from $45 to
              $35 per therapy hour.

August 6   Dr. X and his second wife separate.

August 9   First incident of sexual intercourse between Dr. X and
              Carolyn occurs.

October 7   Third patient to eventually file suit against Dr. X for
              sexual misconduct enters therapy with him.

1977

January 28	Dr. X's divorce is finalized.
July 12	Final incident of sexual intercourse between Dr. X and Carolyn takes place.
August 9	Carolyn terminates therapy with Dr. X.
August 25	First patient to eventually file suit against Dr. X enters therapy with him.
November 17	Single incident of sexual intercourse between first patient and Dr. X occurs; she terminates treatment immediately.

1978

February 7	In a taped conversation with an abused client, Dr. X states that he would deny her charges in a malpractice suit, to protect his license.
March 7	First complaint is filed with the state licensing board for psychologists.
May 2	Second complaint is filed with the state licensing board for psychologists.
July 19	Psychological evaluations of the two complainants are received by counsel so that both parties may consider damages.
August 2	Two malpractice lawsuits are filed in the district court charging professional negligence, assault and battery, fraud and deceit, deceptive trade practice, breach of contract, and gross negligence.
August 4	Dr. X denies all allegations made in the plaintiffs' petitions.
September 14	Dr. X is sent a list of interrogatories questioning his conduct in therapy with two complainants and other patients in order to identify witnesses.

September 26   "I cannot remember any specific dates, but we did have sexual intercourse several times. Carolyn may have been charged for the session but was never charged for the time intercourse took place."
—Dr. X answering an interrogatory

October 12   Plaintiffs are deposed for the first time.

October 17   Dr. X seeks motion for a protective order, objecting to the interrogatories on grounds of relevancy and the violation of his constitutional right of privacy.

November 13   "There's been very little consistency [in media coverage]. There's not been a sustained day-by-day effort put on this situation to cause people to keep . . . this case in . . . mind . . . The impact, as far as [electronic] exposure, has not been anywhere near saturation."
—Witness for the plaintiffs in a pretrial deposition

November 15   The judge orders Dr. X to jail for contempt, but releases him on bond while awaiting appeal of the ruling to the state supreme court. The question of privileged communications and confidentiality between psychologists and their patients will be tested.

November 18   "I felt there was a relationship other than professional developing between us . . . At the time I thought it was emotionally beneficial to both of us . . . I attempted to compartmentalize our relationship on a professional and on a personal level."
—Dr. X at a hearing before the state licensing board for psychologists

December 12   The defendant requests a motion for a change of venue.

December 19   "Our position is that he admitted sexual intercourse with the other two women but will deny it in this case."
—Attorney for Dr. X. responding to the press after third lawsuit is filed

1979

January 2   In the state supreme court, the plaintiffs argue against Dr. X's application for writ of habeas corpus.

January 16   Of the registered voters polled, 45% have heard of Dr. X, 54% have not. Dr. X can get a fair trial in the county.
—Public opinion survey to determine the need for a change of venue

January 15   Second hearing before the state licensing board for psychologists. Three former female patients of Dr. X's testify that he never made improper advances toward them. One woman states, however, that she had dated Dr. X twice after her therapy was terminated and that they had had intercourse on one of those dates.

"Dr. X admits point blank that he was wrong . . . he has consistently told the truth. If he had lied he might not be here today."
—Attorney for Dr. X at hearing before the state licensing board

Members of the state licensing board for psychologists vote unanimously to revoke Dr. X's license and certificate for unprofessional conduct.

January 24   "Should he appeal, the Board will consider it carefully. It's always possible a person might be reconsidered [for reinstatement]. Some rehabilitation may be required. Dr. X can reapply for a license in a year."
—Chairman of the state licensing board for psychologists

January 31   The state supreme court refuses to overturn the contempt judgment against Dr. X.

February 1   Dr. X still refuses to answer questions concerning possible sexual contact with his patients, asserting that the contempt judgment violates his and his patients' rights of privacy guaranteed by the United States Constitution and common law.

February 23   "I cannot recall a situation where people knew more about a particular individual."
—Witness on behalf of Dr. X in a pretrial deposition

"In light of my experience in selling products and political candidates, this case has not received a substantial amount of attention."
—Advertising and Public Relations consultant in a pretrial deposition

"County juries do not reflect the same make-up as registered voters in the county."
—District judge

Judge orders a change of venue.

March 6	Annette Brodsky, Ph.D., is chosen as the expert witness for evaluating psychological damage to the plaintiffs.
April 30	U.S. district judge upholds contempt ruling.
May 24	Dr. X appeals the contempt ruling to the U.S. Circuit Court of Appeals.
October 9	The plaintiffs are deposed a second time, for current information regarding their personal lives.

1980

February 6	Dr. X's appeal is heard in the U.S. Court of Appeals.
August 29	"[A dual relationship] muddies the water. I'm not sure I can explain it and I see no purpose in explaining it. . . . It was not specifically unethical. Later [the state board of examiners] added that to make it specifically unethical. . . . I have never witnessed it to be harmful in my experience." —Dr. X in a deposition taken by Brown and Whitehurst
September 30	The Circuit court of appeals denies Dr. X's appeal, charging that he "should remain under obligation to this Court to answer the questions propounded to him, and [is] in contempt for failure to do so." Dr. X is ordered to surrender himself to the sheriff.

October 9   "The Circuit has left us back at square one in this matter."
—State district court judge in letter to plaintiffs' and defendant's attorneys

December 1   Dr. X is detained at the courthouse and then placed under "house arrest" by the sheriff. His lawyers again ask the high court for a writ of habeas corpus, alleging that he no longer needs to comply with the district judge's order because of a 1979 state law that renders information about mental patients confidential.

December 2   The petition for a writ of habeas corpus is allowed by the state supreme court, granting Dr. X bail.

"At the time I did not believe there was any problem with being someone's lover and therapist at the same time. Punishing someone has never served to reduce the incidence of the problem. There appears to be a growing interest in helping rather than . . . taking [the professional] out behind the woodshed and beating the hell out of him. Professionals are people who have the same kinds of money, emotional and sexual problems as anyone else. And the sooner that they and lay people stop perceiving them as gods, the better."
—Dr. X in an interview in a local newspaper

December 3   The State supreme court frees Dr. X on a $1,000 bond, agreeing to consider whether the contempt citation should be overturned.

1981

January 21   "Two years ago Dr. X attempted to hide his wrong-doing behind the constitutional rights of patients, now he comes to this court in an effort to hide behind the statute passed in the interim. The 1979 law does not create an absolute privilege for psychotherapists like the attorney–client privilege."
—Bill Whitehurst, attorney for the plaintiffs, before the state supreme court

"We want to know whether Dr. X had kissed, touched, fondled or had any sexual contact of any type, including sexual intercourse with any other client or former patient. We need the information to demonstrate the horrendous pattern of conduct that existed in his practice.
—Suzanne Brown, attorney for the plaintiffs, before the state supreme court

March 18   In a 5–4 decision, the state supreme court rules that a 1979 state law making therapist–patient matters confidential is retroactive. Dr. X does not have to reveal the names of other patients with whom he may have been intimate.

October 3   Dr. Brodsky meets the complainants for psychological evaluation.

1982

March 15   A District court judge denies the plaintiffs' motion to reconsider the change-of-venue decision.

August 26   Another district court judge grants Dr. X's motions to consolidate the three cases against him.

September 9 An attorney for Dr. X deposes Dr. Brodsky, expert witness for the plaintiffs.

October 10 The case is settled out of court.

1984

June 15   In a hearing before the state licensing board for psychologists, a 29-year-old woman states that from June until August 1983, sexual intimacy with Dr. X took place during therapy sessions. During this time, Dr. X was under the board-ordered supervision of a licensed psychologist.

Dr. X denies her charges before the state licensing board for psychologists and states that the board has no jurisdiction over him and should not hear the case.

September 13   The state licensing board for psychologists votes unanimously to revoke Dr. X's certificate to practice psychology, determining that he had violated nine principles established for the practice of psychology in the state, including a rule that sexual intimacies with a patient are unethical.

September 14   "Dr. X may ask for a re-hearing. If the Board does not respond to the request, Dr. X may challenge the revocation in District Court."
—Chairman of the state licensing board for psychologists

"I cannot find [Dr. X] guilty [of Principle 6a] because I feel I have unsubstantiated evidence."
—Boardmember of the state licensing board for psychologists

1985

January 4   Dr. X sues the state board for licensing psychologists, claiming that their latest formal hearing dealing with a patient's complaint against him was unfair, "denying" him the right to full and meaningful prehearing discovery by denying him sufficient time in which to obtain a list of [her] sexual partners since January 1982, her income tax records for 1983, a picture of herself, and her medical records.

June 4   Dr. X and his supervisor are sued by a 29-year-old ex-patient who alleges that Dr. X engaged in sexual intercourse with her during the course of her therapy with him.

August 30   The state board for licensing professional counselors issues a final order revoking Dr. X's professional counselor's license, opening the way for Dr. X to seek a judicial review of the decision.

October 3   Dr. X sues the state board for licensing professional counselors, stating that "the board's findings, inferences, conclusions, and decisions concerning him are unlawful and improper because they . . . were arbitrary and capricious to reach [their] conclusion . . . for they knew of *no* underlying facts to support [the complainant's accusations]" and that the hearings were simply unfair.

1986

February 27   Dr. X's attorney, who represented him in his latest defense against a patient's civil suit, withdraws as his council.

October   Dr. X and his supervisor settle Dr. X's latest civil suit out of court.

1987

February 12   The firm representing Dr. X in his most recent lawsuit files a suit against Dr. X himself for a due and unpaid bill amounting to $15,488.63.

March 19   The county grand jury indicts Dr. X on a second-degree felony charge for using physical force to compel a teenage patient to submit to sexual advances. The victim is a 17-year-old who was seeing him for marital counseling.

March 26   Dr. X is arrested, his bond is set at $20,000, and he is released on personal recognizance.

April 14   A judge rules that Dr. X's ex-attorneys may recover from him $17,227.72 in owed bills and interest.

April 21   Dr. X files a motion for a psychological and psychiatric examination of the woman charging him with sexual assault, asking for the full names of men and women whom she had earlier identified to him, probably in the context of therapy.

May 5   The court dismisses Dr. X's suit against the state board
                   for licensing psychologists for want of prosecution.

November 13   Dr. X pleads guilty to second-degree felony charge of
                   sexual assault before the district court.

        1988

January 9   Dr. X receives a 10-year probated sentence and a
                   $10,000 probated fine as punishment for the charge
                   of sexual assault. The final stipulation of his probation
                   statement is that he not "practice any type of counsel-
                   ing during" the 10-year probation period.

Appendix 2: If Sex Enters into the Psychotherapy Relationship

This brochure has been prepared to help you, the patient of a psychotherapist, to understand what is appropriate for you to do if sex enters into your relationship with your therapist and what recourses you may have if this occurs. Although this pamphlet may raise issues that you have not considered before, it will help you to understand that

- Most psychologists who practice psychotherapy are ethical persons who adhere to professional standards and who care about their patients; however, a very small percentage of psychologists behave unethically and do not think about what is best for their patients.

- Out of concern for you as a patient, a large percentage of psychologists feel that it will help you, the consumer of therapy services, if inappropriate behaviors are brought to your attention so that you can decide what to do if you ever have to confront such situations.
- Not all psychologists are psychotherapists and not all psychotherapists or counselors are psychologists. Many professions—psychiatry, social work, nursing, the clergy, and others—train mental health workers. Some therapists may not be affiliated with any profession. Although this pamphlet has been prepared specifically to explain circumstances and issues as they relate to psychologists, the issues raised also apply to any mental health worker who practices psychotherapy and counseling.

Is it ethical for a therapist to have sexual contact with a patient?

Professionals in the mental health field, and therapists in particular, are generally required to adhere to standards and codes of behavior that are more or less consistent from one profession to another. It is important for you to know that sexual contact between therapists and their patients is specifically prohibited by the ethics codes of the American Psychological Association, the American Psychiatric Association, and the National Association of Social Workers, as well as other associations representing a variety of professions that conduct psychotherapy as part of their practice.

Why is sexual contact bad for a therapy relationship?

Although therapists who engage in sexual contact with patients represent a very small percentage of all therapists, each one is committing an act that is unethical and potentially harmful to patients. A therapist engaging in sexual contact with a patient is breaking one of the most basic rules of a therapy contract, because such sexual contact destroys the objectivity that a therapeutic relationship should have, and it can damage the patient's trust not only in the therapist but also in other people. It is not a legitimate form of treatment. It can never be of help to you, no matter what your problems may be, for your therapist to have sexual contact with you. Most therapists who attempt to introduce sex into a therapy relationship do so more than once, and with more than one patient. Very few people whose therapists have had sexual contact with them have emerged from the experience feeling that they have benefited by it or feeling better about themselves. Moreover, although the negative impact may be apparent almost immediately, it is often not apparent until later.

What is sexual contact in therapy?

Keep in mind that sexual contact can refer to a wide range of behaviors beside sexual intercourse. A relationship can be made sexual in a variety of ways, from making verbal remarks intended to arouse sexual feelings; through erotic hugging and kissing; to manual, oral, or genital contact. Some forms of physical contact between you and your therapist—such as a comforting hug when you are especially sad or a congratulatory pat on the back when you have achieved a success—need not concern you. Usually when touching occurs in therapy, it is nurturing and caring and feels that way to you, and you should be able to talk about it with your therapist. Moreover, there will be times in your therapy when it might be both appropriate and valuable, even if very uncomfortable for you, for you and your therapist to discuss your feelings and concerns about sex. Such discussions may be not only ethical but essential if you are to benefit from your therapy.

However, sexual contact between you and your therapist is not in your best interest. Such contact has been reported to be clearly harmful to therapy patients in almost every case studied. If your therapist touches you in a way that seems sexual to you, but he or she says that this is a perfectly "friendly" or "nurturing" touch, you are the best judge of its effect on you. If you feel shamed or pushed to touch or be touched in therapy, your therapist may be sexualizing the relationship.

An ethical therapist will want you to discuss anything he or she does that makes you uncomfortable so that both of you can understand what is happening in the relationship and so that he or she can desist from personal conduct that creates discomfort for you. Your therapist should respect your feelings of discomfort without challenging them. If he or she doesn't stop when you report feeling uncomfortable, the therapist is probably acting inappropriately. Regardless, first discuss your feelings with the therapist. It is possible that you may be misinterpreting your therapist's intentions; however, after this discussion, if you are still uncomfortable and the therapist persists in his or her actions, you should take additional steps (explained later in this pamphlet) to change the situation.

What about your falling in love with your therapist?

It is normal for people undergoing therapy to have feelings of love, affection, and even sexual attraction toward their therapists. (This reaction is so common that there is even a psychological term for the process—*transference.*) After all, a good therapist shows you caring and gives you support. Thus, you probably will develop positive feelings in response. And such feelings can be intense. But a good, caring therapist knows that it could be harmful to you if she or he were to exploit those feelings by involving you in a sexual relationship. Instead, a good therapist will want you to talk about your feelings and will help you do so. At the same time, your therapist will want to help you find other people in your life with whom you can develop loving, caring, mutually fulfilling relationships.

Should you end therapy in order to have a sexual relationship with your therapist?

Ending therapy to have a personal relationship with your therapist is never a good idea. If either you or the therapist cut things short in order to enter a personal relationship, you will not get the therapy you need. Moreover, your therapist can never completely relinquish the influence he or she has over you, and you will always remember that you met this person when you needed help. If you and your therapist are considering entering or continuing a sexual relationship, then you need to change therapists. End the personal relationship with your former therapist. Your former therapist needs to consult his or her supervisor or personal therapist immediately.

What can you do if you feel uneasy about your therapist's sexually oriented behavior toward you?

If you are uneasy about any element of your therapy, regardless of its nature, first raise your concerns with your therapist. Remember that useful discussions of your sexual feelings can be an important component of your therapy, and, although such discussions can be intensely uncomfortable for you, in the end they are helpful in resolving problems. In situations such as these, your therapist should be able to help you understand the difficulties and discomfort you feel in the context of the overall issues with which you are dealing. However, if your therapist comments about his or her being attracted to you or having sexual fantasies about you or appears to be using forms of verbal and physical sexual seduction, your therapist is not helping you work through your own difficulties with sexuality. If your therapist persists in initiating discussions of his or her own sexual feelings and activities instead of encouraging you to deal with *your* concerns about sexuality or persists in physical contact and does not alter such behavior when you point out that it makes you uncomfortable, it is likely that you have reason to be concerned about your therapist's motives.

What are your options if you feel that your therapist has not acted appropriately?

If your therapist continues to behave inappropriately and will not openly discuss your concerns, there are alternative actions that you can take. These include finding a different therapist and filing various types of complaints. Regardless of what you eventually decide to do, you need to assess for yourself the risks and benefits involved. Inaction is the one "wrong" reaction, but there is no one "right" course of action. Although choosing to take action is sometimes painful and difficult, people who have pursued some of the courses of action discussed here find that taking action often leaves a person feeling more at peace and more complete as a person. What is important is that *you* be the person who decides what to do, and that you do so in a manner and at a pace that reflect your needs, feelings, and interests.

At first it may be painful to contemplate the fact that your therapist eventually will know that you are bringing a complaint about him or her. You may worry about his or her job, reputation, or marriage. However, very often therapists who have sexual contact with their patients take advantage of a person's natural desire not to harm another person; they will tell the patient that she or he is being trusted by the therapist and that this trust must not be betrayed. This approach is self-serving and is designed to protect the therapist from responsibility for his or her inappropriate behaviors. In fact, if a therapist has taken advantage of you in this way, the person who has been betrayed is *you*. Also, be aware that if no one reports the therapist's unethical behavior, the therapist is likely to harm others as well.

If discussion with your therapist fails to satisfy your concerns, then you may wish to deal with the situation in another way. Some of those ways, listed more or less in order of complexity, include the following:

• You can go to a different therapist. Ending therapy is your right and privilege, but it is best to seek the services of another therapist in order to complete your therapy. At the same time, you may wish to consider taking action against your original therapist for his or her behavior with you.

• If your therapist is employed in an agency, you can request a meeting with his or her supervisor or the agency director in order to raise your concerns. No matter where your therapist works, you can also take any of the steps listed here.

• If your therapist belongs to a licensed or regulated profession, you can report the therapist to the state licensing board. A licensing board is the part of the state government responsible for reviewing the credentials of a professional to determine that individual's entitlement to offer his or her services to the public for a fee. The licensing board is also empowered to investigate complaints of unlawful conduct and to enforce sanctions against the professional, including loss of licensure when such unlawful behavior has been proven. Whereas all states license psychologists, not all states license all types of therapists, and some types of therapists are exempted from licensing (e.g., an institution may not require that a staff member be licensed to use the title "psychologist"). You may have to investigate on your own to find out the profession and organizations to which your former therapist may belong. One source of information is professional directories and registers.

• Licensing boards have different names and are operated under different departments in each state, but it is likely that you can find the office of the licensing board by contacting the department that issues the license (e.g., department of health, education, or commerce). Local crisis lines, family service organizations, and mental health centers also may be able to give you the precise name of your state's licensing body. If your former therapist has represented himself or herself to you as a psychologist but is not licensed to practice in your state or is in an exempted category, then the state board may be able to investigate the therapist for misrepresenting himself or herself as a psychologist, or for illegally practicing psychology, as well as for the charges leveled in your complaint.

• You also might want to report the behavior of the therapist to the state's professional association. Such groups can tell you if your therapist is a member, and, if so, might conduct their own investigations or refer you to their ethics committee. State professional associations do not license their members to practice; however, they can impose penalties on an unethical therapist, such as expelling that person from membership in the organization. Such an action might make it more difficult for the therapist to get or keep a license to practice, at least in that state.

• If the therapist is a member of a national association, you also can report his or her behavior to the ethics committee of the appropriate national organization. Each of the major organizations listed below has such a committee.

American Psychological Association
1200 Seventeenth Street, N.W.
Washington, DC 20036
(202) 955-7729

American Psychiatric Association
1400 K Street, N.W.
Washington, DC 20005
(202) 682-6000

National Association of Social Workers
7981 Eastern Avenue
Silver Spring, MD 20910
(301) 565-0333

American Association
for Counseling and Development
5999 Stevenson Avenue
Alexandria, VA 22304
(703) 823-9800

If you contact a national or state organization, verify whether your therapist is a member of that association. If so, ask about the procedure for filing an ethics complaint against a therapist. At this point, you are free not to reveal why and for whom you are asking these questions, and you can maintain your confidentiality until you actually file a complaint. The national or state organization will advise you further about the procedure. Your hesitation in inquiring about or reporting a complaint of sexual misconduct will be understood and taken very seriously. Professional organizations want to know about such breeches of ethics when they occur in order to intervene and prevent them from happening again. There are a variety of steps they may take against an offending member therapist if your charges are confirmed.

• You might consider filing a civil complaint or requesting that the criminal prosecutor file a criminal complaint against the therapist. Most such cases go to civil court in the form of lawsuits for damages. In a few states sexual contact by a therapist with his or her patient is a criminal offense. You also should note that in some states there is a statute of limitations that prohibits filing a malpractice or personal injury complaint after two or three years have passed. You will need to consult an attorney experienced in either personal injury or malpractice law for advice on how to proceed in a legal arena. In fact, you also might decide that you want the advice of an attorney when bringing a complaint to a licensing agency or a professional organization. If so, take the time to find an attorney with knowledge and experience in this kind of case.

If mental status becomes an issue in a civil or criminal case, such status is no longer covered under the rules governing patient/therapist confidentiality. Under such circumstances, you may have to reveal personal and, sometimes, very sensitive information about your treatment to the court, and, at times, courtrooms are open to the public.

What can you do to resolve your emotional concerns about taking action against your former therapist?

Bringing an action against a therapist can be a long and difficult process, often taking several years in the case of a lawsuit. If you take such a step, at times you may feel as if you've been caught up in a system that is trying and difficult. It is common for people bringing actions against therapists to feel discouraged, overwhelmed, and angry. Thus, during the process, it is essential for you to have support from those around you and to have advocates on whom you can depend. Such support can come from friends, a support group, a new therapist, or an attorney. Whatever you do, don't try to go it alone. You are more likely to feel secure and firm in your resolve if you identify the support systems you may need before you initiate the complaint process.

What can you do to resolve your emotional concerns about your experience?

Either before, during, or after you begin to develop your strategy for action, you might decide that you would find it helpful to see another therapist in order to deal with the problems that have surfaced as a result of your previous therapist's unethical sexual conduct. It is very common for people who have been sexually involved with a therapist to feel confused about what has happened and, sometimes, to feel simultaneously in love with and enraged at the therapist. Given your previous experience, it also can be very frightening to seek out another therapist. In spite of your concerns, or rather because of them, be a careful consumer. Look for a therapist who has had experience working with victims of therapist abuse and who will support you and understand the situation with which you are dealing. State or local professional organizations may have a referral list of such specialists.

Other options may be open to you as well. In some communities, there are self-help and support organizations formed by patients whose former therapists have abused the therapy relationship. In other communities, sexual assault or rape crisis centers are sources of help for people sexually exploited by therapists. If you are unsure about where and how to find such a group, you can consult the Women's Program Office at the American Psychological Association (202/955-7767) or find a list of consumer groups that might guide you to local resources.

Whatever you decide to do, it's important to remember these points:

• Sexual relationships between therapists and their patients are never the fault of the patient. No shame or blame attaches to you if this has happened to you. This is true even if you were the one who first felt and expressed attraction for the therapist. It is your therapist's responsibility not to exploit your feelings of love and attraction. It is because such a relationship is exploitative that it has the potential to harm you.

• Sexual relationships between therapists and their patients are never an appropriate or helpful way of dealing with your problems. Often, they are a source of greater pain and confusion. For your therapist to suggest sexual involvement, or to have done so in the past, is evidence of his or her lack of ethical and professional concern for you.

• Even though some therapists may engage in such actions under the influence of alcohol or drugs or during a life crisis of their own, the responsibility for their actions is not removed from their shoulders. Regardless of the circumstances, because of your position of vulnerability and trust when you are a patient, despite any personal feelings of blame or guilt, or your seemingly willing participation in sexual contact, you still have the right to address the issue with your therapist. You also have the right to take whatever formal action you believe to be appropriate and necessary to remedy the misconduct on the part of your therapist.

• Finally, give yourself credit for being willing to deal with this complex and painful issue. It takes both strength and courage to take such an action.

It is the hope of ethical, caring psychologists and other mental health workers that the information in this pamphlet will be a source of support and encouragement for you as you make your decision.

RESOURCES FOR FURTHER READING

The publications listed below may be of use to you as you consider your course of action. Publishers' addresses are included for your convenience. (Inclusion of a publication in this list in no way implies that the American Psychological Association endorses it.)

Pamphlets

Advocates Against Psychic Abuse. (1983). *Prevention and protection guide: Psychiatric and psychological mental service.* San Diego, CA: Author. (Available from Advocates Against Psychic Abuse, 8860 Miramar Road, Ste. 144, San Diego, CA 92126.)

Written by a woman who successfully brought suit against a psychiatrist who had exploited her sexually. Contains information on therapist qualifications, guidelines for detecting inappropriate therapist behaviors, and relevant excerpts from various ethical codes.

Fisch, S. C. *Choosing a psychotherapist: A consumer's guide to mental health treatment.* Waterford, MI: Minerva Press. (Available from Minerva Press, 6653 Andersonville Rd., Waterford, MI.)

A brief consumer guide with a useful reading list. Price $0.79 plus $0.50 postage and handling. Bulk rates available from the publisher.

National Coalition for Women's Mental Health. (1985). *Women and psychotherapy: A consumer handbook.*

Contains information regarding client rights in therapy, descriptions of the various kinds of therapists, information about the effects of sexism or racism on therapy, and suggestions about what to do if you have a complaint against a therapist.

Books

Friedman, S. S., Gams, L., Gottlieb, N., & Nesselson, C. (1979). *A woman's guide to therapy.* Old Toppen, NJ: Prentice-Hall. (Available from Prentice-Hall, 200 Old Toppen Road, Old Toppen, NJ 07675.)

Raises some cogent points about power, its legitimate use, and its potential abuses in psychotherapy. Although the resource list in this book is very dated, the annotated bibliography is useful.

Hall, M. (1985). *The lavender couch: A consumer's guide to psychotherapy for lesbians and gay men.* Boston: Alyson Publications. (Available from Alyson Publications, 40 Plympton St., Boston, MA 02118.)

Contains information similar to that given in the pamphlets above, but in greater detail. Although aimed at the special concerns of sexual minorities, many of the issues apply to all therapy patients.

Lerman, H. (1985). *Sexual intimacies between psychotherapists and patients: An annotated bibliography.* Washington, DC: American Psychological Association. (Available from Patricia S. Hannigan, Department of Counseling, California State University, Fullerton, CA 92634.)

The most complete collection of data regarding research and writing on the topic of sexual contact between therapists and patients. Invaluable for educating your new therapist, your attorney, or as a personal resource. Contains citations to both legal and mental health literature.

Minnesota Department of Corrections. (1985). *Report of the task force on sexual exploitation by counselors and therapists.* St. Paul: Author. (Available from Minnesota Department of Corrections, 300 Bigelow Bldg., 450 N. Syndicate Ave., St. Paul, MN 55104.)

Contains an excellent overview of the nature and extent of sexual exploitation, as well as a copy of Minnesota's model law regarding reporting processes and criminal penalties for sexual contact between therapists and their patients.

References

American Psychiatric Association Committee on Education of Psychiatrists on Ethical Issues. (1987). *Sexual contact between psychiatrists and patients: Ethical issues* [videotape]. Washington, DC: American Psychiatric Association.

American Psychological Association. (1981). Ethical principles of psychologists. *American Psychologist, 36* (6), 633–638.

American Psychological Association. (1987). Report of the Ethics Committee, 1986. *American Psychologist, 41,* 694–697.

American Psychological Association Insurance Trust. (November, 1986). *Letter.* Washington, DC: Author.

Belote, B. J. (1977). Sexual intimacy between female clients and male psychotherapists: Masochistic sabotage. *Dissertation Abstracts International, 38* (2-B), 887.

Bennett, B. E. (1987). *Information about your professional liability program* (letter). Washington, DC: American Psychological Association Insurance Trust.

Bouhoutsos, J. C., & Brodsky, A. M. (1985). Mediation in therapist–client sex: A model. *Psychotherapy: Theory, Research, and Practice, 22* (2), 189–193.

Bouhoutsos, J. C., Holroyd, J., Lerman, H., Forer, B. R., & Greenberg, M. (1983). Sexual intimacy between psychotherapists and patients. *Professional Psychology, 14* (2), 185–196.

Brodsky, A. M. (1977). Sex and the student therapist. *The Clinical Psychologist, 30,* 12–14.

Brodsky, A. M. (Producer). (1979). *Sex fair psychotherapy stimulus films. Series 1: Relationships between clients and therapists* [videotape]. Educational Media, University of Alabama.

Brodsky, A. M. (1980). Sex role issues in the supervision of therapy. In A. K. Hess (Ed.), *Psychotherapy supervision: Theory, research and practice* (pp. 509–522). New York: Wiley.

Brodsky, A. M. (1984). *Issues in the litigation of a sexually abusive therapist.* A symposium presented at the annual convention of the American Psychological Association, Toronto, Canada.

Brodsky, A. M. (1985). Sex between therapists and patients: Ethical gray areas. *Psychotherapy in Private Practice, 3* (1), 57–62.

Brodsky, A. M. (1986). The distressed psychologist: Sexual intimacies and exploitation. In R. R. Kilburg, P. E. Nathan, & R. W. Thoreson (Eds.), *Professionals in distress.* Washington DC: American Psychological Association.

Brodsky, A. M., & Hare-Mustin, R. T. (Eds.). (1980). *Women and psychotherapy: An assessment of research and practice.* New York: Guilford Press.

Brodsky, A. M., Holroyd, J., Sherman, J., Payton, C., Rosenkrantz, P., Rubinstein, E., & Zell, F. (1975). Report of the task force on sex bias and sex role sterotyping in psychotherapeutic practices. *American Psychologist, 30* (12), 1169–1175.

Butler, S. E., & Zelen, S. L. (1977). Sexual intimacies between therapists and patients. *Psychotherapy: Theory, Research and Practice, 14* (2), 139–145.

Callanan, K., & O'Connor, T. (1988). *Staff comments and recommendations regarding the report of the Senate task force on psychotherapist and patients sexual relations* (pp. 10–11). Sacramento. CA. (Available from Board of Medical Quality Assurance or Board of Behavioral Science Examiners.)

Chesler, P. (June 19, 1972a). The sensuous psychiatrists. *New Yorker,* 52–61.

Chesler, P. (1972b). *Women and madness.* New York: Doubleday.

D'Addario, L. J. (1978). Sexual relations between female clients and male therapists. *Dissertation Abstracts International, 38* (10B), 5007.

Dahlberg, C. C. (1970). Sexual contact between patient and therapist. *Contemporary Psychoanalysis, 6,* 107–124.

Deutsch, H. (1945). *The psychology of women.* New York: Grune & Stratton.

Forer, B. (1980). *The therapeutic relationship: 1968.* Paper presented at the annual meeting of the California State Psychological Association, Pasadena, CA.

Freeman, L., & Roy, J. (1976). *Betrayal.* New York: Stein & Day.

Gartrell, N., Herman, J., Olarte, S., Feldstein, M., & Localio, R. (1986). Psychiatrist patient sexual contact: Results of a national survey. I. Prevalence. *American Journal of Psychiatry, 143,* 1126–1131.

Glaser, R. D., & Thorpe, J. S. (1986). Unethical intimacy: A survey of sexual contact and advances between psychology educators and female graduate students. *American Psychologist, 41* (1), 43–51.

Gluck, M. (Personal Communication, 1988). Citation of Klopfer, B. (1955). *Transference as Freud and Jung looked at it.* San Francisco, CA: Division 12 of the American Psychological Association Postdoctoral Institute.

Gonsiorek, J. C. (1987). Intervening with psychotherapists who sexually exploit clients. In P. Keller & S. Heyman (Eds.), *Innovations in clinical practice: A source book* (Vol. 6, pp. 417–427). Minneapolis, MN: Walk-In Counseling Center.

Hare-Mustin, R. T., & Hall, J. E. (1983). Sanctions and the diversity of ethical complaints against psychologists. *American Psychologist, 38* (6), 714–728.

Holroyd, J., & Brodsky, A. M. (1977). Psychologists' attitudes and practices regarding erotic and nonerotic physical contact with patients. *American Psychologist, 32* (10), 843–849.

Holroyd, J. C., & Brodsky, A. M. (1980). Does touching patients lead to sexual intercourse? *Professional Psychology, 11* (5), 807–811.

Jones, E. (1957). *Life and work of Sigmund Freud* (Vol. III). New York: Basic Books.

Kardener, S. H., Fuller, M., & Mensh, I. V. (1973). A survey of physicians' attitudes and practices regarding erotic and nonerotic contact with patients. *American Journal of Psychiatry, 130* (10), 1077–1081.

Keith-Spiegel, P. (1979). *Sex with clients: Ten reasons why it is a very stupid thing to do.* Presented at the meeting of the American Psychological Association, New York.

Masters, W. H., & Johnson, V. E. (1976). Principles of the new sex therapy. *American Journal of Psychiatry, 133,* 548.

McCartney, J. L. (1966). Overt transference. *Journal of Sex Research, 2,* 227–237.

Murray, J. R. (November, 1986) *Letter to insureds.* Washington, DC: American Psychological Association Insurance Trust.

Perry, J. (1976). Physicians' erotic and non-erotic physical involvement with patients. *American Journal of Psychiatry, 133,* 838–840.

Pope, K. S. (1987). Preventing therapist–patient sexual intimacy: therapy for a therapist at risk. *Professional Psychology: Research and Practice, 18,* 624–628.

Pope, K. S., & Bajt, T. R. (in press). When laws and values conflict: A dilemma for psychologists. *American Psychologist, 42.*

Pope, K. S., & Bouhoutsos, J. C. (1986). *Sexual intimacy between therapists and patients.* New York: Praeger.

Pope, K. S., Keith-Spiegel, P., & Tabachnick, B. G. (1986). Sexual attraction to clients: The human therapist and the (sometimes) inhuman training system. *American Psychologist, 41,* 147–158.

Pope, K. S., Levenson, H., & Schover, L. R. (1979). Sexual intimacy in psychology training: Results and implications of national survey. *American Psychologist, 34* (8), 682–689.

Pope, K. S., Tabachnick, B. G., & Keith-Spiegel, P. (1987). Ethics of practice: The beliefs and behaviors of psychologists as therapists. *American Psychologist, 42,* 993–1006.

Schoener, G. (1988). Assessment and development of rehabilitation plans for the therapist. In G. Schoener, J. Milgrom, J. Gonsiorek, E. Luepker, & R. Conroe (Eds.), *Psychotherapists' sexual involvement with clients: Intervention and prevention*. Minneapolis: MN: Walk-In Counseling Center.

Schoener, G., Milgrom, J., & Gonsiorek, J. (1983). *Responding therapeutically to clients who have been sexually involved with their psychotherapists* (unpublished manuscript). Available from the Walk-in Counseling Center, 2421 Chicago Avenue South, Minneapolis, MN.

Sell, J. M., Gottlieb, M. C., & Schoenfeld, L. (1986). Ethical considerations of social/romantic relationships with present and former clients. *Professional Psychology: Research and Practice, 17*, 504–508.

Shepard, M. (1971). *The love treatment: Sexual intimacy between patients and psychotherapists*. New York: Peter Wyden.

Smith, S. (1982). *The sexually abused patient and the abusing therapist: A study in sadomasochistic relationships*. Paper presented at the meeting of the American Psychological Association, Washington, DC.

Taylor, B. J., & Wagner, N. N. (1976). Sex between therapists and clients: A review and analysis. *Professional Psychology, 7* (4), 593–601.

Index